Problematic youth group inv

PROBLEMATIC YOUTH GROUP INVOLVEMENT AS SITUATED CHOICE

Testing an integrated conditions-controls-exposure model

LIEVEN PAUWELS
WIM HARDYNS

international publishing

Published, sold and distributed by Eleven International Publishing
P.O. Box 85576
2508 CG The Hague
The Netherlands
Tel.: +31 70 33 070 33
Fax: +31 70 33 070 30
e-mail: sales@budh.nl
www.elevenpub.com

Sold and distributed in USA and Canada
International Specialized Book Services
920 NE 58th Avenue, Suite 300
Portland, OR 97213-3786, USA
Tel.: 1-800-944-6190 (toll-free)
Fax: +1-503-280-8832
orders@isbs.com
www.isbs.com

Eleven International Publishing is an imprint of Boom uitgevers Den Haag.

ISBN 978-94-6236-593-3
ISBN 978-94-6274-363-2 (E-book)

Printed in The Netherlands

ACKNOWLEDGMENTS

This book is the result of a personal research project which started a couple of years after the defence of the PhD of Lieven Pauwels on Social Disorganization Theory and juvenile delinquency and the PhD of Wim Hardyns on Collective Efficacy Theory. Both of us are interested in criminological theories and the relationship between theory and empirical research. Both of us also share an interest in theoretical integration and the search for intervening mechanisms in order to increase our understanding of a phenomenon. The present book is the result of cooperation during many years of studying ecological effects and integrates our interest for theoretical elaboration and empirical testing. We found it very inspiring to combine our expertise. Two books were especially influential, both from a theoretical perspective and with regard to the structure of the book: (1) the book by Esbensen et al. (2010), *"Youth violence. Sex and race differences in offending, victimization, and gang membership"*, on youth violence which focuses on the role of gang membership, and (2) the book by Wikström et al. (2012), *"Breaking rules: The social and situational dynamics of young people's urban crime"*, on the social and situational dynamics of adolescent offending. Both books combine theory, an overview of studies and empirical results in a way that is appealing as these books contain straightforward analyses and complex models.

The ideas outlined in this book are strongly influenced by many interesting discussions we had, especially the discussions during the Eurogang meetings. We thank professor Finn Esbensen (University of Missouri-St. Louis) and professor Cheryl Maxson (University of Southern California) for the comments on our work which has been presented in preliminary form at the Eurogang meeting in Stavern, Norway (2014). This special event could not have taken place without the help of professor Tore Bjørgo. Special thanks also goes to Dr. Frank Weerman (The Netherlands Institute for the Study of Crime and Law Enforcement) and Associate Professor of Sociology Dr. Robert Svensson (Malmö University), who took their time to read the entire manuscript and provide their valuable comments. Finally we would like to thank Professor Per-Olof Wikström (University of Cambridge) and Professor Gerben Bruinsma (The Netherlands Institute for the Study of Crime and Law Enforcement), for many inspiring discussions on the philosophy of causation and critical realism. Discussions on research programs and the values of scientific realism and emergentist systemism have been very fruitful.

Lieven Pauwels and Wim Hardyns would like to express their gratitude to their wives, respectively Cédrique Walthoff-Borm and Jill Roesbeke, for enduring support and allowing us to spend many hours during weekends on this project. A last word of thanks goes to the publisher, Eleven International Publishing and in particular Joris Bekkers and Tom van der Meer, for their interest in this topic and their fruitful editing work.

Ghent, 03-11-2015
Lieven Pauwels and Wim Hardyns

TABLE OF CONTENTS

List of Figures and Tables

1 | INTRODUCTION

1 STUDY BACKGROUND

Problematic youth groups of all kinds – often referred to as street gangs – have been a classic theme in criminology for a long time. From the early days of criminology, the existence of such groups has been subsequently explained by the social disorganization perspective of the Chicago School (Thrasher, 1927), the strain and subcultural (Cohen, 1955; Cloward & Ohlin, 1960; Miller, 1958) control theories (Hirschi, 1969; Kornhauser, 1978) to lifestyle/routine activities theories (Riley, 1987: 339-354). Previous research on gangs or 'troublesome youth groups' has been the subject of study in the US especially (Decker & Weerman, 2005; Klein & Maxson, 2006; Tita, Riley & Greenwood, 2002) and has become the subject of study in some European countries as well (Bjørgo & Haaland, 2001; Decker & Weerman, 2005; Haaland, 2000; Pauwels & Svensson, 2013). Comparative studies have also been conducted (Esbensen & Weerman, 2005; Klein, Weerman & Thornberry, 2006; Pauwels & Svensson, 2013). Despite observed differences between characteristics of 'street gangs' in the US and in Europe, we can no longer deny the existence of small numbers of juveniles involved in some kind of 'troublesome youth group' in European cities, although it is worthwhile to repeat that none really meet the stereotype criterion of 'boys from the hood' controlling a neighborhood. This has previously been documented by Maxson and Klein (1995) and Klein, Weerman and Thornberry (2006). In the past ten years, the scholarly activities of the Eurogang working group have been expanding, resulting in numerous publications from numerous scholars within and outside Europe (e.g. Esbensen et al., 2010; Sharp, Aldridge & Medina, 2006; Esbensen & Maxson, 2011). A vast number of studies have been conducted in the US and in many European countries as well. The study of street gangs has grown internationally, thanks to the enduring activities of the Eurogang working group. This international group of scholars have been using the term *troublesome youth groups* in their empirical works. While we fully agree with the conception and definition of troublesome youth groups, we have decided to use the term *problematic youth groups* for one main reason: the measurement instrument we have used is not identical to the Eurogang measurement instrument. While we will go into definitional issues later, we thought this was important to already stress this at the beginning of the book. In older work, we have used the term violent youth group involvement, but this term is misleading and suggests that violent youth groups only (or mainly) commit violent acts. The idea of specialization among young persons who participate in problematic youth groups is rather supportive for the idea of versatility.

However, research on problematic youth group involvement, young people's offending, and its causes is a research tradition that is still nascent in Belgium. The main sources of information on juvenile delinquency come from police register data and official statistics of juvenile delinquency based on the juvenile court statistics. Although Belgium was a pioneer in the study of criminal statistics in the 19th century with the famous professor Quetelet, it should be noticed that Belgium quite early lost its interest in crime statistics in general and data on juvenile delinquency in particular. It was the late professor Josine Junger-Tas who conducted the first self-report study in Belgium in the 1970s, with a small-scale survey in Brussels on self-reported substance use. Belgian criminology was at that time not preoccupied with the issue of crime and its causes but rather interested in the study of inequality and the criminal justice system. In the period between 1980 and 1995, self-reported delinquency studies were highly exceptional (De Witte, Hooghe & Walgrave, 2000). Recently, this situation has changed. A full overview of published Belgian self-report studies can be read elsewhere (Pauwels & Pleysier, 2009). Regarding the research topic of this book, it is important to notice that Belgium participated in the second wave of the international self-report study, which included questions on troublesome youth group involvement (Pauwels et al., 2011). It seems that the millennium shift has brought about a renewed interest in self-reported delinquency studies and victims surveys in Belgium. Scholars have regained interest in questions that involve the patterns of offending and the offering of explanations of these patterns. Recently, Pauwels (2007) tested the key assumptions of social disorganization theory, fleshing out individual and ecological patterns of offending in the urban context of Antwerp, and Op de Beeck (2011) tested key assumptions of Agnew's strain theory using data from the Flemish JOP-monitor, a representative survey of youth that contains questions on self-reported offending and covariates.

However, very few academic studies have explored the prevalence and patterns of offending and problematic youth group involvement in Belgian cities before 2008. Belgian research into youth and delinquency has primarily focused on the social and judicial reaction toward delinquent behavior of minors as well as the treatment of delinquent youth, i.e. the juvenile justice system (Christiaens, De Fraene & Delens-Ravier, 2005). Research documenting the existence of problematic youth groups in the context of Belgian metropolitan areas is therefore relatively scarce, and existing research does not go beyond a documentation of official registers such as police data. Only one Belgian self-report delinquency study has documented the presence of high-frequency offenders and the different clusters of adolescent offenders based on problem behavior. Another study focused on disorder caused by youth groups using the Public Prosecution files in Brussels (De Wree, Vermeulen & Christiaens, 2006). Cammaert et al. (2005) focused on the monitoring of alternative measures toward hardcore recidivist youth. In short, there is a lot of research being conducted on juvenile delinquency, but information is not systematically gathered in the same way as it is in our neighboring countries, such as the UK and the Netherlands. Furthermore, it is difficult to compare results because research has focused on different age groups and different samples.

So far, no previous Belgian study has incorporated a measurement instrument explicitly designed to measure violent youth group involvement. In an attempt to bridge this gap in Belgian criminological research, the measurement instrument to identify problematic youth group affiliation used by Heitmeyer et al. (1995) was introduced in a large-scale urban survey of young adolescents that was conducted in 2005. That survey was the Antwerp Youth Survey, which is introduced in chapter six. So far, data on problematic youth group involvement were presented during conferences, and only a part of the findings have been published (Pauwels, 2008; Pauwels, Hardyns & Van de Velde, 2010).

The present study largely builds upon our previous work on adolescent offending and problematic youth group involvement and takes the basic principles of theoretical integration as a starting point for offering an integrative explanation for the involvement of young adolescents in problematic youth groups and individual differences in offending. Much inspiration has been found in the book by Wikström and Butterworth (2006) on the role of lifestyles in the explanation of offending and in the book by Esbensen et al. (2010). The basic idea we have adopted from Wikström and Butterworth is that the major direct causes of adolescent offending are their crime propensity and exposure to criminogenic moral settings. In the present study, problematic youth group involvement is the ultimate dependent variable and the focus will be on a series of causal risk factors in key contexts such as the street-level and the school, family position, and structure, social bonds, dispositions, and exposure to criminogenic moral settings (as measured by their lifestyles). In the present book, we present an extended version of an integrative framework that stresses the importance of informal controls as causes of the causes of offending and problematic youth group involvement and lifestyles as direct situational mechanisms in the explanation of individual differences in problematic youth group involvement. An earlier version of that framework was presented at a number of conferences (the ESC conference in Tübingen in 2006, the Stockholm Criminology Prize Conference in 2008 and the Eurogang Conference held in Stockholm in 2013, the Eurogang Conference held in Stavern in 2014). The ideas presented here are thus not new, but are the result of an ongoing work in the integration of control theories and routine activities theories (Pauwels & Svensson, 2013; Pauwels & Svensson, 2014). Of special interest in the present study is the question to what extent the explanation of individual differences in problematic youth group involvement parallels the explanation of individual differences in offending and to what extent there exists a relationship between problematic youth group involvement and offending, controlling for a number of potential common causes of the causes. It has been noted before that there exists substantial overlap between the risk and protective factors of problematic youth group involvement and self-reported offending (Esbensen et al., 2010). While the Antwerp Youth Survey, a survey that was exclusively conducted among individuals in their early adolescence, has been used before to test key assumptions derived from Social Disorganization Theory (Pauwels, 2007; 2012) and Situational Action Theory (Svensson & Pauwels, 2010; Pauwels & Svensson, 2014), these rich data are up to now not fully explored. The questionnaire of the Antwerp Youth Survey contained questions on troublesome youth group involvement and was based on previous work of the Eurogang working group and Heitmeyer et al. (1995). In December 2004, Dr. Frank Weerman, member of the Eurogang network and senior researcher at the NSCR, suggested that the inclusion of the core questions of the 2004 version of the measurement instrument would create a unique opportunity to test hypotheses on problematic youth group involvement in a setting that did not study the topic of problematic youth group involvement empirically at that time. The decision to include these questions was the beginning of a new journey through academia, unraveling troublesome youth group involvement in the urban context of Antwerp, the largest city in the Flemish part of Belgium.

2   BALANCE BETWEEN THEORY, RESEARCH, AND POLICY

Why is affiliation with problematic youth groups more prevalent in some social groups than in others, and what factors make that some individuals are drawn to such groups or pushed toward such groups? These questions remain fundamental for crime causation theory as science and criminal policy. These questions are often studied separately, but they can be studied together, as it is highly plausible that a set of common denominators is detected. We submit that it is important for theory and policy to study these phenomena together. It is important for theory that we understand possible common causal factors and causal routes to offending and problematic youth group involvement. The answer to these questions affects the way reactions toward crime through criminal policy, social, and situational crime prevention. Policy measures need to be accurate. Effective prevention of crime and problematic youth group involvement, i.e. a prevention that succeeds in reducing crime and problematic youth group involvement as a social phenomenon, needs to target mechanisms through which external conditions or events that are differently perceived are related to crime and problematic youth group involvement. Therefore, we strongly believe that policy measures need to address factors that are causally related to crime and problematic youth group involvement and which are backed up by empirical research. Precisely because it is so difficult, if not impossible to adequately demonstrate causation, the role of theorizing should be given a more prominent place in empirical studies of crime and problematic youth group involvement.

Unfortunately, the state of criminological theorizing is somewhat problematic. Criminology is characterized by the problem of having too many theories, which sometimes have conflicting ideas about causes and effects. Criminological theory therefore needs to be improved. In a state of theoretical normlessness, where policy makers can pick up their favorite theory to justify some policy measure, the role of theory becomes trivial. Theory becomes an excuse to do whatever one wants to stress in criminal policy and crime prevention. During several decades, the development of etiological theories existed relatively independent of the empirical analysis of phenomena. Classicist and biological, psychological, and sociological positivist theories provided preliminary explanations for the differences in offending at the societal and individual level. The empirical analyses that were carried out in these early days were characterized by several methodological constraints. This means that a gap existed between theory and empirical analysis. Fortunately, more recently formulated theories are resulting from new research findings and empirical developments. The aim of this chapter is to present a framework that may contribute to the bridging of the gap between abstract theory and research. After all, what is the point in using theories that lack empirical fundaments? We emphasize that theories of problematic youth group involvement just like theories of offending should have strong empirical grounds, i.e. they should be strongly rooted in the social reality. The role of social theories is precisely to improve our understanding of the social world around us. "Without a theory, empirical research often lacks wider significance, and without empirical research, sociological theory easily turns into fictitious storytelling" (Hedström, 2005: 114, see also Elster, 1989: 7-8).

We strongly believe that criminology as a discipline can benefit from a balance between integrated theories of the middle-range and semi-general theories, empirical research, and criminal policy. When theory, research, and policy are out of balance, we encounter one of the following problems (Pauwels, Ponsaers & Svensson, 2010): (1) If we emphasize theory too much and thus neglect empirical research and criminal policy, scientific activity will be reduced to *l'art pour l'art* or 'exercising the art of science merely for its own purpose'; hence, criminology will be reduced to prosaic texts. A theory-driven criminology that lacks empirical grounds, and policy relevance, depicts the scientist as an estranged individual, incarcerated in an 'ivory tower.' (2) Putting too much emphasis on empirical research, and hereby ignoring theory and policy, leads to blind empiricism, the reification of science as number crunching and fetishism of the number. Science is then reduced to a collection of data that are carefully ranked and reported in a book of results but without meaning or social and policy relevance. The result is a patchwork of observations that grows endlessly, without direction, meaning, and use. This was the fate of the multiple-factor approach. (3) Science that is too narrowly related to policy is also a reification. In this situation, science is reduced to a technical instrument of criminal policy that takes over implicitly existing and perhaps wrong policy theories without trying to empirically test their original underlying hypotheses. Science then is merely a technical instrument, an application of confirmed hypotheses that were formulated long time ago. Criminological research such as the study of crime and problematic youth group involvement should be relevant for policy, not per se supportive of policy. To be relevant, we need well-developed theories that are strongly supported by data.

3   AIM OF THE RESEARCH: KEY QUESTIONS AND CONSTRUCTS

The overall goal of this research is to contribute to a better understanding of youths' involvement in problematic youth groups and crime in early to mid-adolescence. We aim to achieve this by studying the relationships between self-reported offending, problematic youth group involvement, and a number of key risk factors identified in previous studies. This study has a specific focus on the ecological contexts (the social-ecological structure of neighborhood, the micro-ecological structure of the 'street segment,' and the school), the family social position (family disadvantage, family structure, and immigrant background), their external locus of control or subjective powerlessness, the adolescents' social integration (family and school bonds), their dispositions (low moral beliefs and low self-control) and lifestyles (as implicated by their peers' delinquency, their own unstructured routine activities, and substance use), and how these risk factors relate to their involvement in a problematic youth group and crime as offenders. We have conducted the present study from a general integrative theoretical framework, which focuses on the role of different kinds of controls and lifestyles, and tested its applicability to the explanation of problematic youth group involvement and adolescent offending. Our integrative 'micro-place conditions-controls-exposure model' will be used as a guideline to make sense of the large number of correlates of problematic youth group involvement and to distinguish between distant factors and proximate factors, or in other words, mechanisms that bring about involvement in a problematic youth group. The integrative conditions-controls-exposure model hypothesizes that low moral beliefs, low self-control, and lifestyle risks (and their interactions) are key proximate causes of problematic youth group involvement and offending and that micro-place conditions, especially micro-place disorder, are only indirectly related to problematic youth group involvement through several intervening mechanisms, especially, social bonds and external locus of control. The theory is meant as a framework. Thereby, we mean that conditions, controls, and exposure are important concepts in the development of crime and problematic youth group involvement; the conception of conditions, controls, and exposure are variable and depend on the age structure and developmental phase in the life course. The causal structure of the theoretical framework will be fully outlined in detail later. At this point, it is sufficient to point to the fact that we make a distinction between a life course exposure model that explains why people have acquired certain belief systems that are conducive to problematic youth group involvement and supportive of offending and lifestyles and a situational model that explains why people that have acquired certain belief systems become situationally exposed and triggered to offend and become involved in a problematic youth group.

We are especially interested in the much debated role of the community context, especially neighborhoods and micro-places (street segments). The study of problematic youth group involvement practically grew out of the social disorganization theory, with Thrasher (1927) being the first to apply the core theoretical model of weakening social controls in disorganized neighborhoods to the explanation of the emergence of gangs and informal groups in Chicago, almost hundred years ago. The neighborhood tradition has undergone a massive evolution, especially since the study of ecological mechanisms became possible through the application of new methodologies to capture the social processes of social ties, collective efficacy (neighborhood social trust and the residents' ability to intervene), and adults' supervision on the behavior of peer groups and through the widespread use of newer statistical techniques to assess neighborhood effects.

However, the picture is far from clear, and neighborhood studies continue to struggle with key problems, especially the definition and measurement of neighborhoods as a unit of analysis. For several years, scholars have raised questions to the use of adjacent 'neighborhood clusters' in studies on juvenile delinquency and a number of scholars have suggested to focus on micro-units such as street blocks (Weisburd, Groff & Yang, 2014). In this study, we will keep this critique of neighborhood studies in mind and reassess the impact of neighborhood effects by gathering data on the neighborhood where the survey participants live and by combining these data with the measures of ecological processes at several levels of analysis.

4   OUTLINE OF CHAPTERS

Chapter two deals with the theoretical risk factors of problematic youth group involvement used in the present study. The aim is not to be comprehensive as many excellent overview works exist, but to give a summary and thereby stressing the different domains that are at the heart of the theoretical model that is presented and tested in this book. Chapter three deals with the origins of the theoretical framework that is used throughout this book. The reader should therefore not expect a list of all possible theories of violent youth group involvement. On the contrary, the basic idea was to give an overview of the major developments in the traditions that lay at the heart of the integrative model. Chapter four provides a useful meta-theoretical framework within which it is possible to arrive at multiple theories, not just the integrative model that is tested in this book. This is an attempt to hold a plea for an integrative life course developmental and situational meta-theoretical framework that can be used to build theories of action and theories of the causes of the causes of action. The basic idea is that meta-theoretical frameworks are useful toolboxes to develop different integrative theories or even families of theories. Chapter five contains the explicit formulation of what we have called an integrative conditions-controls-exposure model. Chapter six deals with the multi-method approach that guided the empirical research in the urban context of Antwerp. Chapter seven describes crime patterns of young adolescents who are involved in a violent youth group. We present the results in four different subgroups: nonimmigrant and immigrant boys and nonimmigrant and immigrant girls. It is only seldom that attempts are made to describe crime patterns in such detailed subgroups. Chapter eight describes the relationship between family social position and problematic youth group involvement. Chapter nine describes the community context of problematic youth group involvement. Attention is paid to the neighborhood level and the micro-place level by using observational measures of micro-places. Chapter ten describes some important individual characteristics and their relationship with problematic youth group involvement. Attention is paid to informal controls (social bonds, monitoring, integration) and individual beliefs (low moral beliefs and external locus of control) and the ability to exercise self-control. Chapter eleven then describes the relationship between lifestyle differences and problematic youth group involvement. Chapter twelve describes the test of the integrative model in the overall sample and in subsamples by gender and immigrant background. Chapter thirteen contains a summary of the results of the present study.

PREVIOUS RESEARCH ON RISK FACTORS
OF PROBLEMATIC YOUTH GROUP INVOLVEMENT

1   INTRODUCTION

In the present chapter, we give an overview of the several risk factors in subsequent domains that are involved in this study and argue that it is of major importance to the field to move beyond the study of risk factors. Furthermore, we outline the different theoretical frameworks that are centered on the risk factors that are studied in the present study of problematic youth group involvement and offending. The key elements in a integrative conditions-controls-exposure model (hence, CCE theory) finds its origin in social disorganization theory, control theory, and lifestyle theory. The theoretical development of each of these perspectives is thoroughly discussed and key findings from these perspectives are discussed. Finally, we present an conditions-controls-exposure model of problematic youth group involvement.

2   THE IMPORTANCE TO STUDY EARLY ADOLESCENCE

This book is about crime and problematic youth group participation of young adolescents. Why is it important to study the rule-breaking behavior of individuals in early adolescence? It has been shown in predominantly U.S.-based studies that involvement in a problematic youth group on average starts at age 14 (Curry, Decker & Pyrooz, 2003). Thus, it should be studied if and to what extent violent youth group participation exists in early adolescence. Apart from that, early adolescence is an interesting period. These years are an exciting time of many varied and rapid changes. This rapid development can be a confusing time for both children and parents and can produce side effects, e.g. breaking rules to find out how far they can go. In general, developmental psychologists argue that from ages 11 through 14, a child develops in different life domains (see Martens, 1990)

- *Physical development*. Adolescence is a time of change throughout the body. A growth spurt usually occurs near the time of puberty.
- *Cognitive development*. This is how the brain develops the abilities to think, learn, reason, and remember. Children in early adolescence start to understand that what they do and how their present deeds can have long-term effects. In early

adolescence, children start understanding that issues are not just clear-cut and that information can be interpreted in many different ways.

- *Emotional and social development.* When moving away from childhood into adolescence, children feel the urge to be more in control and less depending of parents' decision making. Usually, peers replace parents as a source of advice. When at home, adolescents may prefer spending time alone instead of being part of the family. Still, family support is important to help adolescents build a high self-esteem, self-control, and internal locus of control.
- *Sensory and motor development.* Young adolescents' brains are adjusting to longer physical developments.

Early adolescence is a time of many physical, mental, emotional, and social changes. Hormones change as puberty begins. In early adolescence, teenagers are confronted with peer pressure to use alcohol, tobacco, and illegal drugs, to violate general moral standards, and to have sex. Other challenges can be eating disorders, depression, learning disabilities, and family problems. At this age, adolescents are allowed to increasingly become independent from parents in the processes of choosing friends, leisure time, time spent with friends, time spent on school work, and developing their own personality and interests. The above-mentioned arguments make it clear why offending in early adolescence deserves to be studied in its own right as it is related to many developmental changes, within the person and its environment. Adolescent offending continues to be an issue of major concern to parents, teachers, police, and local and state governments and is a significant cost to the community. As not all rule-breaking is recorded by the police, it is valuable to measure adolescents' own reports of their rule-breaking (Kivivuori, 2011). Self-reported measures allow questions to be answered about the types, rates, and patterns of adolescent offending and the degree to which such behavior results in police contact. Better understanding of these behaviors can contribute to the development of both theory development and prevention approaches.

3   RISK FACTORS FOR PROBLEMATIC YOUTH GROUP INVOLVEMENT
         AND OFFENDING

Greater understanding of the course and causes of adolescent offending can inform early intervention and prevention efforts. This is best done using panel data. However, cross-sectional studies, which compare adolescents of differing ages at a single time point, can provide a snapshot of general trends and developmental trajectories, e.g. by comparing different groups of offenders (Moffitt, 1993; Moffitt & Caspi, 2001). Insufficient resources and a limited time were the main reasons why a cross-sectional research design was chosen. While the issue of the advantages of longitudinal designs over cross-sectional designs are sometimes debated, especially within the framework of the study of situational causes of offending (see Gottfreddson & Hirschi, 1990;

Wikström et al., 2012), the cross-sectional design leaves us with no opportunity to unravel the relationship between problematic youth group involvement and offending. The relationship between offending and problematic youth group involvement can be explained from different angles (selection, causation, amplification), and this cannot be assessed in the present study.

Risk factors are conditions in the individual or environment that can predict an increased likelihood of becoming engaged in offending and problematic youth group involvement. Several studies have identified causes or risk factors that, if present for a given individual, make it more likely he or she will break rules, including joining a problematic youth group (Thornberry et al., 1993; Howell & Egley, 2005). Although research has not yet clearly identified unique risk factors for problematic youth group involvement, in general, it is predicted by the same risk factors as general forms of adolescent offending. However, youth with elevated risk for joining a problematic youth group tend to have more risk factors than youth at risk for general delinquency. Why is knowledge of risk factors important? Many actors in the field of crime prevention call for an integrated or holistic approach incorporating not only intervention and suppression efforts but prevention and early intervention as well, i.e. a continuum of program options. One of the purposes of this type of approach is to identify conditions in the environment and in the child that increase the risk of problem behavior early in childhood/adolescence and predict delinquency and youth group involvement later on. The intent is that prevention and early intervention programs address and reduce these risk factors. However, we must keep in mind that risk factors cannot be equated with causes. Most risk factors are merely attributes or markers, but some can be considered as causal factors, i.e. factors that are capable of bringing about something, in the present study that is problematic youth group participation.

4   CLASSIFICATION OF THE RISK FACTORS IN THE PRESENT STUDY

In today's world of prevention and treatment of social problems, the term risk factor refers to individual or ecological hazards that increase an individual's vulnerability to negative developmental outcomes. As also Esbensen et al. (2010) have stressed:

> we have been accustomed to hearing about risk factors associated with heart disease and cancer and therefore the transition from health issues to crime was an easy one. While the study of risk factors identified with offending and violent youth group involvement has played a major role in criminology, the problems associated with the risk factor approach are numerous: some risk factors are mere attributes, some are symptoms of offending and some can be identified as possible causes of offending and violent youth group affiliation.

A risk factor approach assumes that there are multiple, and often overlapping, risk factors in an individual's background that lead to adverse outcomes. Furthermore,

Table 1   Risk/promotive factors in the present study by domain

Risk factor domain	Risk factor	Theoretical perspective(s)
Neighborhood (ecological risk factors)	Disadvantage, street crime, disorganization, residential stability, immigrant concentration	Social disorganization theory, collective efficacy theory, broken windows theory
Micro-place ecological risk factors	Perceived social trust, perceived informal control, observed unsupervised youth groups, observed disorder	Social disorganization theory, collective efficacy theory, broken windows theory
Social support and social control promotive factors	Parental attachment, school social bond, classroom integration, parental monitoring	Social Control Theory, Social Support Theory
Cognitions and dispositions	Legal cynicism (normlessness), low self-control, subjective powerlessness (lack of personal control, external locus of control)	Social learning theory, social bonding theory, self-control theory, routine activities theory
Lifestyle domain risk factors	Peer delinquency, problematic youth group involvement, unstructured routines, substance use (being drunk and cannabis use)	Lifestyle theories, routine activities theories
Demographic and structural/ positional risk factors	Redo a school year (academic failure), family disadvantage, family disruption (one-parent family), immigrant background, gender, school failure	These factors are considered to be attributes, but in some sociological perspectives (especially strain theories), they play an indirect role

it posits that "it is the accumulation of risk in the life course that is most strongly related to adversity." (Thornberry, 1998). Risk factors are often grouped into five developmental domains: individual, family, school, peers, and community (Howell & Egley, 2005). The present study adopts a theory-driven approach and is guided by the principle of end-to-end integration, i.e. the integration between distant and proximate causes in the explanation of offending and problematic youth group involvement. Yet, before adopting a conceptual framework in the present study, we classify the various factors that will be studied in the present study by different theoretical domains, i.e. the theoretical domains they initially were considered to be part of. We will discuss each of the risk factors in the subsequent chapters. In Table 1, we present the different risk factors by theoretical perspective to document one of the key problems in criminology: some risk factors belong to more than one theoretical perspective. We need to sort this problem out if we are to enhance our understanding of offending. As mentioned above, risk factors of juvenile delinquency and problematic youth group involvement have been identified in five major domains: community, individual, family, peers, and school. The U.S. Office of Juvenile Justice and Delinquency Prevention has adopted this approach specifically with regard to problematic youth groups and 'gangs' (Curry, Decker & Pyrooz, 2012; Esbensen et al., 2010).

The major problem for criminological theory is that there is considerable overlap between different theories regarding their key concepts. The major difference between theories is the explanatory mechanism that relates the risk factor to offending and problematic youth group involvement. Let us briefly discuss the risk factors associated with different domains and theories of offending/gang membership that will be studied in this book and presented in an integrated theory.

Neighborhood ecological risk factors. Neighborhood disadvantage has been a classic risk factor in studies of offending and problematic youth group involvement (Curry & Spergel, 1988; Pappachristos & Kirk, 2006). Several community or neighborhood risk factors predict problematic youth group involvement. Youth groups tend to cluster in high-crime, socially disorganized neighborhoods, where many youth are in trouble, feel unsafe, and are less attached to others in the community (Bjerregaard & Lizotte, 1995); thus, illegal gun ownership and carrying are key predictors of gang membership. Gang involvement also significantly increases the probability of subsequent gun carrying (Lizotte et al., 2000).

Indicators of disadvantage, crime, and poor social climate have by and large been subject to social disorganization theory, while especially disorder has been the key variable in broken windows theory (Bruinsma et al., 2013). That crime and disorder are somewhat related at the ecological level is without doubt. Scholars mainly disagree about the causal relationship between both (Sampson, 2012; Steenbeek & Hipp, 2011). Scholars in general tend to share the view that it is neighborhood structural characteristics that set the stage for crime and disorder.

Micro-place ecological risk factors. We have separated observed micro-place disorder and perceived collective efficacy from the true ecological measures as they are somewhat different. If neighborhood characteristics are to be of importance in explaining individual differences in offending and problematic youth group involvement, the signals that they produce need to be perceived by our senses. Without these perceptions, there simply cannot be any influence at all. It is important to notice that these perceptual measures could have easily been placed under the individual domain, as these perceptions are related to the individual. It is the individual youth who perceives signals of low collective efficacy, crime, disorder, etcetera, and individual perceptions may be different across youths and social groups. However, as these perceptions ultimately refer to ecological conditions at the micro-ecological level, we have decided to place them under the denominator of ecological risk factors. There is however another serious difference between true ecological and perceptual risk factors: true ecological risk factors have been identified at different levels of aggregation. While neighborhood studies belong to one of the oldest traditions of research on the causes of crime, these neighborhood studies have been plagued by problems of aggregation bias and neighborhood definition. It is highly plausible to assume that

perceptual measures refer to smaller ecological units of analysis, probably street segments, because it is quite impossible to adequately oversee large ecological units such
as neighborhoods or other huge areas consisting of some administrative units of a
couple of thousand inhabitants. We will go more into detail on that matter in the chapter on community factors and problematic youth group involvement and offending.
The problem of defining the right unit of analysis is well known in studies of ecological processes in neighborhoods and schools as units of analysis. Social disorganization theory and collective efficacy theory have been applied to the school level as well,
and in European studies, the school level variation seems to be somewhat larger than
the neighborhood level variation in offending and problematic youth group involvement. We will go more into that issues when evaluating the role of these true ecological and perceptual measures of disorganization and organization.
Within the *social support/social control domain*, researchers have pointed to the school
social bond, classroom integration, parental monitoring, and parental attachment
(Esbensen et al., 2010). Risk factors that fall under that denominator differ from the
ecological school-related risk factors in that they refer to the individual rather than
the school as a unit of analysis. Most of the school-related risk factors in the present
study associated with offending and problematic youth group involvement are
derived from social bonding theories. That is the case for the school social bond
and integration in the class one attends.

Cognitions and trait-related risk factors. Cognitions and dispositions are significantly
related to offending and problematic youth group involvement. The number of individual-level risk factors is huge and ranges from attitudes to traits (e.g. self-control;
see Hope & Damphouse, 2002; Katz & Fox, 2010; Kissner & Pyrooz, 2009). A first
series of individual risk factors can be categorized as cognitions. Within the field
of criminology, much attention has been given to attitudes favorable to the violation
of law. Such attitudes have been labeled as antisocial values, antisocial potential,
delinquency tolerance/legal cynicism (Sampson & Bartusch, 1998), and normlessness. Similar to moral values, moral feelings are related to offending and problematic youth group involvement: feelings of shame and guilt have been reported to
correlate with problematic youth group involvement (Esbensen et al., 2010), but
measures of moral feelings are not available in the present study. These moral feelings however do correlate quite strong with moral values (Svensson et al., 2013;
Wikström & Butterworth, 2006). There is a lot of empirical evidence for the relationship between low self-control and offending and also some evidence for the relationship between low self-control and problematic youth group involvement (Hope &
Damphouse, 2002; Katz & Fox, 2010; Kissner & Pyrooz, 2009; Pauwels & Svensson,
2013; Pauwels et al., 2011). Studies differ in the magnitude of the relationship.
It is plausible to assume that the magnitude of the relationship is in itself a consequence of differences in measures that are used (behavioral versus attitudinal):

subdimensions of self-control such as volatile temper, impulsiveness (immediate gratification), and the tendency to seek thrills or to take risks.

The concept of *subjective powerlessness/external locus of control* has been studied less frequent as risk factor for offending and problematic youth group involvement in comparison to the other aforementioned domains. External locus of control or subjective powerlessness is the belief that one's fate is determined by chance or outside forces that are beyond one's personal control. This strategy can sometimes be healthy when one is to cope with disease or unexpected loss. Subjective powerlessness/external locus of control is the experienced gap between what one would like to do and what one feels capable of doing. It is synonymous for a strong belief in fate. In early gang theories, belief in faith or external locus of control is a key characteristic of street corner gang members. Miller (1958) attempted to explain the behavior of members of adolescent street corner groups in lower-class communities as being based around six focal concerns: trouble, toughness, smartness, excitement, fate, and autonomy. Albert Cohen (1955) also pointed to external locus of control as a characteristic of street corner groups. The concept of external lack of control seems to be overlooked or neglected in contemporary theories of offending. We found only one study that related lack of personal control to offending (Ross & Mirowsky, 1987). We will go into the role of external control when we discuss the theory of alienation as outlined by Ross and Mirowsky.

The risk factors that we will study in the lifestyle domain are *peer delinquency* and *problematic youth group involvement*. Exposure to delinquent peers is one of the strongest predictors of individual differences in offending (Thornberry et al., 1993). In many studies, exposure to peer delinquency is also a significant predictor of problematic youth group involvement, but results from more complex analyses in recent studies are less supportive, suggesting a more dynamic relationship. By comparison, youth group involvement is observed to be a significant predictor of individual offending, even when controlling for exposure to peer delinquency or the number of delinquent peers (Battin et al., 1998; Thornberry et al., 2003). It is exactly this finding that has led scholars to conclude that youth groups are distinctly different from just associating or socializing with delinquent peers. Associations with aggressive peers during early adolescence is a predictor of youth group involvement, but this "may reflect a selection effect, i.e. a general tendency for antisocial youths to associate with one another" (Lahey et al., 1999: 274). Indeed, some studies have observed that delinquent youths affiliate with one another beginning in childhood, and this pattern of deviant friendships continues through adolescence. 'Associates' of youth group members are also part and parcel of a community's youth group problem because they are more actively involved in delinquency than nongang youth (Curry, Decker & Egley, 2002). *Unstructured routines and substance use* are indicators of a *risky lifestyle* that exposes youths to what can be referred to as criminogenic moral settings (Wikström & Butterworth, 2006). Empirical studies have found a lot of support for the relationship between unstructured routines and substance use as risk factors for delinquency and offending.

Finally, we discuss a number of characteristics that refer to the *social position of the individual (and the family)* that have been associated with problematic youth group involvement and offending (although mainly in studies that use official statistics on offending): the *family disadvantage* and *family structure*. Traditionally these characteristics have been related to offending from the basic idea that indicators of disadvantage produces goal blockage, an idea that has failed to find a lot of empirical evidence. Among the structural factors exhibiting a significant relationship with problematic youth group involvement are family poverty, family disruption (not living with both biological parents), and low levels of parental education. However, these characteristics are often found to influence family process variables and thus are typically only indirectly associated with youth group involvement. Among the social process variables associated with youth group involvement are poor family management, including low parental monitoring and attachment to and involvement with the child; attitudes and child maltreatment. Sibling antisocial behavior is also a significant predictor. The youth group serves as a sanctuary for troubled youth from troubled families (Fleisher, 1998). For girls, in particular, finding relief from a violent family life and personal protection are major motivations for gang joining (Miller, 2001). It has been suggested that youth groups provide street socialization where the family leaves off or when social service agencies fail youths (Vigil & Hanley, 2002). *Family structure* has been brought in relation to offending and problematic youth group involvement for another reason, namely the idea that the growing up in a broken home, or split family, may have consequences for informal control, especially monitoring. However, the broken homes literature has also resulted in inconclusive results. Relative deprivation has been taken into account in the present study to enable us to find out whether objective social position risk factors and subjective satisfaction with one's objective situations interact in the explanation of adolescent offending and problematic youth group involvement. School failure (i.e. redoing a school year) is an individual characteristic that has been identified in studies of offending and problematic youth group involvement and has been named in early subcultural theories (Cohen, 1955). Low achievement in school and having learning problems are among the strongest school-related predictors of youth group involvement. Related risk factors include low academic aspirations, low school attachment, low attachment to teachers, low parent expectations for their children's schooling, low commitment to school, and general academic failure, at least as early as the elementary school-level in the Seattle study (Hill et al., 1999). These deficits may be amplified by labeling processes by teachers (Esbensen & Huizinga, 1993) and corresponding low parent expectations (Thornberry et al., 2003). Early youth gang theories have hypothesized a relationship between different measures of school failure and gang membership: school failure was supposed to be of paramount importance in Cohen's subcultural theory, mainly because it leads to status frustration among lower-strata youth and reaction formation. In the present study, we use a proxy of school failure, namely having repeated a class, but we will come to that later. School failure may be of relevance because it may produce additional strains in Agnew's general strain theory. School failure may also be of importance for offending because school failure is strongly related to IQ, a risk factor in itself for offending and problematic youth group involvement. Herrnstein and Wilson summarize this argument when they state that "a child who chronically loses standing in the competition of the classroom may feel justified in settling the score outside, by violence, theft and other forms of deviant illegality" (Herrnstein & Wilson, 1985: 148).

A cumulative effect (in general or by domains) means that the greater the numbers of risk factors that are present, the greater the likelihood of problematic youth group involvement. Hill et al. (1999) found in the Seattle study that children with seven or more risk factor indicators were 13 times more likely to join a gang than children with none or only one risk factor indicator. Nevertheless, only 32% of these youths joined a gang. The presence of risk factors in multiple developmental domains appears to increase the likelihood of problematic youth group involvement even more. Rochester researchers investigated the predictive power of risk factors in multiple domains (Thornberry et al., 2003), finding that a majority (61%) of the boys and 40% of the girls who scored above the median in seven risk factor domains (area characteristics, family sociodemographic characteristics, parent-child relations, school, peers, individual characteristics, and early delinquency) were gang members. In contrast, approximately one-third of the boys and one-fifth of the girls who experienced risk in four to six domains joined a gang. This has led to the argumentation that the prevention of problematic youth group involvement not only should address multiple risk factors, they also need to address a number of risk factors in multiple developmental domains. While many studies pay attention to the additive study of risk factors, we will also pay attention the cumulative and independent effects of risk factors in different domains (such as the accumulation of micro-place conditions and social bonds).

5   SEX AND ETHNICITY AS RISK FACTORS

Sex and race/ethnic backgrounds are covariates of offending and problematic youth group involvement that have been consistently reported in delinquency studies. It is well established that males and immigrants commit more offenses and more serious offenses than females and natives in bivariate and multivariate studies of both self-reported and officially recorded delinquency (e.g. Loeber & Stouthamer-Loeber, 2008). One important task facing criminology is that of developing theoretical frameworks in which both gender and immigrant background differences may be understood and explained. Most traditional theories focus explicitly on male delinquency and several researchers have concluded that more research is needed to test the gender gap in these theories (e.g. Bruinsma & Lissenberg, 1987; Liu & Kaplan, 1999; Svensson, 2003). Immigrant background is often a more complex definable concept than the biological sex of respondents. Ethnic differences are often defined as racial differences in U.S. studies (Sampson & Laub, 2003), while this is usually not the case in Europe. European studies often differentiate between first-, second-, and third-generation immigrant background. However, regardless of the definition used, immigrant background is a rather stable bivariate correlate of delinquency in general, while its strength largely depends on the data used for analysis.

It is however often ignored that gender and immigrant background, although they may be important structural conditions setting the stage for behavioral outcomes, never can be seen as real causes, as neither gender nor immigrant background can bring about behavioral effects. Structural background variables may be important because they place adolescents in different social segments of the population, each of which generates different restrictions for living standards (Skarðhamar, 2005). It is not uncommon in criminological inquiries for attributes like sex and race to be included as predictors. In the case of sex, some researchers even (wrongly) claim that it is the best predictor of criminal involvement. The problem with the common practice of including attributes as predictors is that they may confuse our search for causes and explanation of crime, and even more worryingly, they may make people think that the fact, for example, that someone is male or black could be a cause of his or her crime involvement.

We argue that it is important to distinguish between causes and correlates and instead focus on the general nature of an assumption of how causal processes affect offending. Precisely because prediction does not equal causation, it is of utter importance for criminologists to make a strong argumentation that a factor possesses the ability to initiate a causal process that produces the effect (e.g. being involved in a problematic youth group or commit a crime). This does not mean that characteristics or experiences that are relevant for the study of offending and problematic youth group involvement might not be more prevalent among males (such as, for example, poor ability to exercise self-control), but the point is that it is these characteristics or experiences that we should focus on as causal factors in our explanations rather than the fact that the person is male (see Wikström, 2007 for a thorough discussion). Wikström (2007) has argued that if one can measure the real causative factors, there is no need to include attributes (such as sex and immigrant background) that at best are *markers* of the real causative factors among the predictors in our studies.

A key issue that is often misunderstood by practitioners is that while the correlation between attributes and crime involvement can be explained, attributes cannot explain why people commit acts of crime (Wikström, 2007). It is possible to explain why males commit more crimes overall than females, or why certain ethnic groups are more or less involved in gang violence, but an individual's sex or ethnic status cannot explain why he or she participates in gang crime. In the former case, differences in crime involvement by attribute is the outcome (what is to be explained) while, in the latter case, attributes are (mistakenly) treated as potential causes of an individual's gang participation (what explains).

This very important insight has significant implications for how research should be conducted (e.g. what research questions can be posed) and what conclusions for policy and practice can be drawn from research findings about correlations between attributes, gang involvement, and offending. The fact that a person's sex or race to some degree may predict his or her crime involvement does not mean that his or her sex or race causes his or her crime involvement. At best, it can be a marker of causes associated with a particular attribute. Wikström (2007) therefore suggests to avoid including attributes as causes in models that aim to explain what causes people's crime involvement and pathways in crime. The exception to the rule is risk prediction, when the aim is predicting (future) recidivism based on a number of static and dynamic predictors. In the present study, we are not interested in prediction, rather in statements derived from theories. Statistics are just a tool to answer the hypotheses derived from the integrative perspective that is developed here.

Studies that analyze differential effects of risk factors by gender or by immigrant background are not common (Esbensen et al., 2010). Differences in the relationship between risk factors and problematic youth group involvement still tend to attract some scholars in guiding their empirical work. With regard to sex differences, Wong (2012) found little evidence for the hypothesis that different causal processes are at work among males and females. It would be strange to see that causal mechanisms operate in a different way for males and females and for ethnic minorities and majorities. However, it may be possible that there exist differences in males and females and ethnic majorities and minorities in risk factors in the aforementioned domains. The present study is based on a very large sample of urban youths, allowing to split up the total sample by gender and immigrant background. While previous work has been conducted from the perspective of sex and ethnic differences, only very few studies have gone beyond that and studied the relationship between risk factors from different theories in subsamples that are made up of specific combinations of gender and ethnic background. The present study will contribute to the literature by additionally testing the general integrative theoretical framework of problematic youth group involvement and offending in combined subsamples of sex and immigrant background.

| # Origins of the integrative conditions-controls-exposure model

1   Introduction

Theories serve as a guideline for explaining whatever that is in need of an explanation. It is not difficult to imagine that there are many ways through which one might consider and choose to become involved in a problematic youth group, just like there are many ways that may affect a person's perception of seeing an act of crime as a viable action alternative., e.g. social bonds (Hirschi, 1969; Sampson & Laub, 2003), moral beliefs (Hirschi, 1969; Akers, 2008), preferences (Opp, 2009), opportunities and unstructured routines (Osgood et al., 1996; Felson & Boba, 2010), and developmental and ecological social influences, e.g. neighborhoods, schools, and peers. All these factors may shape a person's beliefs and preferences that give rise to offending as action and participating in a problematic youth group as what we call a situated choice. A situated choice is the result of processes of deliberation in a given context.

2   Some notes on theoretical integration

Rather than seeking some single or dominant model of a problematic youth group participation, which focuses exclusively on structural mechanisms (at the meso- or macro-level) or which focuses exclusively on social psychological mechanisms (at the micro-level), criminologists increasingly acknowledge in their empirical work that there are multiple pathways, and the standard practice in contemporary crime causation studies is to theorize and build integrative models by specifying why and how individual differences in offending and problematic youth group involvement can be best explained. Early examples are the attempt of Johnson (1979) to develop an integrated approach and the classic book on integration by Messner et al. (1989). There is significant practical utility to an integrative approach. Taking this further, we can state that theory can – and arguably should – provide a foundation for systematic inquiry and even for the development of conceptual models, though the relevance of theory is sometimes underdeveloped or explicitly rejected in applied social/behavioral research, as social psychologist Kurt Lewin (1951) famously said, "There is nothing so practical as a good theory." Mutatis mutandis we argue "nothing is so practical as a good integrative theory." Regarding traditional theories of offending, Elliott

(1985) argued more than two decades ago that theoretical reliance on a single explanatory variable to explain criminal behavior has resulted in theories that are capable of explaining only a small percentage of the variance in crime or criminal behavior. Nowadays, that statement seems equally true for problematic youth group involvement. The suggestion of Elliott (1985) that something needs to be done in order to adequately account for the complexity of such behavior resulted in widespread attempt of theoretical integration for the better or the worse: criminologists were not all in favor of attempts to integrate theories that strictly spoken came from totally different backgrounds with conflicting assumptions about the nature of crime and human nature. Thornberry (1989) defined theoretical integration as the act of combining two or more sets of logically interrelated propositions into one larger set of interrelated propositions, in order to provide a more comprehensive explanation of a particular phenomenon. Theoretical integration generally serves three purposes. The first purpose of integration is theory reduction. Some scholars have made a clear point that scientific progress has been made virtually impossible because there are too many theories competing against one another in an effort to essentially explain the same type of behavior with a series of concepts that actually can be differentially interpreted from different angles (Bernard, 1990). Consequently, an abundance of theories impedes their development by diffusing research attention (Bernard & Snipes, 1996). Theory reduction is proposed as one way to decrease the number of criminological theories, allowing scholars to focus on a smaller number of promising theories. The second goal is to increase explained variance. Most theories are capable of explaining, at best, about 20% of variance in criminal behavior (Elliott, 1985). This is more like a practical and anti-theoretical way of dealing with restrictions in theories. The third purpose of theoretical integration is theory development through the clarification and expansion of existing propositions and theoretical concepts. Alternatives to theoretical integration include theory competition and theoretical elaboration. Theoretical competition involves the intellectual competition of two theories against each other in an empirical test that determines which theory's variables have the most explanatory power (Hirschi, 1979). The results of theory competition, however, are seldom definitive. Messner et al. (1989) have correctly observed that it is rarely the case that one theory is discarded in favor of another. The principle of falsification, which was meant to be applied when testing theories and comparing results of tests of theories, has never been successfully applied in criminology. Theoretical competition has merely led to an endless set of tests, sometimes favoring theory A and many other times favoring theory B. That approach has been largely criticized in contemporary criminology. The endless testing of theories in absence of falsification and the discarding of one approach have generated an enormous body of research that yields inconclusive results. Theoretical elaboration has been considered more fruitful. It involves the expansion of a current theory with the end goal of building a more comprehensive and more well-developed theoretical model than was proposed by the original theorist (Thornberry, 1989). This is typically done through the clarification of original propositions, as well as the addition of new concepts that may or may not be 'borrowed' from existing theories or disciplines. Conceptually integrated theories are theories that combine the concepts and central propositions from two or more prior existing theories into a new single set of integrated concepts and propositions. Integration can take several forms. Conceptual integration involves an absorption strategy, arguing that concepts from one theory have the same meaning as concepts from another theory and combining them into a common language and set of concepts. Conceptual integration faces enormous challenges, given the state of the field and conceptual anarchy that exists. By that we mean that scholars have used countless scales and measures to measure concepts and use these concepts in tests of theories. The results of the conceptual 'anarchy' is of course that it increases the difficulty to evaluate our integrated theories. End-to-end integration, if conducted by following a clear and concise deductive logic, entails the sound integration of mechanisms that play a role in differing theories so that the dependent variables of some theories become the independent variables of the integrated theory (Hirschi, 1979). A prime example of this type of integration is Thornberry's (2003) Interactional Theory. Thornberry integrates control and learning theories in an end-to-end fashion. Thornberry (2003) speculates that individuals with weak social bonds have a higher likelihood of associating with delinquent peers, which increases their probability of engaging in delinquent behavior. The commitment of acts of crime, in turn, further weakens attachments to social bonds and increases associations with delinquent peers in a reciprocal manner.

The present study, an attempt to develop and test an integrative model, has undergone a lot of influence of some of the major theoretical perspectives on adolescent offending and street gang research. The selection of risk factors that were measured in this study was by and large guided by different theories and empirical research. In the following paragraphs, we therefore outline the major theoretical perspectives that we are indebted to. In evaluating traditional criminological paradigms and frameworks (families of theories) for possible inclusion in an integrated-interactive theory of crime, two criteria were considered: empirical corroboration and facility of integration. Theoretical frameworks accruing a reasonable amount of empirical support and demonstrating amenability to conceptual end-to-end theoretical integration were selected for inclusion in the integrated theoretical framework outlined in this book. The following theoretical traditions were judged to contain important concepts and testable hypotheses while also sharing a possibility of conceptual and end-to-end integration: social disorganization tradition, social bonding theories, alienation theory (locus of control theory), routine activities lifestyle theory, and self-control theory. From these theoretical frameworks, the key concepts that are eligible for integration were selected. Conceptual integration was considered to be a valuable approach, contrary to the vision that was predominant in the 20th century, namely that "separate and unequal was better" as argued by Hirschi (1979). The major drawback against conceptual integration was the argument that all theories had different visions on human nature and social order. However, Agnew (2011) has successfully demonstrated that none of these classic visions on human nature and social order were correct. Thus, one major drawback against integration has thereby been overcome. We will dig into that at the end of this chapter, when the major theories have been presented.

Basically our theoretical integration results in a model that rests on some semi-general mechanisms. It is an attempt to understand the role of proximate and distal factors in the explanation of offending and participation in a problematic youth group as situated choice, i.e. how social and ecological influences affect our control beliefs and moral beliefs about the legitimacy of offending and how moral beliefs, individual capacities, situational exposure, and their interactions as proximate predictors of action affect both problematic youth group involvement and offending. In other words, the present chapter presents theories that have developed concepts which we have borrowed to construct our integrative framework.

As we have tentatively labeled our integrative framework, a 'conditions-controls-exposure theory,' we need to pay attention to different theories that served as inspiration for the conceptual building blocks of the theory. Conditions referred in this study to micro-place conditions and conditions are seen as external social contexts, which, through developmental exposure, may affect individuals' control mechanisms (hence, controls) such as social integration, control orientation, moral belief systems, and the capacity to withstand temptation and provocations. Exposure refers to situational exposure and is supposed to moderate the effects of personal controls.

3   FROM SOCIAL DISORGANIZATION TO COLLECTIVE EFFICACY
     AND FROM NEIGHBORHOODS TO MICRO-PLACES

3.1   *Shaw and McKay and the theory of neighborhood disorganization*

The core of the traditional argument is that social organization of a local community will become conceptually disconnected from the individual organization of a person. Social disorganization is in this way ultimately equated to poor self-regulation of a community: a reduction in the influence of existing conventional rules on behavior rules on the individual group members (Pauwels, Hardyns & van de Velde, 2010). Social disorganization in urban neighborhoods is studied as a social phenomenon (an aggregate). Weak self-regulation in a local community is considered as the context within which the overriding of prevailing rules becomes possible for the individual. In contemporary urbanized societies, characterized by strong mobility and in which neighborhoods have lost their influence as a means of socialization, the urban sociology of the Chicago School may be seen by some as naive. However, this is not the case when viewed in the context of the time in which it was written. Urban sociology arose during a period in which thinking about causes of offending was dominated by individual biological and psychological positivism. In the light of the dominant concept of that time, this theoretical approach must have been innovative and revitalizing. The idea that crime and juvenile delinquency were characterized by a spatial dimension was articulated clearly in the criminological writings of Shaw and McKay (1942). Shaw and his colleague were the first to empirically illustrate the zonal model developed by Park, Burgess and Mckenzie (1984 [1925]) based on data that referred to the places where delinquents lived. They worked with several large fact files in which the coding and analysis, in an era before computers and statistical processing packages, were not straightforward at all. The strong empirical documentation of neighborhood characteristics that correlated with the geographical concentration of places of residence of delinquent young people allowed the authors to make an abstraction of these characteristics. From this, they were able to formulate a rudimentary theoretical declaration. Neighborhood characteristics in this category were numerous but could be broadly divided into three groups. The first set falls under the general heading of economic deprivation or disadvantage. The proportion of low rents, low incomes, the degree of unemployment in the neighborhood, the number of households receiving government support, and so on all showed a strong and stable consistency with the geographical concentration of delinquent young people. The second set refers to the geographical concentration of minority groups: the presence of different groups of immigrants. The third group of characteristics referred to population turn-over (or the absence of residential stability) in the neighborhood. Not only were these correlations stable throughout the period of their research, the findings were also replicated in other cities. Shaw and McKay argued that social control ceased to function in disorganized areas. Traditional norms and standards of the conventional community would weaken and disappear. Resistance on the part of the community to delinquent and criminal behavior therefore decreased, and offending was tolerated and became accepted and approved. In the conflict of values between different groups, the traditional cultural and social controls of the larger society tend to break down. This, together with the fact that there are few constructive forces at work to re-establish a conventional order, makes for continued social disorganization. In this state of social disorganization, community resistance is low. Delinquent and criminal patterns arise and are transmitted socially just as any other cultural and social pattern is transmitted (Shaw et al., 1929).

3.2   *Frederick M. Thrasher and gangland*

Frederick M. Thrasher was one of Robert Park and Ernest Burgess's students in the 1920s Sociology Department of the University of Chicago. His dissertation, *The Gang: A Study of 1313 Gangs in Chicago* (Thrasher, 1927), became the seminal work on the topic, and theoretically his group process perspective remains influential today. Thrasher concluded that:

> gangland represents a geographically and socially interstitial area in the city. Probably the most significant concept of the study is the term interstitial – that is, pertaining to spaces that intervene between one thing and another. In nature foreign matter tends to collect and cake

in every crack, crevice, and cranny – interstices. There are also fissures and breaks in the structure of social organization. The gang may be regarded as an interstitial region in the layout of the city. (1927: 20)

For Thrasher, gangs originate from the spontaneous effort of boys to create a society for themselves where none adequate to their needs exist (Thrasher, 1927). What boys get out of such associations that they do not get otherwise under the conditions that adult society imposes is the thrill of participation in common interests, more especially in corporate actions, such as in hunting, capture, conflict, flight, and escape (Thrasher, 1927). According to Thrasher, by being in a gang, a young man acquires a personality and name for himself; he acquires a sort of status and has a role to play. The gang not only defines for the adolescent his position in society but it becomes the framework of personal identification. The gang becomes the youth's reference group, that is the group from which he obtains his main values, beliefs, and goals.

Thrasher's findings suggested that gangs are geographically and socially interstitial, occurring in city slums wrought with physical deterioration, transiency, and disorganization. Gangs also exist along economic and ecological boundaries as well as political frontiers. Thrasher contended that the basic causal variable for the structural issues and gang formation is weak controls. Social disorganization – as defined by Thrasher, the weakness or breakdown of established institutions – destroys the basis of social order. The gang is thus seen as an elementary form of social organization that is reactionary to the order that has become nonexistent as a result of social breakdown. Boys form gangs to enable a chaotic environment by establishing order and structure. Bursik and Grasmick (1993: 119) argue that Thrasher's work is "the most important processual definition for understanding the relationship between neighborhood dynamics and gang behaviour." Thrasher's work established that gangs were more likely to arise in poor and unstable neighborhoods, thereby contributing to the scholarly dialogue concerning the nature of controls and, most importantly, social disorganization. Thrasher's work exemplifies three linked strengths and weaknesses of the Chicago School: (1) an ecological but ethnically neutral theory; (2) a lack of analysis of girls' lives; and (3) an understanding of male gang and delinquent behavior based in spontaneity, social disorganization, and group processes, thereby ignoring intervening individual mechanisms. These issues will be dealt with in the empirical chapters.

3.3   *Criticisms of the original model of neighborhood disorganization*

There are many reasons why the ecological tradition has been declining in importance. The rise and the success of other theories are only partially responsible. Theoretical and methodological shortcomings within the tradition itself have played a larger role. These shortcomings have already been described exhaustively elsewhere (Bursik, 1988;

Pauwels, 2007). To understand the contemporary evolution of social disorganization theory (as a theory of offending), it is important to understand these criticisms.

The traditional Chicago School placed too much emphasis on urban development as a result of natural processes (e.g. the struggle for space). The role of political decision making in creating unequal spatial patterns of deprivation is ignored because of this. The possible role of the historical, cultural, and political context was thus overlooked. It became apparent later that this was a mistake because the impact of urban planning and housing on the ecological spacing of crime has been repeatedly highlighted in literature (Wikström, 1991).

The extent to which borders of census tracts coincided with local communities was hardly explored. The increased levels of mobility apparent since the World War II have further undermined the links between administrative neighborhood borders and actual communities. Living, working, and free time are less likely to be organized within the geographical setting of the residential neighborhood.

Early ecological studies were not sufficiently skeptical about using official statistical instruments. In other words, Shaw et al. (1929) made the observation that the crime statistics of the police and judicial agencies could not account entirely for delinquent behavior, but also noted that there is no evidence to show that children living in areas of low rates are involved in such serious behavioral difficulties as larceny and burglary. The research of Shaw and McKay led to some important conceptual misunderstandings concerning the dependent variable in ecological research. This conceptual misunderstanding arose partly from the imprudence of the authors, who themselves stated that ecological studies should start with an analysis of the places where 'delinquency occurs.' It is therefore not surprising that in the first empirical tests of the findings of Shaw and McKay, it seemed that the concepts 'place of residence' and 'place of commission' were mutually interchangeable. The seeds for future confusion were irrevocably sown (Morris, 1957). Delinquents' places of residence and the places where they committed their offences are not mutually interchangeable.

An additional and important substantive problem is that Shaw and McKay's explanation has a contextual character. Readers of the traditional ecological theory would be hard pressed to consider neighborhoods as anything other than hotbeds where delinquency slumbered as a consequence of social disorganization. This contextual interpretation was premature and cannot be assumed from the empirical results of aggregated research. This criticism is the consequence of the ecological fallacy, a problem described by Robinson for the first time (1950), that had fascinated scientists for many years. That is why ecological studies were unpopular in the 1950s. Ecological fallacies occur when a relationship found at the aggregate level is assumed to exist at an individual level. In his methodological contribution, Robinson (1950) explicitly referred to the working method of Shaw and McKay. Contextual fallacies occur when ecological correlations are mistaken for contextual effects, for instance, when the ecological correlation between the offender rate and economic deprivation at the neighborhood level is interpreted as follows: deprivation in the neighborhood influences the behavior of the young people who live there. The findings of Shaw and McKay also suggested ecological stability. In their analyses of official figures, high-crime areas appeared to show a relatively stable character over a long period. According to Morris (1957), this finding frees the way for ecological determinism. Processes of suburbanization that were already going on during the 1950s have shown a more dynamic picture of the geographical distribution of offenders (Bursik, 1988). More-over, the traditional studies failed to empirically distinguish social disorganization from the structural characteristics that caused disorganization (Bursik, 1988). From the analysis of the empirical studies of the ecological school, we can indeed see that social disorganization was considered to be an unmeasured mechanism rather than a real variable. The ecological school was also criticized because of the pejorative over-tone of the disorganization concept.

3.4   Collective Efficacy Theory

The theory of community collective efficacy has been of major influence on the eco-logical study of crime-related outcomes. Sampson and his colleagues highlighted the relationships between dimensions of social capital that were already mentioned in systemic models of cohesion and crime that were built in the 1980s and 1990s (e.g. Bursik & Grasmick, 1993). Collective efficacy theory stresses the importance of a com-munity being able to solve its commonly identified problems, such as crime and safety.

Collective efficacy is defined as "social cohesion among neighbors combined with their willingness to intervene on behalf of the common good" (Sampson, Rauden-bush & Earls, 1997). This definition makes the link between 'social trust' on the one hand and 'informal social control' on the other more clear. Social and mutual trust in a community is an essential condition for fostering informal social control in the community and thus the willingness to intervene for the common good. Therefore, communities characterised by a strong collective efficacy are resistant to high local concentrations of crime, victimization, and fear of crime. In this view, local collec-tive efficacy is important because it avoids collectively defined problems and it guarantees security in the community (Sampson, Morenoff & Gannon-Rowley, 2002). Collective efficacy can be seen as the 'local social eyes' in the community. Thus, it should be clear that the collective efficacy theory cannot be applied to all types of crime; instead it focuses mainly on visible property crime and violent crime. As the unstructured activities of youths in a problematic youth group may also be visible in the local communities, the collective efficacy approach may as well be applicable to the phenomenon. Collective efficacy is an important self-reg-ulating mechanism in the community and consists of collective supervision of the behavior of children and adolescents and intergenerational closure, the ties between different generations (for children and adults that live in the same area). Generally, collective efficacy is based on shared norms and values in the commu-nity (Sampson, Raudenbush & Earls, 1997; Sampson, Morenoff & Gannon-Rowley, 2002).

3.5   *Problems in neighborhood contextual research*

While the aggregate association between community organizational processes and offender rates and gang activities has been observed many times in the US, Canada, and European cities (Bruinsma et al., 2013; Papachristos & Kirk, 2006; Papachristos, Hureau & Braga, 2013; Pizarro & McGloin, 2006), the unique contribution of neighborhoods (as units with nonoverlapping boundaries) in the explanation of individual differences in offending has always been part of a strong debate, with opponents and believers. As early as 1986, Simcha-Fagan and Schwartz argued that neighborhoods do not contribute much to the explanation of individual differences in adolescent offending (Simcha-Fagan & Schwartz, 1986). To be more precise, their neighborhood measure explained 1% in the variance of offending. While that finding predates the age of multilevel modeling, it was highly suggestive for the fact that neighborhoods, conceived as (large) geographical areas (although homogeneous) do not add much to the explanation of individual differences of offending. This debate has also taken place in European studies, where some scholars have concluded that neighborhood contextual effects on adolescent offending are lacking (e.g. Pauwels, Hardyns & van de Velde, 2010). Only very few European studies report the existence of contextual effects of neighborhood level variables on self-reported delinquency (Oberwittler, 2004). An overview of studies of contextual effect can be found in Oberwittler, Rabold and Baier (2013). Coincident with the advent of multilevel modeling, the neighborhood effects literature has conceptualized neighborhoods using various definitions, namely geographically nonoverlapping units thathave become smaller over time (Hipp & Boesen, 2013).

There are several theoretical reasons and methodological reasons for the explanation of the inconsistency of research findings on neighborhood contextual effects: (1) aggregation bias; (2) neglecting the role of perception; and (3) failure to distinguish between short-term and long-term effects. We submit that these problems stimulated the development of new traditions that focused on micro-places and their situational characteristics and neighborhood studies that started to distinguish between developmental influences in the life course and short-term situational influences. As no study of behavior can be complete without taking into account context, we delve into the criticism of neighborhood research.

(1)   *Aggregation bias*

Most studies of contextual effects on offending, be it multilevel studies that use hierarchical regression models or less-advanced regression methods, rely predominantly on areas of residence and use neighborhood clusters as ecological units of analysis. The boundaries used for neighborhoods must be relevant to the mechanism being tested. However, data constraints mean that theoretical considerations of this nature are often abandoned or even violated. Dietz (2002) observed that neighborhood definitions have typically not been formed by thoughtful theoretical considerations. Rather neighborhood delineation has been defined by the limitations of an available data sets. Scholars that study neighborhood effects have pointed to the importance of beneficial organizational features of neighborhoods, such as collective efficacy and negative community routines such as unsupervised youth (Bruinsma et al., 2013), as a formal of 'negative community capital' (see also Kubrin & Weitzer, 2003). Attention should also be paid to cultural characteristics (Kirk & Papachristos, 2011), which were largely ignored due to the one-sided interpretation of cultural perspectives by Kornhauser in his seminal work in (1979). Wikström and Sampson (2003) have argued that neighborhood may probably more fruitfully be studied as *activity fields*. An *activity field* is a part of the environment that can be perceived by our senses (Wikström et al., 2012). Large geographical areas can, even if they are rather homogeneous, therefore not automatically be considered as part of the individual's activity field, which may be one of the most important explanations for the fact that characteristics of large ecological units of analysis such as neighborhood clusters do not yield any substantial effect on offending. Some ecological units of analysis are simply too heterogeneous to be potential candidates for serving as a behavioral setting. Sizes and boundaries have thus become key issues in contemporary studies of neighborhood effects. Scholars who study the geographical distribution of crime have recently also provided strong empirical evidence for the fact that there exists tremendous variation between neighborhood clusters and even between census tracts (Jean, 2008; Weisburd, Groff & Yang, 2014).

(2)   The role of perception and observation of events in micro-places
Another reason for the inconsistency of findings of neighborhood effects on offending is the fact that neighborhoods and their characteristics are perceived differently by individuals who are exposed to these behavioral settings (Sampson, 2012). To fully understand any neighborhood effect, it may be fruitful to consider an additional link between objective characteristics of small ecological settings and what could be called 'psychological neighborhoods.' Neighborhoods may foster a sense of community, just like they may provoke offending by sending signals that 'nobody cares' in the neighborhood. But, in order of a neighborhood to be conceived, it must be small enough to be caught by our sense. This way of theorizing and analyzing does not conflict with collective efficacy theory and theories of neighborhood structure, disorder, and problematic youth group involvement.

Just like social geographers argue that people develop their own sense of place, we are convinced that an adolescent (or any individual) develops his or her sense of informal control, collective efficacy, and disorder. Neighborhood inhabitants and users can thus see such a small geographic unit, a street corner, as either a place of safety or a risk to be avoided. A potential offender can see the street corner as an attractive place of criminal opportunity. Youth gangs find street corners attractive as they are used to mark as their turf by spraying graffiti on walls and leaving signs of who is really in control of the area. It is vital to understand the individual's perceptions, because that very perception is required for neighborhood disorder to be able to act as a neighborhood incentive, while neighborhood social control can be viewed as a neighborhood disincentive, at least with regard to the processes of decision making. The famous theorem of Thomas that stated "if men define situations as real, they are real in their consequences" is often used by scholars in the relativist perspective in criminology to argue that objective conditions do not exist and therefore deserve not to be studied in criminology. We follow the viewpoint that individual differences in perceptions may be explained from both subjective and objective conditions. Objective conditions in neighborhoods (from 'bricks and walls' to informal control and neighborhood routines) must be perceived in order to exhibit an effect on the behavior and attitudes of individuals. Therefore, it is plausible to expect that living in an area that signals that offending goes unpunished or is tolerated by the inhabitants may provide individuals (both inhabitants as neighborhood users, bystanders who just walk by) with some *observational* and *interactional learning mechanisms*. The observational and interactional learning principles are therefore crucial to understand the link between neighborhoods and individual differences in attitudes and actions. Without exposure to external conditions, a personal 'sense of local community' or sense of informal control cannot be acquired. Thus, if the individual fails to perceive his or her environment as being high or low in informal social control, then that individual cannot not be affected by it. To adapt one's norm to the situation is to adapt one's norm to the situation that can be perceived.

The weak effects of neighborhood characteristics in multilevel studies that use a nonoverlapping geographical definition of place on individual-level offending are therefore probably not only caused by differences in size and boundaries, and differences in exposure, but may just as well be caused by the fact that not all individuals living in a neighborhood perceive it similarly. In the context of social disorganization theory and broken windows theory, the assertion is that the individual's perceptions of informal social control are vital al in explaining whether one is deterred from offending (Wikström & Treiber, 2007). Lynam et al. (1993; 2000) and Jones and Lynam (2009) therefore coined the expression that neighborhoods are partially in the *eye of the beholder*. There exists a vast and still nascent amount of studies that have empirically demonstrated that objective neighborhood characteristics are related to individual-level perceptions of informal control and cohesion). Thus, how individuals perceive informal control and observe disorder in the direct ecological environment, the street-corner or street-segment, is an important factor to consider, especially in the absence of more valid definitions and boundaries of small ecological settings. If micro-place social processes such as the presence of unsupervised youth groups or disorder are to act as an additional learning mechanism that stimulates offending, the individual must perceive it as being high (Moffitt, 1993; Wikström & Treiber, 2007). The use of perceptions of neighborhood conditions (that refer the area in the immediate surroundings of the individual) is fully consistent with Hipp and Boeser's redefinition of neighborhoods as egohoods, geographically overlapping small areas in which the individual is seen as the 'centroid' of the area. According to Hipp and Boeser (2013), this reconceptualization of neighborhoods with blurred boundaries is more in line with the fuzzy reality of the concept of neighborhoods. In the present study, we will therefore explicitly study the relationship between neighborhood measures that consist of micro-places' units and observational and perceptual neighborhood measures of small areas in which the inhabitant is seen as the centroid.

(3)   *The failure to distinguish between short-term situational effects and long-term developmental effects*

Another possible explanation for the inconsistency of results of neighborhood contextual effects is the failure of correctly distinguishing between short-term and long-term enduring effects (Wikström & Sampson, 2003). One of the key arguments of Wikström and Sampson (2003) was that neighborhood effect may differ depending on the explanandum. They argued for differentiating between crime (action) and criminality (the development of propensity) when assessing the effects of neighborhood characteristics on individual outcomes. Indeed, on the one hand, one may hypothesize that there exist short-term situational effects of neighborhood characteristics on spontaneous (or momentary) induced offending, while on the other hand, one may hypothesize long-term development of criminality. Neighborhood characteristics that may trigger adolescents to actually commit an act of crime at a specific moment in time and space, without necessarily influencing an individual's propensity to offend over the longer term, are referred to as *opportunity structures*. These characteristics are related to absence of control. Long-term neighborhood influences on adolescent development are resources (e.g. an on-going lack of neighborhood resources or enduring poverty and disadvantage) together with neighborhood rules, the overwhelming presence of normative beliefs supportive of rule breaking.

This is an important theoretical issue that needs to be taken up in both theorizing about the causes offending and empirical studies of causes of offending and problematic youth group involvement. We argue that integrative theories of street gang involvement should definitely benefit from such an effort to separate models that explain criminality and models that explain acts of crime. In contemporary criminology, there are very few examples that explicitly distinguish these two aspects. One example is situational action theory that distinguishes between direct causes of crime as action and causes of the development of the propensity toward offending (Wikström et al., 2012). We will dig deeper into that theory later. This distinction is currently not made in theories of street gang involvement.

Based on the aforementioned criticisms of the disorganization approach, the present study builds on the reconceptualized micro-place definition and will make use of observational measures of disorder and crime and perceptions of social trust and informal control (the two key dimensions of collective efficacy).

4   FROM SUBJECTIVE ALIENATION THEORY TO LOCUS OF CONTROL
           THEORY

4.1   Alienation theory

Control orientation is an important concept in our general model. Therefore, it is of importance to understand its historical foundations. During the 1950s, sociological theories were characterized by a strong interest in the consequences of normlessness and subjective powerlessness. Powerlessness and normlessness have been technically defined by Srole (1956) and Seeman (1959). Seeman (1959: 787) was the first to provide a definition for the concept of powerlessness as "the expectancy or probability held by the individual that his own behaviour cannot determine the occurrence of the outcomes, or reinforcements, he seeks." A person suffers from alienation in the form of 'powerlessness' when he or she is conscious of the gap between what one would like to do and what he or she feels capable of doing. Powerlessness has become synonymous for an external locus of control, a belief in fate and destiny and a belief one has no grip over one's own future.

According to Seeman (1959), powerlessness is a generalized expectation that outcomes of situations are determined by forces external to one's self, such as powerful others, luck, fate, or chance. Instrumentalism, its opposite, is a generalized expectation that outcomes are contingent on one's own behavior. In the former, the individual believes that he or she is powerless and is at the mercy of the environment, while in the latter, the individual believes that he or she can master, control, or effectively alter the environment. Subjective powerlessness often represents an awareness of objective conditions. By continually experiencing failure in the face of effort, a person learns that his or her efforts are unlikely to affect the outcomes of situations (Pauwels & Svensson, 2014). Sociological theory indicates that the prolonged and regular experience of failure and lack of control are inherent in objective conditions of powerlessness.

Normlessness (or what Durkheim referred to as anomie) relates to a situation in which the social norms regulating individual conduct have broken down or are no longer effective as rules for behavior. This aspect refers to the inability to identify with the dominant values of society or, rather, with what are perceived to be the dominant values of society. Seeman (1959: 788) adds that this aspect can manifest in a particularly negative manner:

> The anomic situation [...] may be defined as one in which there is a high expectancy that socially unapproved behaviours are required to achieve given goals.

Normlessness is the sense that social norms regulating individual conduct have broken down or are no longer effective as rules for behavior. Normlessness is a relative term in two senses. First, it refers to a weakening of socially approved norms. Everyone is guided by rules of behavior, but the rules may not be socially approved.

Second, normlessness refers to one end of a continuum that ranges from low to high levels of normlessness. Even people at the high end of the continuum are not absolutely normless.

The concepts of powerlessness and normlessness are especially relevant for theories of problematic youth group involvement. Seeman's concept of alienation can be traced down to both Marx and Durkheim. The element of subjective powerlessness was a key element in Marxist interpretations of the negative consequences of capitalism on the satisfaction of the working class, while the concept of alienation was described by Durkheim as anomie or a state of relative normlessness or a state of norm erosion. A norm is an expectation of how people will behave, and it takes the form of a rule that is socially rather than formally enforced. Anomie describes the breakdown of the moral bond between an individual and the community: this may lead to a rejection of conformity. Perceived normlessness brings about the effect that societal norms become less binding for individuals. Individuals thus lose the sense of what is right and wrong. Subjective alienation theory argues that crime is caused by alienation. The concept of alienation is found in many theoretical perspectives. This is of no surprise as both Marx and Durkheim have studied alienation as a source of crime and social unrest in societies. Subjective powerlessness is a major component of alienation and deals with an individual's expectation of reinforcements (outcomes) following behavior. Subjective powerlessness flourished in the 1960s as a theory to explain individual differences in involvement in left-wing political extremism (Gurr, 1970), a theoretical concept more or less vanished in the 1980s. One possible explanation is the fact that it was picked up in other disciplines under another name and thus started to live on in different disciplines.

4.2   Locus of control theory

Basing his ideas on social learning theories and on the sociological writings of Seeman and others in the alienation tradition, Rotter (1966) suggested that the probability that one engages in a behavior to satisfy a need rests on the expectation of a specific reinforcement and the value attributed to this reinforcement. He also pointed out that this expectation depends much more on the person's attitude toward the situation than on the situation itself. This attitude is shaped by people's perceptions of their capacities to influence the outcome of the desired reinforcement. Some people believe that they can have a certain impact on the course of events, whereas others believe they have little ability to influence situations:

> When a reinforcement is perceived by the subject as following some action of his own but not being entirely contingent upon his action, then, in our culture, it is typically perceived as the result of luck, chance, fate, as under the control of powerful others, or as unpredictable because of the great complexity of the forces surrounding him. When an individual interprets the event in this way, we have labeled this a belief in external control [emphasis

added]. If the person perceives that the event is contingent upon his own behavior or his own relatively permanent characteristics, we have termed this a belief in internal control. (Rotter, 1966: 1)

To have an internal locus of control indicates that an individual believes that the reinforcements in his or her life are contingent upon his own behavior. On the other hand, to have an external locus of control indicates that an individual believes that the reinforcements in his or her life are a consequence of luck, fate, or chance (Rotter, 1966). Research has shown that locus of control is an important aspect of self-development, and the perception of personal control is a result of feeling competent in controlling one's environment (Lefcourt, 1982; Rotter, 1966). The sense of external control is vital to consider as it relates very much to many maladjusted behaviors such as neuroticism and extreme forms of social withdrawal and introversion. Locus of control theory has been applied to a vast array of subjects and on very different population. For example, it has been studied among adults in the work-place setting, while it has been studied among adolescents in the school context. Within the framework of this book, it is important to discuss the role of external locus of control in the context of problematic youth group involvement and adolescent offending. During adolescence, the need to master an increasingly complex environment is especially strong and urgent (Lau & Leung, 1990). This requires an internal locus of control. But what if an individual does not develop an internal locus of control and rather beliefs that he or she is not able to make a difference? Lau and Leung (1990) posed this question a couple of decades ago and have argued that it is important to empirically study the negative effects of an external locus of control. It has been difficult to find many studies of juvenile delinquency that have empirically assessed the role of locus of control. Surprisingly, the concept regularly pops up in theoretical essays without being empirically tested and integrated in existing theories.

Previous results on the relation between delinquency and locus of control are inconsistent. Some have found delinquents to be more external in control (Duke & Fenhagen, 1975; Ransford, 1968); others have found no relation (Jurkovic, 1980; Parrot & Strongman, 1984). Past research on delinquency and locus of control relied primarily on the vague comparison of delinquents and nondelinquents. The groupings of delinquents (usually institutionalized subjects) and nondelinquents are often very arbitrary and may be confounded by unknown factors. Therefore, these previous studies might have made the difference in locus of control less clear or stable. Studies show that children's relations with parents and school have significant effects on their development of locus of control (Hess & Holloway, 1984). In particular, parents perceived as warm and supportive are conducive to children's development of internal control (see Lefcourt, 1982). The relationship between school-child relations and locus of control is however unknown as very little research is done in this area. Past studies tend to focus on locus of control as an antecedent of academic achievement.

4.3   *Locus of control in Mirowsky and Ross' conditions-cognitions-emotions model*

In contemporary sociology, Mirowsky and Ross' conditions-cognitions-emotions theory (CCE theory) can be seen as a contemporary application of Seeman's alienation
theory of distrust. Ross and Mirowsky have contributed to the development of a conditions-cognitions-emotions theory and have extensively tested their model with
regard to normlessness, mistrust, and distress in a series of empirical studies.
Mirowsky and Ross' conditions-cognitions-emotions model combines insights from
the social disorganization/collective efficacy tradition with Seeman's alienation concept and relates subjective powerlessness and normlessness to neighborhood social
climate to a series of cognitions (perceptions of powerlessness and normlessness),
which in turn seemed to have consequences for distress and distrust. According to
Ross and Mirowsky (2009), observations and experiences of disorder may promote
distressing views of human nature, social relations, and individuals' own ability to
navigate life unharmed. Following the CCE theory, subjective alienation (i.e. both
subjective powerlessness and normlessness) is the cognitive link between the perceived social environment and psychological distress (Mirowsky & Ross, 2003).
Mirowsky and Ross (2003) argue that neighborhood disorder may promote the view
that people are by nature rapacious, untrustworthy, and unhelpful, and that life is
essentially chaotic, alienating, and beyond personal control. Similar arguments about
the detrimental effects of neighborhood conditions can also be found in Broken Windows Theory). Neighborhood disorder signals the potential for harm. Graffiti, noise,
vandalism, dirty streets, public drinking, and run-down buildings are cues. These
cues tell residents about themselves and the world they live in. They indicate the
breakdown of social control and order. Through exposure to threatening social conditions residents may learn that they are relatively powerless and that normlessness
reigns, coming to mistrust others and remaining isolated from them.

4.4   *The importance of alienation for theories of problematic youth group involvement*

Guided by both classic ideas from prominent scholars in gang research and the more
recent work by Ross and Mirowsky that linked observations of disorganization and
disorder to negative outcomes, especially moral beliefs about rule breaking, we argue
for a renewed attention towards external locus of control as a mechanism that may
increase the likelihood of moral beliefs that are supportive of rule breaking and
thus play an important role as one of the causes of the causes of offending and problematic youth group participation. External locus of control may form a the cognitive
bridge between a threatening social environment and normlessness. Adolescents
who have developed an external locus of control believe in fate and are more likely
not to withstand from delinquent peers and are vulnerable to join youth groups as
they have the feeling that they have nothing to lose by joining a problematic youth
group. In the present study, we bring in external locus of control as an overlooked
intermediate mechanism by which micro-place conditions promote moral beliefs that

are supportive of rule breaking in the study of problematic youth group involvement and offending. The concept of alienation can also be interpreted as a source of perceived strain (Agnew, 2011).

The interest of early gang theorists in the phenomenon of external locus of control can probably be explained by the popularity of studies of perceived powerlessness in sociological studies of the 1950s; after all, Walter Miller and Albert Cohen developed their theories in the same time frame.

In our study we are influenced by alienation theorists in two ways: first, by borrowing the concept of external locus of control (subjective powerlessness) and by borrowing the concept of legal cynicism. Sampson and Bartusch (1998: 782) conceived of legal cynicism as a component of anomie, "a state of normlessness in which the rules of the dominant society (and hence the legal system) are no longer binding in a community." While the concept of legal cynicism has been used in a number of studies (Emery, Jolley & Wu, 2011; Kirk & Matsueda, 2011; Reisig, Wolfe & Holtfreter, 2011) the concept of legal cynicism has not been widely used in studies of problematic youth group involvement, with some exceptions (Pauwels & Svensson, 2013; 2014). Finally, Mark Colvin's theory of coercive control should be mentioned (Colvin, 2000). Colvin's theory is a theory of why individuals become persistent offenders and he stresses a key variable in his theory: coercive control. While we acknowledge the importance of controls, we do not want to stress coercive control as the only key mechanism or the most important variable to use his own words (Colvin, 2000). We have no objection to the study of coercion, we merely state that coercive control theory places too much attention on coercive control, while social bonds as such are equally important (Colvin, Cullen & Van der Ven, 2002). However, Colvin argued that coercive control leads to the installation of an external locus of control. In his theory coercive control affects control orientation and additionally affects low self-control.

Sociological locus of control theories have their roots in (neo-)positivistic ideas on human nature: the individual is causally affected by structural constraints in the environment, but there is no deterministic interpretation of causation. Although a general theory of causation is lacking, it is fair to argue that the probabilistic theory of causation is used.

5   SOCIAL BONDING THEORIES

Social bonding theories gained prominence during the 1960s. It was during this period that Travis Hirschi (1969) put forth his version of control theory, a theory built upon existing concepts of social control as developed by early theorists such as Albert Reiss (1951), who developed the idea of personal and social controls as key explanatory concepts in the explanation of conformity and compliance. Hirschi built upon the ideas of early control theorists and developed a very popular version of control theory: his theory of the social bond: in his social control theory, Hirschi asserts that ties to family, school, and other aspects of society serve to diminish one's propensity for deviant behavior. As such, social control theory posits that crime occurs when such bonds are weakened or are not well established. Control theorists argue that without such bonds, crime is an inevitable outcome. Unlike older positivist theories that seek to explain why people engage in deviant behavior, control theories take the opposite approach, questioning why people refrain from offending. Control theorists have generally assumed that the motivation for engagement in criminality is a constant for all individuals within society, avoided only by those who dispose of social ties to conventional society. While we do not support the idea that only controls are variable and motivation is not, we argue that control theory plays an important role in integrative theories of offending and problematic youth group involvement, as a lack of controls pave the way for the development of unstructured routines and lifestyles and unstructured socializing with deviant peers. Weak social bonds may also have consequences for the installation of negative learned belies, such as an external locus of control. *Attachment* is the emotional component of the social bond. *Commitment* is 'the rational component in conformity' (Hirschi, 1969: 20). Not only can one be committed to conformity by what he or she has obtained, but the hope of acquiring goods through conventional means can reinforce one's commitment to social bonds (Hirschi, 1969: 186).[1] *Involvement* in conventional activities comprises the component of involvement in structured routines. Hirschi believed that involvement in conventional activities would keep someone's time too occupied to allow him the indulgence of crime. The thinking that "idle hands are the devil's workshop" is the reason Hirschi (1969: 187) stated "the child playing ping-pong, swimming in the community pool, or doing his homework is not committing delinquent acts." *Belief* refers to the existence of a common value system within the society whose norms are being violated (Hirschi, 1969: 197). A person is more likely to conform to social norms when he believes in them. Hirschi recognized that individuals vary in the depth and magnitude of their belief, and this variation is reliant upon the degree of attachment to systems representing the beliefs in question. An overview of empirical studies by Kempf (1993) has revealed that the relationships between the elements of the social bond and self-reported delinquency are rather stable. There is one exception to that rule: involvement did not seem to correlate well with delinquency measures. The relationships between the elements of the bonds were never really discussed in the original contribution made by Hirschi. That should not surprise us, as the book predates the age of statistical modeling and thinking in terms of causes, mediators, and effects. Sequential effects of social bonds have been demonstrated earlier (Johnson, 1979).

While Hirschi's control theory may be seen as an overly simplistic vision on offending, somewhat biased toward minor rule breaking, the idea that strong bonds to conventional society restrain individuals from offending, has been reconceived and revived through the linking of the social bonding theory with the social capital perspective (Sampson & Laub, 2003). In their influential book *Crime in the Making*, Sampson and Laub (2003) draw on the life course framework and present their

---

1. Note that Hirschi makes use of the learning mechanism of reinforcement in this statement.

age-graded theory of informal social control, which emphasizes the importance of social bonds *at all ages*. Sampson and Laub's work has been especially of importance to this study as it provided us with the generalized idea that social bonds should be interpreted as social capital and that social capital is being accumulated in the life course in a number of domains. Therefore we have re-interpreted social bonds as a cumulative fact, something that is acquired through the life course. For children it encompasses attachment in the family, parental monitoring and the school social bond. According to their theory, the strength of a person's bonds to social institutions (e.g. family, school, work) will predict criminal involvement over the entire life course. Thus, social bonds in adulthood stemming from life events will explain persistence in or desistance from crime despite early childhood propensities or antisocial behavior (Laub & Sampson, 2003). Contemporary theories, such as Cullen's social support theory (Cullen, 1994), are still much influenced by the old control theories. Cullen stressed the importance of both promotive ties and parental monitoring.

In the present study, we are influenced by the social control perspective in the following way: we borrow the concept of informal controls that have an external source, i.e. social bonds as social ties in different life domains that affect the young adolescent (integration in school, commitment to school, parental attachment, and parental monitoring), but we do not borrow the concept of internal social controls, i.e. Hirschi's rather general and vague concept of beliefs, but instead we borrowed Sampson and Bartusch's concept of legal cynicism, as we have explained in the previous paragraph. We submit that this concept is conceptually compatible with the tradition of control theorists. Indeed, both Sampson and Bartusch and early control theorists such as Hirschi are intellectually influenced by Durkheim. Additionally, control theories start from the idea that humans have agency, and thus not from deterministic visions, as was the case in positivism (Laub & Sampson, 2003). Although a general theory of causation is lacking, it is fair to argue that soft determinism (probability theory) is used in Hirschi's theory, while Laub and Sampson (1993) combine actor causation (i.e. the idea that actors bring about things by doing things) with a probabilistic theory of causation.

6   SOCIAL (COGNITIVE) LEARNING THEORY

In our integrative framework, we occasionally draw on learning mechanisms, e.g. the development of moral beliefs, but we also draw on learning mechanisms to point to the effects of being exposed to criminogenic conditions in micro-places.[2] We mostly refer to cognitive processes. Social environments can only be related to individual differences in involvement in a problematic youth group if they encourage or discourage joining a problematic youth group but also because social learning is the cognitive mechanism by which individuals learn about conditions in neighborhoods. In

---

2.   Subcultural theories are also often used to explain actions of all kinds of criminal groups. However, it is unclear whether these theories should be treated separately, as both theories use learning mechanisms.

criminological theory, Akers' social learning theory has been the version of learning theories that has been referred to mostly.

The four components of Akers' (1991) influential social learning theory of crime were differential association, differential reinforcement/punishment, definitions of behaviors, and imitation. Most recently, Akers (1998) has integrated certain social structural considerations and a person's differential position in the social structure into his social learning theory of crime. Akers' main contribution was the introduction of reinforcement in Sutherlands' model of differential association.

- *Differential reinforcement* refers to the balance of actual or anticipated rewards and costs, both social and nonsocial, that follow a behavior. This notion of reinforcement is important for understanding the role of symbolic social rewards and punishments as consequences of being in a problematic youth group and for understanding habituation, i.e. the development of habitual offending. However, the most important reinforcements tend to be social (resulting from interactions with peer groups and family members). In later reformulations of the theory, Akers explicitly refers to the principle of the matching law (Herrnstein, 1991) and the generalized matching law. According to the matching law, choice (i.e. relative preference) may be understood by studying the relative rates of reinforcement associated with each option. In this conceptual framework, relatively dense sources of reinforcement will feature relatively higher rates of behavior.[3]
- *Imitation* refers to engagement in behavior after observing similar behavior in others who have meaning to the individual.
- *Definitions* refer to one's own attitudes that define the commission of an act of crime as right or wrong, justified or unjustified. Definitions are the cognitive part of the learning process and refer to the content, i.e. deviant or extremist-prone scripts (e.g. the acceptance of violence to reach goals).
- *Differential association* refers to direct and indirect exposure, via associations with others, to patterns of behavior as well as to patterns of norms and values.

Of great importance to our understanding of social learning is the social cognitive learning theory of Bandura, who played an important role in the transformation of behaviorist learning theories toward integrative learning theories that included

---

3. The Matching Law Theory is based on the principle of hyperbolic discounting and the principle of melioration. Hyperbolic discounting means that given two similar rewards, humans show a preference for one that arrives sooner rather than later. Humans are said to discount the value of the later reward, by a factor that increases with the length of the delay. Melioration is a form of matching where the subject is constantly shifting its behavior from the poorer reinforcement schedule to the richer reinforcement schedule, until it is spending most of its time at the richest Variable Interval Schedule. According to rational choice theory, humans act in a manner that seeks to maximize the overall achievement of subjective utility. By contrast, melioration theory asserts that the driving force underlying decision making is not the attempt to maximize global utility but rather a process of continually shifting behavioral preferences towards alternatives with higher local rates of reward. Melioration theory relaxes some of the assumptions made in RCT-models (Sims et al., 2013).

cognitive elements. Bandura argued that learning involves the teaching of problematic styles of conduct, the lessening of restraints on violence, desensitization and habituation to violence, and the shaping of images of reality on which people base their actions. In his later work, Akers has incorporated elements of Bandura's theory.

6.1   *Some problems of cause and effect in social learning theories*

Learning theories are useful in so far as they explain how learning happens, and thus learning mechanisms actually play a role in most theories, even without acknowledging this. What is it then, that makes some scholars not to use learning theories as an overall theory, under which all other theories can be placed, as Akers suggested (Akers, 2008). One of the major criticisms of social learning theory pertains to its principal concept that increased associations with deviant peers increases the likelihood that an individual will adopt attitudes and values favorable to criminal conduct through the mechanism of rewards and punishments. The critique centers around the temporal ordering of the adoption of deviant attitudes and behaviors and the association with other deviant peers. Social learning theory is premised on the idea that it is association with others (family and friends) that contributes to the learning and subsequent acceptance of deviant behavior and problematic youth group involvement. It has instead been suggested that young people may develop these deviant attitudes and values without prior exposure to it and then seek out peers with similar attitudes and behaviors (Weerman, 2011). Gottfredson and Hirschi (1990) argued that an individual's propensity to crime is stable throughout the life course and it is the opportunities for crime that change. Thus, high propensity youths are not expected to have conventional friends. The problem is a causal one. That is, the cause of delinquency, from a critic's point of view, is not associations with deviant peers. Instead, delinquent behavior or attitudes favorable to it are established before group contact. From this perspective, individuals with low self-control seek out similar peers. Social learning theorists have responded to this criticism by stating that development of delinquent attitudes and behavior prior to association with deviant peers is not inconsistent with the theory because group associations still influence behavior (even if delinquency precedes the group membership) (Akers & Sellers, 2004). In addition, longitudinal research has shown that, in addition to the persistence of delinquency, peer group associations are related to the onset of delinquent behavior. Whether one likes social learning theory or not, it is hard not to notice that a significant number of tests of the social learning model has been conducted on substance use (Akers, 2008). which is probably more than other types of rule-breaking behavior subject to anticipated rewards, due to the chemical components in addiction.

6.2   *The problem of tautology*

Also, Akers' version of social learning theory has been accused of being tautological. Operant conditioning is based on the idea that reinforcement is anything that strengthens a response and that behavior is reinforced; therefore, the idea that behavior is strengthened by reinforcement is true by definition (Akers, 1998: 45). However, Akers (1998: 45) responds to this criticism by arguing that the principles of operant conditioning can be stated in a way that is not tautological. The tautology claim is not valid as (anticipated) rewards and punishments can be measured independent of offending and problematic youth group involvement.

6.3   *The narrow vision of human nature in social learning theories*

Another strong criticism, probably the strongest criticism, of Akers social learning theory is the narrow vision on human action as simple the result of (operant) learning processes, thereby ignoring the role of agency and choice-processes. In behaviorism, choice is regarded as the distribution of behavior to reinforcement alternatives. In this sense, a 'choice' is nothing more than the emission of a particular response instead of other responses. Every instance of operant responding represents the choice to engage in that given behavior at that moment in time, whether due to positive or negative reinforcement (Herrnstein, 1991). Given the provocative result of that humans are apparently no more rational than pigeons, a large number of empirical and theoretical studies have attempted to either disprove or further elucidate the role that melioration plays in human choice (Reed & Kaplan, 2011). Indeed, because of the introduction of mechanisms of operant conditioning, social learning theory has been criticized for being too deterministic, in large contrast to Sutherland's Differential Association Theory. Learning theories have relevance for theories of offending and problematic youth group involvement in several ways: in examining the role of anticipated rewards and punishments in a given context or environment and in explaining the development of moral norms and moral emotions.

We submit that learning processes are not incompatible with choice processes, and if one ignores the extreme positions once taken by strict behaviorism, one recognizes the importance of social learning mechanisms. It cannot be ignored that there are similarities between learning theories and rational choice theories: learning theories explain behavior in terms of rewards and punishments, while rational choice/opportunity/deterrence theorists explain behavior using costs and benefits. We will discuss our position more in detail when we present the integrative model.

7   SELF-CONTROL THEORY AND ITS EVOLUTION

7.1   *The concept of low self-control in Gottfredson and Hirschi's theory*

Another influential theory that has partially shaped our model is self-control theory. As in 'Causes of Delinquency,' 'A General Theory of Crime' purports that other theories pay insufficient attention to the facts about the nature of crime, which are that all crimes are committed in the pursuit of pleasure/self-interest and avoidance of pain.

As with Hirschi's former theory of criminality, self-control theory has had an enormous influence on the field of crime causation theories, although the theory has flaws and has seriously been criticized. The authors provide their own definition of crime as, *acts of force or fraud undertaken in pursuit of self-interest* (Gottfredson & Hirschi, 1990: 15). The authors purport that their concept of self-control is not deterministic (Gottfredson & Hirschi, 1990: 87). They also note that people involved with crime also engage in analogous behaviors that provide short-term gratification (Gottfredson & Hirschi, 1990: 91). Smoking, drinking, gambling, irresponsible sex, and speeding in cars are examples of risky analogous behaviors that may be manifest in criminal individuals who seek instant gratification. As originally conceptualized by Gottfredson and Hirschi (1990: 232), low self-control is argued to be *the individual-level cause of crime*, i.e. low self-control is theorized to be the primary explanation for criminal behavior. Individuals with low self-control are more vulnerable to temptations of the moment because they fail to consider the negative or painful consequences of their acts and therefore are more likely to engage in acts of crime. The effects of all other theoretical constructs to explain offending are spurious when self-control is entered into the equation. While several scholars have issued critiques of the theory (for an overview see Lilly, Cullen & Ball, 2014), it also attained considerable empirical support. Low self-control has consistently been found to be a modest to strong correlate of both crime and analogous acts of deviant behavior.

7.2   *The reformulation of the general theory of crime*

Gottfredson and Hirschi have reconceptualized the general theory to address some of the criticisms, such as the unclear relationship between the social bond and self-control. Hirschi (1969) redefined self-control as "the tendency to consider the full range of potential costs of a particular act" (p. 543). This definition departs from the original conceptualization in which self-control was termed to be "the tendency to avoid acts whose long-term costs exceed their momentary advantages" (Gottfredson & Hirschi, 1990: 3). The redefined self-control encompasses both short- and long-term costs, instead of merely long-term costs of deviant acts. Self-control, as redefined by Hirschi (2004), seems more akin to rational choice theories, as decisions are made within the moment of an act and less attuned to persistent trait-like, individual differences. Hirschi (2004) further notes that self-control is a "set of inhibitions one carries with one wherever one happens to go" (Hirschi, 2004: 543). These inhibitions are linked to social bonds (attachments, commitments, involvements, and beliefs) that Hirschi (1969) identified as part of social control theory. The more 'bonded' an individual is or the more inhibitions a person has, the higher level of self-control the person exhibits. The reconceptualization lies primarily in the development of the challenging thought that self-control may be *causally prior to the social bonds*. Traits representing propensity to engage in delinquency suggest that the causal effect of social bonds on offending may merely be artificial: low self-control, as a propensity established early in life, may have negative effects on the development of social bonds later in life. The person with low self-control may be less likely to form and maintain stable friendships, more likely to associate with others who lack self-control and who are similarly delinquent, less able to adjust to the demands of school, and less likely to place high value on conventional ties.

7.3   *Some criticisms*

The relationship between self-control and crime
Scholars have been critical of the general theory of crime's circular argument regarding the relationship between low self-control and crime (Siegel & McCormick, 2006). As Akers and Sellers (2004) suggest, the general theory of crime seems to suggest that "propensity toward crime and low self-control appear to be one and the same" (Akers & Sellers, 2004: 125). As such, the theory suggests that low self-control and criminality are always linked. *Nature versus nurture?*
Ineffective child-rearing (inconsistent and harsh parenting) is proposed as the major cause of low self-control according Gottfredson and Hirschi. Self-control is established early in life as a consequence of the socialization process. Gottfredson and Hirschi stress the importance of parental supervision, monitoring, discipline, and affection. Thus, the authors follow a pure socialization hypothesis, which states that

> when socialization is effective, norms will be internalized and, as a consequence, an individual's conscience, or superego, will be well developed. If the level of attachment to parents is poor, however, it is hypothesized that the internalization of norms and the development of conscience will be adversely affected. (Svensson, 2004: 479)

Some theorists have argued that there is strong evidence that self-control and its development are biologically informed (Beaver, Ratchford & Ferguson, 2009; Boisvert et al., 2012; Vazsonyi & Huang, 2010; Wikström & Treiber, 2007).
These scholars have challenged the idea that social bonds and parenting mechanisms do not add anything to the explanation of self-control if genetic characteristics are taken into account. This is a provocative thought. If the genetic hypothesis is correct, then the relationship between self-control and social bonds has been modeled wrongly in most criminological inquiries. Empirical evidence has however been presented for both hypotheses: self-control → social control and social control → self-control. However, only a minority of studies presented empirical documentation for the mediating effect of social bonds on the relationship between low self-control and offending (Longshore et al., 2005). This may of course be due to the fact that scholars have not tested alternative models as the socialization hypothesis by Gottfredson and Hirschi was very influential. Longshore et al. (2005) correctly underscore the importance of further exploring the causal link between self-control and social bonds by pointing to fact that self-control, as a trait established early in life, exerts any influence on delinquency over the life span. However, we take a neutral position and assume that self-control is the result of the interaction between neurological and

environmental characteristics. Piquero, Jennings and Farrington (2009) have provided evidence that self-control is malleable, More importantly, using longitudinal data, Vaszonyi and Huang (2010) show that there are cross-lagged effects of socialization mechanisms (parenting) on self-control using three-wave panel data and thereby controlling for previous levels of self-control.

Moderation effects
Most studies have looked into the direct effects of self-control and thereby ignored interactive or moderator effects. The existence of moderator effects has been remarked earlier. Agnew (2011) has argued that the effects of strains may be moderated by self-control, i.e. that strains have a particularly strong effect in low self-control youths. Wright et al. (2001) found that delinquent peer association promoted crime most strongly among those with low self-control (i.e. a social amplification effect). Empirical studies of the general theory of crime have generally tested the relationship between social bonds and delinquency and have found empirical support for a mediating effect of low self-control in the relation between social bonds and delinquency. The capacity to exercise self-control has also been found to interact with moral beliefs: a comparative study in three countries has shown that morality is stronger related to offending than low self-control (Svensson, Pauwels & Weerman, 2010).
In line with contemporary research, we find it useful to distinguish between the capacity to exercise self-control (the capacity to withstand temptations and provocations) and the actual exercising of self-control (Wikström & Treiber, 2007). However, in the present study we use a measure of the capacity to exercise self-control.

8   The lifestyle/exposure model of offending

Finally, our integrated framework draws heavily on the lifestyle/exposure model that provides the situational element in the explanation of problematic youth group involvement. In fact, the Routine Activities Theory of General Deviance (Osgood et al., 1996) served as the basis of the situational model of problematic youth group involvement and offending. We briefly touch upon the historical roots of the lifestyle model. The integrated lifestyle exposure theory (Hindelang et al., 1978) has been originally developed to explain why the distribution of victimization is unequal and varies by background characteristics. According to the theory, individuals are differentially involved in leisure activities, vocational activities, and professional activities due to their different backgrounds. Such background characteristics that refer to age, race, income, marital status bring about differences in role expectations (what to expect in life) and constraints (what can be achieved given a certain structural reference). Individuals are restricted by their backgrounds in realizing or making possible achievements. Individuals react and thus adapt differentially to the structural conditions they are part of. Such adaptations bring about observable differences in lifestyles. In this classic model lifestyle is seen as an indicator of one's daily routines.

The original theory focused on vocational, professional and leisure related activities. Such activities set the stage for exposure to offending in at-risk situations. Differences in lifestyles cause individuals to be differentially exposed to the environmental settings they encounter. E.g. adolescents who have unstructured routines and spend a lot of their time on streets, in absence of parental or social control are more likely to encounter offenders, as also offenders spend a significant part of their leisure time in these settings. Furthermore, differences in lifestyles lead to different associations with (significant) others. For example, adolescent that hang around on the streets are far more likely to get in contact with crime-prone individuals.

The classical lifestyle model has some weak and strong points. One strong point is the fact that lifestyles are seen as an indicator of exposure to environmental settings in which crime is more likely to occur. Lifestyles are thus seen as one situational concept that contributes to our understanding of victimization. One weak point is that the model is rather vague in how lifestyles are developed and how individual differences in lifestyles are brought about. The classical model overemphasized structural and cultural differences, thereby ignoring the role of individual characteristics, such as an individual's level of propensity to offend. Lifestyles were originally considered of importance as a causal mechanism in the explanation of victimization, while more some recent studies actually suggest that lifestyles are of much more importance in explaining individual differences in offending (Wikström & Butterworth, 2006). Riley (1987) was among the first to document that delinquent behavior is associated with the amount of time spent in groups of young people. One found that the amount of time in social activities with peers (like talking, dating, and partying, but also talking on the phone) as well as the amount of time 'just hanging out' (either alone or with peers) was associated with delinquent behavior. Research also supports the situational nature of crime and how certain 'risky behaviors' increase the likelihood of encountering violent situations. By putting oneself in a risky environment or disorganized neighborhood, youth increase their likelihood of criminal involvement. Engaging in 'risky behaviors' (i.e. alcohol and drug consumption, being out at night, gang involvement, associating with delinquent peers, dating) increases proximity and exposure to violence and increases the likelihood that youth will find themselves in situations where they become perpetrators or victims of violence (Nofziger & Kurtz, 2005; Pauwels & Svensson, 2013). According to Chapple and Hope (2003), low levels of self-control, along with exposure to criminal opportunities and criminogenic situations, are associated with engaging in dating and gang violence, as these youth have a tendency to put themselves in 'risky situations' where they are more likely to be involved in violent encounters. Wikström and Butterworth (2006) also found a strong association between delinquency and the time with peers in public and semi-public places: outside home, in city centers or shopping malls and additionally the reported a strong association between substance use and offending. In fact, previous studies seem to show that lifestyles and unstructured routines are far better able to explain individual differences of self-reported offending than self-reported victimization (Vynckier & Pauwels, 2010; Pauwels & Svensson, 2013). The lifestyle model has undergone change since its development. The concept of lifestyles has been fine-tuned, new measures of lifestyles have been developed that go beyond background variables as proxies and the role of lifestyles has been expanded and incorporated into theories of offending. It has especially been integrated with social control theories, since social bonds have been demonstrated to be important buffers against the development of a 'risky lifestyle' (Hawdon, 1996; Pauwels & Svensson, 2013).

Some criticisms on the lifestyle models
Lifestyle models have traditionally started from a pure rational choice perspective, i.e. they sought to explain delinquency as a consequences of choice made in risky settings. Lifestyle models have traditionally used the classical point of view on human nature and social order. This means that lifestyle theories have traditionally studied behavior from the standpoint of the homo economicus, the individual that performs a cost-benefits analysis. While individuals to a certain degree have agency, i.e. are able to pick between action alternatives, the classical image of the homo economicus has been criticized a lot. Typical of rational choice models, few attention has been paid to the origins of the propensities that may lead to an increased likelihood of offending, or problematic youth group participation. This is a strong rationale to integrate lifestyle theories with propensity theories. Indeed, lifestyle theories generally paid little attention to the development of a risky lifestyle. Self-control theory has argued that the relationship between lifestyles and offending (or between lifestyles and victimization) is spurious and a consequence of low self-control. Lifestyle models have generally not paid much attention to interaction effects. Risky lifestyles do not seem to affect every adolescent in a similar way. Previously, a strong interaction effect has been established between a risky lifestyle and deviant moral beliefs (Pauwels, 2012) and between lifestyle and an overall measure of crime propensity (Svensson & Pauwels, 2010).

9   SITUATIONAL ACTION THEORY AND THE EXPLANATION
OF PROBLEMATIC YOUTH GROUP PARTICIPATION?

We draw heavily on situational action theory (SAT), one of the most recent developed integrative theories. SAT grew out of the criticisms that Wikström has addressed towards the study of the causes of offending. As we found these ideas to be provocative, we found it appealing to apply some of these ideas to the study of problematic youth group involvement. While Wikström's theory was not developed to explain individual differences in problematic youth group participation, we felt that many propositions of the theory should also be applicable to the study of problematic youth group participation, due to its strong historical link with lifestyle theories and control theories. Thus, we detected a gap in the gang literature and try to fill this gap by applying many challenging ideas that are put forward in SAT to the study of problematic youth group involvement. Wikström argued that many separate theories have been unclear to fully address: what crime is (to clearly define what it is the theory aims to explain), what it is that moves people to engage in crime (i.e. to present an adequate action theory), how personal and environmental factors interact in moving people to engage in crime (to properly integrate key insights from personal and environmental explanatory approaches), the role of the broader social conditions and individual development/life-histories (to analyze their influence not as causes but as causes of the causes).

In adapting a general framework of action-oriented theory, Wikström argues that actions of individuals should be seen as a consequence of the behavioral options that actors have and the actual processes of deliberation that they make. Those behavioral options are not chosen in a vacuum, they are a consequence of the interaction between moral attitudes and the social environments to which actors belong.[4] Because of its incorporation of situational elements, one may be inclined to think that SAT takes similar assumptions of RCT models that have been used in criminology. However, that is not the case. SAT differs from Cornish & Clarke's rational choice (RCT) model. The main propositions of Cornish and Clarke's (2008) version of RCT are that people's action decisions, including their decisions to commit acts of crime, are purposeful, intended to obtain a desired outcome, primarily of hedonistic benefit to the actor; freely chosen based on a utilitarian hierarchy of preferences, and rational, involving at least some calculation of expected cost and benefits with the aim of maximizing the utility of both the desired ends and the chosen means. In Cornish and Clarke's version of RCT, committing crimes is the results of a two-step process of criminal decision making – involvement decisions through which a person rationally decides he or she would commit a crime given the right conditions, and event decisions through which a person rationally decides the conditions are right to commit an act of crime and how to go about doing so (Cornish & Clarke, 2008).

SAT merely assumes a reasonable actor and takes a slightly different approach to the study of the situation. In SAT it is stressed that decision-making is different from what RCT assumes. People first decide on which alternatives they consider and then, only if one sees crime as alternative, one can choose to act in a given context. The concept of deliberation refers to the judgment of situations (Wikström, 2004). The capability to act upon an environment in a purposeful (that does not necessarily imply a rational way) way is what is called agency in SAT. Individual characteristics and characteristics of social settings can act as direct or indirect causes of actions that are undertaken, but only if they influence the perception of action alternatives and processes of decision-making. In short, the situation is the interaction between the environment and the individual. As a theory of offending, it is easy to recognize elements that have been present (although not in exactly the same way) in the above mentioned theories,. As the above mentioned theories also have been applied to the study of problematic youth group

---

4. Wikström (2004) attributes theoretical stagnation due to the lack of the use of general action frameworks in criminology. Within sociology and economy, action theories have been around for a long time and have successfully guided research into the causes and causes of the causes of different types of social and economic action. We will say more about the potential use of action theories in the next chapter.

involvement, it is a valid idea to incorporate ideas developed in SAT to the study of problematic youth group involvement. From SAT, we borrow the idea that problematic youth group participation can ultimately be seen as the outcome of a perception-choice process, much in the same way like offending is a result of a perception-choice process.

SAT is an integrated model and as such we expect the framework to have merits in theorizing about problematic youth group participation, especially because there is an overlap in empirical research of problematic youth group involvement and adolescent offending, but also because one can assume that, to a certain extent, it will be possible to detect some common causes (of the causes of offending and problematic youth group participation).

The fundamental arguments of SAT are: *(1) that acts of crime are moral actions and therefore need to be explained as such; (2) that people engage in acts of crime because they come to see such acts as viable action alternatives and choose (habitually or deliberately) to carry them out.* If we apply these ideas to the joining of a problematic youth group, we get: *(1) problematic youth group participation is to be seen as moral action and need to be explained as such, and (2) people engage in problematic youth groups because they come to see the action (i.e. participation in crimes committed by the group) as viable alternatives and therefore they choose to participate.* As not all forms of activities that are executed by problematic youth groups are criminal, we can imagine that this statement may be considered provocative. We recognize this: individuals join gangs for different reasons or motives (Curry, Decker & Pyrooz, 2003). We merely point to the fact that this line of reasoning is applicable to the core 'gang-activities.'

SAT proposes that the convergence (in time and space) between a person's propensity (individual tendency to commit offenses) and exposure to settings initiates a perception-choice process, the outcome of which is an action (or inaction) that can be an offence. We apply this line of thinking to problematic youth group participation and submit that the outcome of this specific interaction may be the participation in activities of problematic youth groups. SAT explicitly states that the individual's propensity and exposure to criminogenic settings interact to determine whether an act of crime is committed. The two causally relevant elements of criminal propensity are low morality (individual moral rules) and a low ability to exercise self-control. Causally relevant characteristics of a criminogenic setting are the amount of time spent with friends unsupervised by adults in settings with poor collective efficacy, and exposure to peer delinquency (Wikström et al., 2012). According to SAT, two types of characteristics define the criminogenic potential of a setting: characteristics that define the moral context, i.e. a seducing physical environment (settings characterized by temptation and provocation), and the lack of norm-regulation (deterrent capacities).

Key principles of SAT

Two key principles in Situational Action Theory that specify the role of moral rules and controls in crime causation are the principle of moral correspondence and the principle of the conditional relevance of controls. *The principle of moral correspondence* states that if a person is motivated to commit an act of crime or to participate in the activities of a problematic youth group and there is a correspondence between his or her personal moral rules and the moral rules of the setting, he or she is likely to do commit the act or to participate in the activities of a problematic youth group if the corresponding moral rules encourage committing an act of crime or joining the activities of a problematic youth group, but unlikely to commit an act of crime or participate in a problematic youth group if the corresponding moral rules discourage committing the act of crime. The principle of moral correspondence has been tested on self-reported offending a number of times and with success (Svensson & Pauwels, 2010; Schils & Pauwels, 2014; Wikström & Svensson, 2008; Wikström et al., 2012).

The principle of the conditional relevance of controls applies in cases where a person is motivated to commit a crime but there is a discrepancy between the guidance by the personal moral rules and those rules of conduct that apply in a particular setting. In such cases controls become causally relevant. The two ideal typical situations are (i) when a person's moral rules discourage committing a crime, but the moral rules dominant in the setting encourage committing a crime, in which case whether the individual commits the crime hinges upon the ability to exercise self-control; and (ii) when a person's moral rules encourage committing a crime, but the moral rules dominant in the setting discourage committing a crime, in which case whether the individual commits the crime depends on the effectiveness of deterrence measures in the setting. The principle of the conditional effect of controls has only been partially tested a couple of times. Some studies have tested the interaction between moral beliefs and self-control (Svensson, Pauwels & Weerman, 2010; Pauwels, 2007). Other studies have found interactions between perceived risk of apprehension and propensity (Hirtenlehner, Pauwels & Mesko, 2014), other studies failed to replicate this interaction (Pauwels et al., 2011).

The causes of the causes

Structural factors like inequality, poverty, racial segregation, and poor social integration are not causes of crime, but are the 'causes of the causes of the causes of offending and problematic youth group involvement,' and should therefore be analyzed and studied as such. Technically, this means that they should be analyzed in regression models that do not have offending or problematic youth group involvement as dependent variables, but rather in models that have morality, low self-control, exposure to criminogenic settings as dependent variables. The same idea applies to aspects of people's life-histories (individuals' development of moral and cognitive skills, executive functions and experiences of life events). Central questions that concern the causes of the causes (of offending and problematic youth group involvement) are: why people have different crime propensities (i.e. moral beliefs and ability to exercise self-control), why settings differ in their criminogenic features (i.e. in moral rules in settings and norm enforcement) and, why some kinds of individuals are exposed to some kinds of settings. This idea is a further application of the idea of distinguishing between situational contexts and developmental contexts as argued by

Wikström and Sampson (2003). This idea is of course not new, but the theoretical rationale that is developed in SAT goes beyond the classic attempts to integrate theories without a clear argumentation of why integrated theories should distinguish between situational and developmental parts of the theory and without clearly framing the bridging functions between the developmental elements of the theory and the situational elements of the theory.

10   CONCLUSION

This chapter has been written especially to explain in depth the different theories that form the origins of the integrative conditions-controls-exposures model. At this point the reader may wonder whether it is a good idea to develop an integrated framework that builds on so many different traditions that all have a different background and different ideas on crime and social order. The different theories of crime causation made different assumptions about human nature and offenders. Therefore, it has been a popular idea for many years not to integrate theories who have different backgrounds and make different assumptions about human nature and societal order, use different conceptualizations of crime, etc.

Positivist theories such as strain theories viewed humans as social creatures, willing to cooperate rather than being selfish creatures. The general positivist theories stressed the fact that humans are somewhat determined because of factors outside the free will. This makes offenders inevitably different from nonoffenders. Control theories and rational choice theories (classicism) viewed offenders as nondifferent from law-abiding individuals, meaning that all individuals have a free will. One is considered to be guided by self-interest. Classicists and control theorists differ from positivists in their view and acceptance of the role of motivation versus control in the explanation of offending. Control theorists have been eager in stressing the role of control and while willing to recognize that people may differ in motivation to offend, control theorists usually considered these motivations as noncrucial in the explanation of offending. Positivists have stressed the importance of motivation, while also recognizing the importance of control. Finally learning theorists have been strong advocates of the blank slate principle, and have therefore even criticized for being too deterministic by relying on principles derived from behaviorism.

As Agnew (2011) has pointed out clearly in his evaluation of different theoretical frameworks that explain individual differences in offending, many of these assumptions that scholars have made in the past are only partially true. We are all born differently (in genetic terms), wired for learning, and ready to learn. It is untrue that the individual is a blank slate. It is untrue that individuals act like rational actors as the classical school thought. Therefore, these different theories need an updated view on human nature. Another possibility is to develop new integrative paradigms and research programs that are adjusted to contemporary insights on human nature and social order.

PROBLEMATIC YOUTH GROUP INVOLVEMENT
AS SITUATED ACTION: A META-THEORETICAL
FRAMEWORK

INTRODUCTION

Previously we have outlined a number of risk factors from influential theories that
have been used to explain individual differences and changes in offending and problematic youth group involvement. In a separate chapter, we explained the key ideas of
the leading theories that guided us to develop an integrated model. We argued that
these different theories sometimes had conflicting ideas of human nature and social
order. It was striking that none of the classic perspectives started from clear meta-theoretical ideas, such as an explicit theory of causation and a clear position on the level
of explanation (macro-micro or integrative). In this chapter, we propose a general
meta-theoretical framework that is useful for the development of theoretical models
of crime causation and problematic youth group participation. This framework will
serve as the foundation for the integrative explanatory model that is capable of both
explaining individual differences in offending and problematic youth group involvement. Theories are important as they often are used to guide ideas about how to pre-
vent youth from getting involved in a problematic youth group and how to restore the
regulatory capacity of neighborhoods and schools so that neighborhoods and the
youths who inhabit them become more resilient and learn to resist the influence that
problematic youth groups may have upon people. The general principles in a theory
of problematic youth group involvement are derived from, and representative of, particular facts about problematic youth groups. To document the importance of theory,
we refer to a famous quote by Karl Popper (Popper, 1959: 59):

> Theories are nets cast to catch what we call 'the world': to rationalize, to explain, and to mas-
> ter it. We endeavour to make the mesh ever finer and finer.

A theory needs to improve our understanding of the phenomenon. An integrative
theory of problematic youth group involvement is a coherent system of ideas
arranged in rational order that produce general principles that increase our understanding and explanation of the fact that some youths become involved in a problematic youth group. Integrated theories of offending represent an attempt to bridge
the ideological differences that exist among various older theories of offending
by integrating concepts and mechanisms from disparate theoretical approaches.

An integrated approach recognizes that offending is a complex, multidimensional phenomenon with multiple causes at multiple levels. By integrating a variety of micro-ecological, sociological (bonds), and psychological (morality, self-control, control orientation) concepts into a coherent structure, the shortcomings of older theories that may be criticized on the grounds of reductionism are partially overcome. Indeed, many older theories of offending argue that one causal variable is predominantly important as a cause of offending. A problem with such an approach is that not all persons exposed to a risk factor (for example, poverty) offend or becomes involved in a problematic youth group. Integrated theories recognize that multiple social and individual factors interact to result in the eventual behavior of individuals, and that we must consider the constellation of factors in an individual's life in order to understand his or her behavior.

Developing an integrated approach of action (the commitment of acts of crime and participating in a problematic youth group), its situational causes (unstructured routines/lifestyles), and causes of the causes that have emerged during the life course (moral beliefs, the capacity to exercise self-control, control orientation, and their causes) is only possible when an inspiring meta-theoretical framework is used.

In this chapter, we present the outlines of a possible framework that may be used to develop theories of problematic youth group involvement and offending. In this chapter, we will provide arguments for the idea that problematic youth group involvement and offending can be fruitfully studied from a modest scientific realist approach that is partially rooted in the fundamentals of analytical sociology (Hedström & Swedberg, 1998; Hedström, 2005), Opp's (2001, 2005, 2009) wide version of rational choice theory and developmental ecology (Bronfenbrenner, 1992). Edling and Hedström (2005: 1) gave following definition to the analytical approach in the field of sociology:

> Analytical sociology seeks to explain complex social processes by carefully dissecting them and then bringing into focus their most important constituent components. It is through dissection and analytical abstraction that the important cogs and wheels of social processes are made visible and intelligible.

Analytical sociology is influenced by scientific realism, today's answer to Popper's critical rationalism (Bunge, 2001, 2004). Scientific realism is about the belief that social reality exist independent of the individual. It would be unjust and wrong to think that scientific realism ignores the fact individuals construct their own realities (i.e. differentially perceived the world out there). We thus defend a standpoint that there is an independent world out there, which is differentially perceived by the people who live in their environments. For us, scientific realism is about understanding while individuals commit acts, perform action, and become members of groups in society while acknowledging the fact that crime and youth groups are socially constructed. Understanding is about providing deep causal explanations (Bunge, 1999). By detecting the mechanisms we increase our understanding of something. If we want to understand the causes and mechanisms of action, fact constructivism is just not the approach that provides a meta-theoretical toolbox to provide causal explanations. In other words, scientific realism provides us with a toolbox to study *the cogs and wheels* of participation in a problematic youth group as well as the participation of offending by young adolescents. We will go into these issues in the following paragraphs.

2   WHY WOULD WE NEED AN ANALYTICAL META-THEORETICAL
        FRAMEWORK?

We propose an integrative analytical meta-theoretical framework to the study of why individuals participate in problematic youth groups and why they offend. An integrative analytical framework should facilitate the study of the actions of individuals, groups (such as problematic youth groups), their actions, the causes of their actions, and the causes of the causes of their actions. This is an ambitious goal. To facilitate the realization of such a scientific enterprise, one must choose an integrative meta-theoretical that suits the multidisciplinary study of the social phenomena. One of the main motivations for thinking in terms of integrative action frameworks is that outdated and poorly justified meta-theoretical ideas about explanation, causation, and the nature of scientific theories have had a damaging effect on sociological research (Hedström, 2005). The question is whether such an approach can be applied to criminology? Criminology is far too broad to realize this. Therefore we suggest to apply this approach to what we call an *analytical crime causation science*. Crime causation science is the interdisciplinary study of crime, its causes (and causes of the causes) and consequences at multiple levels. As crime as action is one of the most important outcomes, it seems plausible to argue for an action theoretical framework. Indeed, action theories seem to very useful, especially if one wants to build and test cross-level integrated theories (e.g. Wikström, 2007). Action frameworks have been around for a very long time (Parsons, 1951), and contemporary sociologists became very much influenced by action theories due to the influential writings of Coleman (1986), who developed a research program (methodological individualism) based on an action theory.[1] However, their exist many action theories, how are we to choose between action frameworks that are useful in studies of crime causation, and, above that, are suitable to explain problematic youth group participation? Individuals are seen as the most important causal agents. Only individuals can bring about something by acting in one way or the other. Ultimately the action of individuals shapes society. It is through their actions that individuals shape society or, in Hedström's words, *make society thick*

---

1. Actions theories disappeared because they were equated with the functionalist approach of Talcott Parsons. Functionalism has been criticized for being too conservative on functions, and while we acknowledge this criticism, we feel that it was wrong to totally dismiss the action theoretical approach. There are many different interpretations of methodological individualism. We refer to Udehn (2002) for a clear overview.

(Hedström, 2005: 5). Theories of action should explain how the action of individuals and cohesive groups as key causal agents bring about their effects. In our analytical framework, we consider individuals as important causal agents, but not as the only causal agents. Next, cohesive groups can act as causal agents. Groups (gangs) can be considered as independently existing causal agents when the group acts together to realize goals (Bunge, 2006).

An analytical approach to a crime causation science as a social science can provide scholars with more theoretically guided, and therefore more profound, insights into the social world around us. Analytical crime causation science emphasizes the study of the social structures within which mechanisms operate to explain individual acts as outcomes of a series of social processes. Precisely because an analytical approach to the study of crime causation is interested in both causes and causes of the causes of crime and related phenomena such as problematic youth group involvement at multiple levels, our approach differs somewhat from the analytical approach in sociology. The analytical approach in sociology mainly studies action as a key dependent variable and in an analytical approach to crime causation, attention is also paid to the study of the causes of the causes of the causes. The idea that we need such integrative frameworks is not new and dates back to the early 1990s, when the first attempts to integrate individual and ecological approaches to crime became visible. The idea of integrating theoretical frameworks at multiple levels (i.e. taking into account the individual and the environment) was further developed in Wikström and Sampson (2003).

2.1   A scientific realist perspective on problematic youth group involvement

In contemporary criminology, theories of crime causation are often (but not exclusively) developed from realist perspectives. As with many meta-theoretical frameworks, there are different kinds of realism, from a naive realism to scientific realism. We submit that a *modest* version of the realist perspective (Psillos, 1999; 2009) is useful to the study of problematic youth group involvement.[2] Scientific realism is of interest because it may bridge a gap between paradigms that may seem to be conflicting, but probably only are conflicting in their most strict dogmatic application. Realism refers in this context to the idea that society exists independent of scientists and the theories that scientists produce. From this angle, scientific realism has its roots in critical rationalism (Popper, 1959; 1972). Scientific realism should not be equated with positivism. Positivism shared a deterministic

---

2.   By modest we mean that a realist approach is seen as an epistemic optimist view that science can and does deliver theoretical truth no less tha it can deliver observational truth. Realists leave open the question whether this can be achieved. Just like Popper we submit that theories may contain error, and are subject to change when being falsified, or when the level of corroboration is too low. Realism is an attitude, it is the belief of a certain degree of correspondence with the world. An interesting discussion of realism can be found in Psillos (2008).

world view and was merely interested in the discovery of social laws. Scientific realism only shares with positivism a devotion to the scientific method and a believe that the differences between the natural sciences and social sciences are somewhat exaggerated: there are fact sciences and formal sciences: both the social sciences and the exact sciences deal with facts in their own way, the realism we propose as a framework is a modest realism, one that recognizes the importance of the Thomas theorem. According to some influential realists the differences between natural sciences and social sciences have been exaggerated by proponents of extreme forms of social constructionism and relativism in the era of the Science Wars or Methodenstreit (Bunge, 2001). A realist approach takes an approach to causation that seriously differs from the positivist approach. It is therefore surprising to see that many scholars confuse realism with positivism (Bunge, 1999). In positivism, causation is nothing more than the Humean successive observation of regularities, i.e. a joint observation, which becomes a habit of the mind.[3] In contemporary scientific realism, causation is about finding mechanisms that link external events, like exposure to conditions, to outcomes. Causation is about the production of events. Indeed, the key features of causation are production (to bring about something) and law-likeness. The bringing about can take the form of energy transfer or triggering (Bunge, 1979; 2006). Scientific realism refutes a variable-based approach. In social sciences, variables are not able to bring about things; actors do. The realist approach takes a generative, difference-making, and capacity-based approach to causation. Thus, contemporary scientific realism has broken radically enough with positivism and empiricism. Realism cannot be equated with causal determinism[4] and realists even accept soft (constructive) constructionism (Hacking, 1999). The concept of crime is by definition in technical terms a social construct as criminalization is needed to technically speak of a crime. Yet, the actions and their consequences are real to offenders, victims and society as a whole and it is the task of an analytical framework to explain why actors do the things they do. It is a very unjust criticism of realism to argue that it discards Thomas' theorem. That is a wrong interpretation of realism and is probably caused by equating realism with Comte's positivism. Scientific realism explicitly recognizes Thomas' theorem, "if men define situations as real, they are real in

3. According to David Hume, when we say of two types of object or event that "X causes Y", we mean that (a) Xs are "constantly conjoined" with Ys, (b) Ys follow Xs and not vice versa, and (c) there is a "necessary connection" between Xs and Ys such that whenever an X occurs, a Y must follow. Unlike the ideas of contiguity and succession, however, the idea of necessary connection is subjective, i.e. it lies in the eyes of the beholder. This idea is the basis of the classic problem of induction, which Hume formulated and which was criticized by realists, such as Karl Popper. Hume's definition of causation is an example of a "regularity" analysis and has become the standard notion of causation in positivism.

4. Causal determination is just one form of determination. Determination has two meanings: it refers to property of characteristics of things and it refers to unique connections. That unique connection need not be causal. The causal category is just one aspect of social sciences. For a detailed overview, see the magnum opus on causation by Bunge (1979[1959]).

their consequences," and even considers Thomas' theorem as one major explanation of why external social conditions are *perceived* differently by individuals
(Wikström, 2007). Analytical crime causation science is realistic about its methodology and the epistemic aims of the social sciences. This is a cornerstone shared
also by scholars who work in the field of analytical sociology (Hedström &
Ylikoski, 2010). Analytical crime causation science is in addition realistic about
explanation. Explanation is about understanding the mechanisms at work. By
explaining things, we increase our understanding of the phenomenon. Criminological theories of crime causation should not be seen as just intellectual construc-
tions useful for making predictions and controlling criminal events. The primary
epistemic goal is to represent the causal processes that generate the observable
phenomena (Ylikoski, 2010). The secondary goal may be to adequately translate
the findings from such research in practice.

One important task of science is to discover how the world functions by looking
for scientific explanations and searching for causes and causes of the cause
(Bunge, 2006). Therefore, we strongly prefer a realist approach when the main
aim is (1) to discover the causes of crime and problematic youth group involvement and (2) to construct integrative theories of crime causation, problematic
youth group involvement and the relation between both. To us it seems that a
realist approach to adolescent offending and problematic youth group involvement is the most fruitful way to study causes at various levels of aggregation, i.e.
from Durkheim's 'social facts' to individuals' actions, such as offending and
problematic youth group participation. This approach is useful because crime
does not exclusively exist in the minds of criminologists, but also happens in
the real world outside. In the real world, crime leads to suffering of victims,
offenders and society. While soft constructivism is accepted and it is acknowledged that crime as and problematic youth groups are theory-laden concepts
that have had different meanings during different periods in human history,
we are strongly in favor of a realist approach and refuse the fact-constructivist
approach[5] as this extreme form of constructivism suffers from the equal validity
these and such philosophy of science is not suited to address problems of causation (Boghossian, 2006). It is perfectly possible to make a distinction between
ontological realism and epistemological soft-constructivism. In fact, that is what
scientific realism is all about.

From a realist approach, causes and explanations are not invented but discovered by
means of deduction but always through empirical research, i.e. based on both corroboration and falsification (Bunge, 2006). A realist approach will therefore never strive
to produce 'grand theories' nor can it be seen as equivalent of 'blind empiricism,' In
short, an analytical approach to crime causation is not eclectic and arbitrary variable-
based approach to crime.

---

5.   Fact constructivism also comes in different forms. The more extreme positions are taken by post-modernist
     approaches.

2.2 *Explanation*

Explanations have an added value compared to descriptions because they answer *why-questions* (Little, 1991). An integrative framework needs to bridge the gap between grand theories and the empiricism of a variable-based criminology. A variable-based criminology runs the risk of getting bogged down in the swamp of the crime and crime-related correlates. A mere theoretical criminology pretends to tell the truth by 'story-telling.' Such truth quickly becomes dogma because it is not subjected to empirical tests. Analytical criminology needs to explain why criminal behavior and events and why social factors differ in time and location between societies and communities. Elster (1989) argued that the focus should be on the explanation by mechanisms, while Hedström and Swedberg (1998:25) argued that a mechanism-based explanation seeks to provide a fine-grained as well as tight coupling between explanans (the explaining causally linked concept) and explanandum (that what has to be explained). The tighter the link, the higher the level of clarity will be. This principle of tightness is very important. If we want to explain why and how it is that adolescents who lack low self-control offend, then we have to explain this link. The explanation should be clarifying. Explaining implies that a series of mechanisms is cited. It is through the explanation that we gain a deeper understanding of the world. Realist tend to see the concept of understanding as the psychological consequence of the explanation (Bunge, 2006).

2.3 *Dissection and abstraction*

Dissection refers to the division of both social phenomena and their causes and causal mechanisms that explain the outcome. These dissections should result in the reduction of social phenomena to their essence. The researcher should abstract this essential information about a social phenomenon theoretically. The dissection of a social phenomenon deals with the measurement of concepts, the translation of theoretical concepts into observable, operational elements. This empirical translation deserves more attention in contemporary criminology. Hedström (2005: 3) argued that "dissection and abstraction are two aspects of the same activity, and they are core components of the analytical approach." Through dissecting and abstracting, our understanding of processes becomes more transparent and clear. One example is the dissection of morality as a central concept of criminology. What does the theorist actually mean by that concept? Is morality a general concept referring to broader societal norms that are related to conforming behavior, or is morality a multidimensional concept that refers to levels of tolerance of moral rule breaking or legal cynicism towards the moral principles stated in criminal law? A careful theoretical dissection of this concept is necessary to improve our insight into the phenomenon and its role in the explication of crime as action.

2.4   Precision and clarity

Precision and clarity should characterize the theory driven hypotheses that are about to be tested by empirical findings. The creation of theory in criminology needs to demystify, not reify or add confusion. Thus, theoretical concepts need to be clearly interpretable, as do the nomological relationships between concepts, and mechanisms that bring about effects. This distinction should already be present at the abstract and theoretical level, i.e. before starting an empirical analysis, but also at the empirical level. Precision and clarity imply a transparent way of measuring concepts in empirical studies.

2.5   The principle of complex parsimony

We are convinced that an analytical approach that takes into account the above principles can improve our knowledge because it forces the theorist to carefully consider why the phenomenon under study should be studied and to explain which conditions and mechanisms should be taken into account and why. The theorist should have a clear vision of the broader and more abstract concepts that deserve attention in an analysis. From this theoretical attention it follows that empirical tests of hypotheses can be interpreted more directly, so that results of analyses are less ambiguous and less ambivalent. By doing so, studies of crime and crime causation at multiple levels of aggregation become more fruitful and provide more profound insights for science and policy makers. Thus, there is less room for discussions about which theoretical concepts really matter in the explanation of crime and which do not. The principles of an analytical approach to the study of crime causation could be considered to be acting against another principle of empirical research: the parsimony principle. Following the principle of parsimony (Ockham's razor), one would keep explanations as simple (parsimonious) as possible. That is however not warranted if we miss some key insight. Scientists that follow the principle of parsimony use as few as mechanisms as possible. We argue that parsimony may impede the development and testing of theoretical ideas of how concepts are related to each other in nomological networks. Indeed, the principle of parsimony may also encourage the criminologist to overlook mechanisms that do not directly operate and influence a dependent variable. We argue that, from a theoretical point of view, it is just as important to gain insights into the 'causes of the causes of crime,' and how they are entertwined at several levels of analysis. E.g. a parsimonious explanation of problematic youth group involvement can explain the phenomenon by referring to social controls alone, or self-control alone; In that case we have a partial explanation that does not inform us about the specific role of control orientation (locus of control). Parsimony cannot be equated with simplicity. Therefore we prefer to talk about complex parsimony.

2.6   Action, its causes, and the causes of the causes

Action is behavior that is guided by a certain motivation. It is behavior that is initiated by agency and stands in sharp contrast to bodily movements or automated movements. Action theories prefer to use of the term action to stress the importance of processes of deliberation. Action theories are designed to explain action, i.e. why people do the things they do. Action theories generally do not explain why people have developed the beliefs, cognitions, and emotions, that have shaped the individual. Action theories were originally developed within the realm of the rational choice paradigm. Although there are several forms of rational choice theory (narrow economic that are based on the principle of utility maximization) and broader versions that consider all kinds of incentives that affect decision making (see Opp, 2009 for a discussion), our analytical approach is, just like analytical sociology, only partially related, but conceptually different from micro-economic rational choice theory. We merely assume that actors are 'reasonable rationally'; this means that they have a certain degree of 'agency' or that they are able to make choices when performing actions. Such a rational action perspective serves only as a framework allowing for the study of action and is indeed useful because it can explain why people make particular choices from a broader variety of options (Goldthorpe, 2000). Human action can and does deviate from the microeconomic standard of global utility maximization while bounded rationality "is consistent with our knowledge of actual human choice action" and assumes that the actor who searches for alternatives, has incomplete and inaccurate knowledge about all the consequences of actions, and chooses action that are expected to be satisfactory (attain targets while satisfying constraints within a given context). The actor is thus subject to 'bounded rationality' in the sense that there are "limits upon the ability of human beings to adapt optimally, or even satisfactorily, to complex environments" (Simon, 1991: 132). We prefer the term 'bounded cognitive rationality,' that is to say, that the human being, to a certain extent, given someone's capabilities and limitations, has agency, i.e. is in a position to think in cognitive relative terms.[6]

2.7   *Mechanisms: the heart of the causal nexus*

Our analytical framework is built on the idea of generative causal determination in the explaining of actions.[7] The productive cause is external and works in on a

---

6. Global rationality "assumes that the decision maker has a comprehensive, consistent utility function, knows all the alternatives that are available for choice," and "can compute the expected value of utility associated with each alternative." The cost-benefit framework is often used in deterrence theory and has been used as a heuristic in situational crime prevention (Cornish & Clark, 2008). However, the utility function and the principle utility maximization have been criticized: the processes of decision making in complex settings sometimes cause behavioral preferences that may seem to be irrational outcomes from an objective point of view. In wide versions of RCT, like the version proposed by Opp, it is acknowledged. Analytical sociologists have ideas that are pretty close to wide versions of sociological rational choice theories, but mainly criticize the instrumentalism in rational choice theory. However, the differences are really small between Opp's version of RCT and the points of view developed in Hedström's manifesto (2005). The most typical criticism are that RCT has problems in explaining actions that are not goal oriented or which are not instrumental. RCT prediction is not always good.
7. Causal determination is not to be equated with causal determinism (Bunge, 1999, 2006).

mechanism that is internal. In the philosophy literature, there are many definitions of mechanisms around. One important reason for the abundance of definitions, is the fact that different disciplines make use of different conceptions of mechanisms. A mechanism (in social science research) should detail the cogs and wheels of the causal process through which the outcome to be explained was brought about. In Hedström's own words:

> The core idea behind the mechanism approach is that we explain a social phenomenon by referring to a constellation of entities and activities, typically actors and their actions, that are linked to one another in such a way that they regularly bring about the type of phenomenon we seek to explain (Hedström, 2005: 65). A social mechanism, as defined here, is a constellation of entities and activities that are linked to one another in such a way that they regularly bring about a particular type of outcome. (ibidem, 181)

Causal mechanisms are expected to be the components of the linkages between events or processes hypothesized to bear a causal relation to each other. Causes are conceived as external events or conditions that under the right circumstances may bring about an effect. In our analytical framework, causation requires (1) production (to bring about something), (2) difference-making (causes should make the difference), (3) lawfulness (to bring about something repeatedly), and (4) the existence of powerful particulars (i.e. characteristics that have the ability to be triggered). By this we mean that it is the capacities of entities (such as actors) that make things happen. Individual and cohesive collective actors (such as groups) possess characteristics (capacities) that are able to bring about an action when appropriately triggered. Mechanisms rather than regularities or necessary/sufficient conditions provide the fundamental grounding of causal relations and need to be at the center of causal research (Hedström & Swedberg, 1998; Hedström & Ylikoski, 2010).

To explain the actions of actors, we can partially rely on Hedström's proposition of DBO theory, which is a micro-foundation of a sociological theory of action. DBO theory stands for desires, beliefs, and opportunities versus constraints as the key mechanisms that bring about action. Following Hedström (2005), we propose to organize explanations of problematic youth group involvement organized around the key concepts of desires (or preferences) to commit a crime or to participate in the activities of a problematic youth group (in relation to tempting or provocative stimuli), beliefs (= moral belief systems), and opportunities/constraints (which exist at multiple levels of aggregation and play a role in the development of crime propensities and equally play a role as parts of the situation in the explanation of acts of crime or problematic youth group participation). Most important, attention should always go to the possible interactions between desires, beliefs, and opportunities/constraints. By centering explanations of problematic youth group involvement in terms of DBO theory, we obtain a deep causal explanation, i.e. one who opens the black box (the intervening mechanisms), and in doing so, we obtain a better understanding of the action to be explained.

Following Esser (1994), Wan (2011) and Wikström et al. (212) we propose to make a distinction between several kinds of mechanisms that are of importance to the study of problematic youth group involvement: (1) situational mechanisms (macro-to-micro mechanisms), (2) micro-to-micro mechanisms (action formation mechanisms-which involves framing, general attitudes and cognitions, moral beliefs, …), transformational mechanisms (micro-to macro-mechanisms), (4) life course developmental mechanisms, and (5) selection mechanisms (social and self-selection).

Desires and beliefs are considered to be *compelling causes*: i.e. it is believed that mental states (i.e. cognitions and emotions that supervene on physical processes) can bring about action, but only under the right situational triggering. In the contemporary philosophy of mind literature and neuropsychology, much of the discussion has centered on whether mental states indeed can be said to cause one another, or whether it is rather the physical properties on which the mental states supervene that cause one another (Hedström, 2005). Just like Hedström (2005) we argue these developments in neuroscience are interesting, but at this moment it is still very unclear to what extent our theoretical approach hinges on which of these positions one adopts. We argue that especially beliefs and perceived opportunities/constraints (in interaction with dispositional characteristics) can be considered to be the *proximate intervening mechanisms* in the relationship between generative (= productive) causes and their effects. It is the specific combination of beliefs and opportunities/constraints that evoke the desire to join a problematic youth group or to commit a crime (in response to temptation and provocation). Our action-oriented approach follows the situational logic of Karl Popper. According to Popper's notion of the situational logic, social situations involve three aspects: (1) the availability of action alternatives to the actors; (2) the restrictions that regulate the choice of the alternatives; and (3) the evaluation of the possible consequences of the choices made (Esser, 1994: 180). With his situational logic, Popper wanted to make an argument against the influence of psychology of action theories. According to Popper, decisions to act in a given context are related to situational cues. We agree with that, but argue against a one-sided interpretation. What kind of action that takes place in a given environment is dependent on what kind of person who is in what kind of setting (the same discussion can be found in Wikström et al., 2012). The concept of situational logic is very interesting, but Popper did not really work this idea thoroughly out. Therefore some scholars have argued that the situational logic in its original conception was too vague to be of major influence to the field (see the discussion in Hedström, Swedberg & Udehn, 1998).

An analytical approach to the study of crime causation and problematic youth group involvement should not only develop theories that focus on the action, i.e. the outcome (offending, problematic youth group participation), but also the causes of the causes, in order to obtain a more thorough understanding of problematic youth group involvement and crime. That implies a thorough integration between different disciplines and is one of the challenges of crime causation theories in the 21st century. A simple example can illustrate our position. Think of moral beliefs and the capacity to exercise self-control (the capacity to resist temptation and provocation). These are two key constructs that play a central role in different theories of crime causation, yet they do not emerge in a vacuum. There is ample evidence for the role of negative events, exposure to adverse ecological conditions in the life course, psychological and genetic factors that are responsible for the observed individual differences in morality and self-control, and in the selection of routine activities/lifestyles.

3   AN EMERGENTIST SYSTEMIST APPROACH OF PROBLEMATIC YOUTH
         GROUP PARTICIPATION

Action theories are typically designed to solve macro-micro questions. Therefore, they are perfectly fit to use as a framework for this book, as it deals with the relationship between micro-places and offending and problematic youth group participation. Micro-macro questions in criminology are a consequence of correlations between social facts, such as structural characteristics of ecological settings and crime rates as social outcomes. Micro-level theories help explaining macro level phenomena, such as why do some areas have a higher proportion of youths who are involved in a problematic youth group? This approach is not new. There are multiple visions of the relationship between macro-level characteristics and macro-level outcome: methodological individualism, structural individualism and emergentist systemism. We submit that systemism is the most fruitful way of studying the causes and causes of the causes of gang involvement.

The *methodological individualist* approach stresses that relationships between macro-level outcomes should be understood by actions of actors and propose micro-level explanations as the most important explanations that can account for macro-level outcomes. Advocates of this approach were Jon Elster (1989, 2007) and James Coleman (1986). Some scholars have argued that methodological individualism leaves little room for contextual explanations and the study of the complexity of society and social action and have therefore provocatively argued for the dismissal of action theories (e.g. Jepperson & Meyers, 2011). However, it would be wrong to think that methodological individualism can be equated with atomism, which leaves no room at all for contextual explanations. Just like it is the case with most research paradigms, there are narrow and wide versions of a paradigm. Boudon's (1989) *structural individual research program*, and Karl-Dieter Opp's (2009) *structural cognitive approach*, take into account contextual effects, but stress the importance of individual level mediators. Opp (2009) successfully applied his approach to the explanation of political violence at the individual level and at the country level. We submit that if we want to increase our understanding of problematic youth group participation, it is necessary to think in terms of causes and causes of the causes (and their interactions), but also in terms of levels: micro, meso, and macro. Thus, while we acknowledge the importance of microfoundations of action, we strongly believe that no explanation can be complete without integrating the individual and the context. In other words, we take a non-reductionist approach that stresses the role of individuals and context and their interactions. One approach that allows for a full-fledged contextual analysis is the meta-theoretical framework of Bunge: *emergentist systemism*. Indeed, Bunge's systemic perspective can be considered as a complex elaboration of structural individualism that focuses on causation at multiple levels and pays attention to the issue of emergence, i.e. the genesis of macro-level social facts as a consequence of the actions and interactions of lower level agents. In this study, those agents are young people who may get involved in problematic youth groups and/or commit acts of crime. The Italian sociologist Manzo (2007) refers to complex methodological individualism, but in essence, both approaches take identical positions with regard to contextual causation. According to the emergentist systemic perspective (e.g. Bunge, 2006), the action of individuals as social actors cannot be understood without taking into account contexts, networks, and even broader structures of individuals. On the contrary, these contexts should be studied together with the forces that drive individual actors. The criminologist who takes a pure environmental approach is wrong because he does not take individual characteristics into account, whereas the individualist is wrong for ignoring the contexts, i.e. the settings to which individuals are (situationally or developmentally) exposed. Individuals are connected with society and its structures at multiple levels. Between the atomism of the individual approach and the determinism of the environmentalist or structuralist approach, there exists a third way: the *systemic approach*. This approach is highly useful to the study of problematic youth groups as such groups are not merely aggregates of individuals but also tight and cohesive units that can act as a group. The systemic approach acknowledged that causation exists at the level of the individual actor (the actor is seen as a biosocial system that is able to deliberate) but stresses that cohesive groups can also act and therefore there is room for causation at multiple levels. Following Bunge, when faced with the task of describing a system, one starts by asking the following four questions: what is it made of (*composition*)? what surrounds it (*environment*)? which are the bonds that hold it together (*structure*)? and how does it work (*mechanism*)?

In short, analytical crime causation science, which is part of an analytical criminology (Pauwels, Ponsaers & Svensson, 2010), strongly adheres to the idea of micro-foundations, while we take a non-reductionist standpoint and accept the idea of autonomous social causation (in the sense of contextual effects, not in the sense of autonomous causation between macro-level units). This position is also strongly related to Little's methodological glocalism (Little, 1998). Emergentist systemism is thus a fruitful starting point for developing and testing theories that explain why individuals become engaged in a problematic youth group, why some people have the propensities that affect their decision making and why some areas have higher levels of gang-activities. A systemic approach avoids the 'atomized' and 'heroic' assumptions of traditional economics as well as the 'causalism' of traditional sociology, because, as Mark Granovetter (1985: 487) has expressed it clearly,

> actors do not behave or decide as atoms outside a social context, nor do they adhere slavishly to a script written for them by the particular intersection of social categories that they

happen to occupy. Their attempts at purposive action are instead embedded in concrete, ongoing systems of social relations.

Emergent systemism admits the ontological status and explanatory role of social entities (as concrete systems), and therefore does not stipulate that *every* causal explanation of social facts has to be restricted to references to the individual level actors. It takes into account both development: context and action. While it is true that it is only actors that can do the acting, this does not mean that the only relevant unit of analysis that can claim to have causal capacities is the level of individuals. It is the nature of the research question that decides how many levels one wants to scrutinize.

What is the consequence of adapting emergentist systemism as a framework for the building of integrated action theories of problematic youth group involvement? Integrated action theories of problematic youth group involvement need different coherent theoretical models: (1) a model that explains why people consider to join a problematic youth group given situational conditions and individual characteristics and (2) a model that explains why people develop (in the course of one's personal life-history or the group's life-history) beliefs systems and experience opportunities and constraints that are related to joining a gang as an action alternative. Emergentist systemism also allows for answering macro-level questions (e.g. why do some neighborhoods have higher rates of gang participation among the youths that inhabit the neighborhood. Complex social processes emerge as a consequence of a series of cross-level interactions at multiple levels between the perceived micro-place context and key individual level characteristics (see Bunge, 2006 for a detailed discussion).

4   A SHORT NOTE ON HUMAN NATURE AND SOCIAL ORDER IN EMERGENTIST SYSTEMISM

Individuals are not born as a blank slate, nor are they completely altruistic or egoistic. The Hobbesian image of human nature and the naïve image as shared by Rousseau, … all of these visions are somewhat unidimensional and reduce the complexity of human nature. Human nature can be seen selfish in the pure *evolutionary* meaning (Walsh, 2014), thus not in the meaning of 'being egoistic.' All individuals are born wired for feelings and ready to learn. Shonkoff and Phillips (2000) come to the following conclusion in their excellent book on human development. The long-standing debate about the importance of nature versus nurture, considered as independent influences is overly simplistic and scientifically obsolete. Scientists have shifted their focus to take account of the fact that genetic and environmental influences work together in dynamic ways over the course of development (Robinson & Beaver, 2009; Beaver & Walsh, 2008). Apart from that, we agree with the position taken by Wikström et al (2012) that humans are rule-guided animals, i.e. they create rules and try to live by them. Social order in complex societies demands consensus on some rules of conduct. However, this does not mean that we deny conflict. The consensus-conflict debate is not fruitful when studying why individuals break rules or join gangs. Just like Agnew (2011) we recognize that there is a lot of conflict in complex societies, but that is merely an empirical observation. Conflict may be the motor for change, but in itself it is not an ideal starting point for keeping social order.

5   DO WE NEED GENERAL THEORIES OR THEORIES OF THE MIDDLE RANGE TO EXPLAIN OFFENDING AND PROBLEMATIC YOUTH GROUP INVOLVEMENT?

Now that we have proposed a general meta-theoretical framework for the study of problematic youth group involvement, we turn to the question what kind of theories that should follow from such an overarching framework. A meta-theoretical framework is not a theory, it is the skeleton of some possible theories. Frameworks provide the logic and the structure of an explanation. Now we need to make the explanation down to earth in a theory of problematic youth group involvement and offending. This brings us to an interesting question. Do we need general theories or do we need theories of the middle range in the study of problematic youth group involvement and crime? Action can be defined at different levels of generality. This has implication for theory and research. We illustrate this by borrowing from Fishbein and Ajzen (2010) and adapted to the context of the study of problematic youth group participation (Table 2).

As can be seen from this table action can be studied at different levels, from the lowest perspective, the individual actor, to higher levels. Therefore, a valid question is: what is the right level of analysis. We submit that the general framework (emergentist systemism) allows for choosing at what level one starts. The research question determines where to start and how to build theories that incorporate multiple levels. Building theories can be done by asking oneself what mechanisms are operating at what level. Thus, one hypothesizes the mechanisms and links the actions of actors (or groups) to the context of development and action. Furthermore, we can distinguish between theories that explain why a single individual comes to join a gang, and in that case we have developed a theory that rests upon the principle of token causation) a single event causes a single action. That is not what would lead to a satisfactory theory. Criminologists are often interested in (semi-general) models Thus,

Table 2   **Action and levels**

Level of generality	Action	Target	Context	Time
Low	Hitting Steve	Steve	Local pub	Yesterday, 02.00am
Intermediate-low	Violence toward persons	Member of a skinhead group	Pubs	Past 30 days
Intermediate-high	Violence	Problematic youth group	Recreational setting	Past 6 months
High	Rule breaking	Problematic youth group	Crime generator	Past 12 months

Source: Fishbein and Ajzen (2010).

emergentist systemism is used to build models that explain the behavior of individuals in systems. It becomes clear from the picture that the higher up the level, the less informative the statements of the theory. But if theories are to be informative, then they require some level of abstraction.

Before going into the discussion of what theories we need, and thus before defending the position taken by us, let us tell a story from outside the realm of criminology.

The possibility and desirability of developing general theories have not only been discussed in the field of criminology, but in a variety of social sciences. In psychology, Fishbein and Ajzen (2010) have been proponents of general theories of behavior. Their basic arguments were that there are too many theories for all different kinds of behavior and that this led to the development of many domain-specific theories and mini-theories within each domain. Fishbein and Ajzen (2010) were interested in identifying general principles that guide behavior. They observed that background variables and even general personality traits (the so-called big five traits) usually do not explain much of the variance in behavior; neither do general attitudes. That should ring a bell for criminologists. This led to a discussion in psychology among theorists. The question was as simple as challenging: is it possible to develop general principles of behavior? Fishbein and Ajzen (2010) went as far as too argue that it might be possible to find key factors involved in a wide array of behaviors, from political protest, job performance, discriminatory behavior, and the decision to vote.

In their book on predicting and changing behavior, Fishbein and Ajzen (2010) report on a conference that was held among theorists. The main aim of the conference was to clarify the differences between theories and the possibility to come up with a "finite list of variables that could be used in any explanation of behaviour." The lesson to be learned is that there was a huge disagreement between scholars. Nevertheless, these scholars (all psychologists) agreed upon a list of general conditions that were required for a behavior to be performed. We give a brief overview of these propositions and comment on them from a criminological perspective:

- *Intention to perform the behavior.* By intention it is not meant that individuals carefully plan their behavior, it is just meant that an intention can develop spontaneously (in reaction to environmental stimuli). Theorists in criminology have debated about that and different extreme positions have been taking in subsequent decades, from a classical perspective that people's behavior is guided by free will over a determinist position that people commit crimes independent of their free will. While much of the 'agency versus free will' discussion takes place outside criminology, in the realms of both philosophy of science and neuropsychology, criminologists who are interested in crime theories should not ignore the findings from this kind of research, as it may have consequences for the axiomatic assumptions in theories.

- *Lack of environmental constraints that make it impossible for the behavior to occur.* This is a position that probably nobody would contradict. It seems a truism and has guided much research in environmental criminology, routine activities theory, and rational choice theory.

- *The acquirement of the necessary skills.* This is a position that is not taken by all theorists of crime causation theories. Especially social learning theorists defended the position that techniques need to be learned in order to be able to commit a crime (Sutherland, 1939). However, much crime does not require technical skills and precise therefore this position has been attacked by control theorists (Gottfredson & Hirschi, 1990; Hirschi, 1969).
- *Beliefs about the advantages of the behavior (anticipated costs and benefits).* Such positions have been taken by rational choice theorists, and of one is willing to accept that perceived rewards versus perceived punishments belong to the same category, then social learning theorists also would defend such a position.
- *The perception of moral pressure to perform the behavior.* Perceptions of moral pressure are seen as an important mechanism in subcultural theories. Members of troublesome youth groups would often commit crimes from an obligation to obey the rules of the group, but in general, learning theories also would accept this idea, as peer pressure has been shown to be related to offending (Warr, 2002).
- *The perception that the behavior is rather consistent with the self-image and the absence of violation personal standards that activate negative self-sanctions.* It is highly doubtable that a strong consensus will be reached among criminologists that the self-image is related to offending. Studies have shown very inconsistent results (Van Damme et al., 2014). On the other hand, personal moral standards is mentioned (under different names) in different theoretical frameworks: social bonding theorists point to normlessness and lack of general beliefs, while learning theories refer to specific deviant beliefs. The position that personal moral standards activate negative self-sanctioning (through feelings of shame and guilt) is also accepted in some theories (Wikström et al., 2012) and documented (Svensson et al., 2013).
- *A positive emotional reaction to performing the behavior.* In fact, this is a statement that may fit social learning theories as anticipated positive emotional reactions can be defined as incentives in rational choice theories and as perceived rewards (reinforcement) by social learning theories. Strain theorists would argue that an anticipated positive reaction would lead to lower levels of strain.
- *The capability to perform the behavior (self-efficacy).* The capability to perform the behavior is not directly mentioned in crime causation theories, but rather, the capability of local community inhabitants is mentioned as a mechanisms of community control in collective efficacy theory (Sampson, Raudenbush & Earls, 1997).

Fishbein and Ajzen wrote that the majority of the psychological theorists found the first three variables to be sufficient for behavior in general to occur. Of course, this position was taken in the 1990s. It is unsure to what extent contemporary psychologists would still agree with these positions taken back then. Suppose that we would apply this to the field of crime causation. Probably not many criminologists would take such a minimalist position.

In sociology, another important discipline that has contributed a lot to the study of crime causation, similar ideas of the usefulness of general theories have been uttered.

In sociology, rational choice theorists (Opp, 2009) have defended such positions. The rationale, provided by theorists that propose general theories usually include the arguments that are summarized by Karl-Dieter Opp.

First of all, Opp argues that the most convincing argument for general theories [to be applied in crime causation studies] is that they are already applied in other domains. The rationale for general theories is taken from the overlap that exists between risk factors of different kinds of crime and problematic youth group involvement.

A second argument for the application of general theories is that they can provide additional evidence for the validity of theories of the middle range. Indeed:

> If a general theory is confirmed and it can be shown that a more specific theory or hypothesis can be derived from the general theory, this is a confirmation of the specific theory. The reason is that it is not possible to derive a wrong statement from a set of true statements (or from a true theory). Thus, the truth value of the general theory is transmitted to the derived theoretical propositions.

A third argument is that the application of general theories leads to changes in theories of the middle-range so that they receive a broader application. Applying a general theory, thus, provides a strategy for finding weaknesses of a special theory. The use of a general theory is not to be applied only to existing theories of the middle range. It should be possible to formulate new hypotheses that were not present in the theory of the middle-range previously. *For example, in order to explain why citizens protest against an authoritarian regime despite severe repression, a general theory could be applied that explains behavior in repressive situations. It is, thus, not necessary to begin from scratch when the issue is to explain certain new phenomena.*

Theories of the middle-range are not always equally informative. The abundance of theoretical perspectives in criminology is a testimony to this. This problem is known as the embarrassment of richness. Theories of the middle range explain broadly a limited range of behaviors such as youth crime, but could be applied in a broader sense and can also try to explain rule breaching amongst adults. We do not want to reject the strategy of testing theories of the middle range because a rejection implies that one throws away a possibility or chance to arrive at theoretical progress.

It should be mentioned that a great deal of skepticism exists on the viability of the development of general theories. The complexity of society is the most common argument. Most sociologists have been influenced by the idea of developing theories of the middle range.

The idea of developing theories of the middle range was already proposed by Merton.

> Middle-range theory is principally used in sociology to guide empirical inquiry. It is intermediate to general theories of social systems which are too remote from particular classes of social behaviour, organisation and change to account for what is observed and to those detailed orderly descriptions of particulars that are not generalised at all. (Merton, 1968: 39)

Merton called at that time for MRT because he had the feeling that sociology was not ready for general theories. He found the idea to create general theories optimistic. For this purpose he made the comparison between sociology and the state of affairs in medicine in the 17th century. Neither were capable to come to generalizations that are needed if we want to have a robust general theory. Therefore, according to Merton, social scientific research had to be like a strategy with two characteristics: by developing special theories from which to derive hypotheses that can be empirically investigated and by evolving, not suddenly revealing, a progressively more general conceptual scheme that is adequate to consolidate groups of special theories (Merton, 1968: 53). For Merton, the formation of theories of the middle range was dependent on the knowledge accumulation created by trial and error. A theory was to provide: "logically interconnected sets of propositions from which empirical uniformities can be derived" (Merton, 1968: 39).

The position taken by us is that we need to find a third way, between the general theories and the specificity of the theory of the middle range. Such theories can be called *semi-general theories*. Semi-general theories deal with mechanisms that may have a very broader applicability, but who are translated locally, so that they are usable to explain specific phenomena.

6   CONCLUSION

In this chapter, we have argued that a integrative meta-theoretical framework may be very useful to adapt in the study of problematic youth group involvement. We have drawn upon ideas of many scholars in contemporary scientific realism, most notably Psillos, Wan and Bunge; we have used ideas that can be traced to Hedström's analytical sociology, and Bunge's emergentist systemism (in a life-course developmental way). This led to the adoption of modest realist approach that focuses on productive causation and intervening mechanisms that uses emergentist systemism as a broad framework to study (1) problematic youth group involvement as situated choice and (2) the factors that make people consider problematic youth group involvement as a viable situated choice (in life course developmental perspective). In the next chapter, we present the integrative model that follows the logic of the meta-theoretical framework that we have proposed here.

AN INTEGRATIVE MICRO-PLACE CONDITIONS-CONTROLS-EXPOSURE MODEL OF PROBLEMATIC YOUTH GROUP INVOLVEMENT

1 INTRODUCTION

In this chapter, we present an integrated model of problematic youth group involvement. The theoretical framework is meant to describe those processes that lead to the likelihood of involvement in illegal activities (actions) and involvement in a problematic youth group. The model is an application of emergentist systemism to the explanation of problematic youth group involvement and adolescent offending, and the crucial questions that will be answered are as follows: (1) what forces determine the probability that a young adolescent will be involved in a problematic youth group? We underscore again that we do not adapt a deterministic approach. We make use of productive, mechanismic, difference-making, and capacity-based philosophical position on causation (Bunge, 2004; Wan, 2011). Causal events exhibit their effects on actions (problematic youth group involvement as situated choice) through a series of mechanisms. Interaction is naturally assumed based on the notion of the INUS condition (Mackie, 1970). An INUS condition means that a causal factor is just one causal factor that is an insufficient but a necessary factor in a series of unnecessary but sufficient series of causal factors. This idea fits criminology well: we do not have necessary and sufficient single causes of problematic youth group involvement but rather a specific combination of factors that when joined are able to produce an effect given a certain likelihood. The model outlined here is not a model that serves to explain how gangs emerge in contemporary cities, nor is it a model that explains what group processes are of relevance for the understanding of problematic youth group dynamics over time.

Our model, however, is incomplete as most of the theories are. It is meant to explain offending and problematic youth group involvement, through a series of mechanisms that together form several plausible routes to problematic youth group involvement and offending. Although our model is an integrated one, we are sure the model can be expanded upon; e.g. it would be fully compatible with group process theories. That is work for the future. The basic idea is that mechanisms should be integrated; this implies learning mechanisms and control mechanisms that are operating in action formation or cognition formation. In that sense, it is wrong to attribute our model the status of a pure control theory or a pure learning theory. This basic version outlined in this chapter aims at explaining individual differences. It should be studied to what

extent the model can also explain within-individual changes. An accumulation of negative micro-place conditions, social controls (i.e. social support and monitoring),
moral beliefs, personal controls (the ability to exercise self-control, locus of control)
and exposure to criminogenic moral settings are the heart of the theory that forms
a logical end-to-end conceptual integration. Routine activities theories generally do
not explain where the individual differences in routine activities come from, and
social control theories generally have not studied how social controls are related to
routine activities. Our model departs from pure control theory and adds elements
from structural approaches (disorganization) and alienation theory. Weak social support sets the stage for low moral standards, but additionally sets the stage for a learned belief, namely external locus of control. The model is based on the idea that the
social structure of micro-places (instead of neighborhoods and larger entities) indirectly affects individual offending and problematic youth group involvement
through a series of mechanisms of control (personal control, low moral beliefs, self-
control) and exposure to criminogenic moral settings, represented by the lifestyle
of individuals. The role of the environment is studied from two points: a developmental view of the exposure to criminogenic moral settings, the development of moral
values and lifestyles and, from a situational point of view, the role of the micro-envi-
ronment in explaining individual differences in problematic youth group involvement. This model of problematic youth group involvement has strong roots in
Osgood's routine activities theory of general deviance and Wikström's situational
action theory, because of the emphasis of exposure to criminogenic settings (represented by lifestyles). As far as we know, no previous study has explicitly incorporated
elements of an action theory into a model of problematic youth group involvement.

2   THE INTEGRATIVE MICRO-PLACE CONDITIONS-CONTROLS-EXPOSURE
        MODEL

The integrated conditions-controls-exposure model holds that involvement in a problematic youth group is a consequence of the conditions to which a person is exposed,
the choices he or she makes in life, and the cognitions he or she invokes in support of
becoming involved in a problematic youth group. The integrated micro-place conditions-controls-exposure model of problematic youth group involvement and offending is a cross-level end-to-end integrated model that starts from the idea that
micro-places, as ecological contexts of moral developmental, differ in terms of organization in favor of, and organization against, crime as collective behavior: thus, social
cohesion, informal control, the presence of unsupervised youths, the presence of
counter-narratives (or frames/schemes), and visual signs of order and disorder operate together to explain setting differences in crime. By focusing on both the organization against crime (control) and in favor of crime, we are convinced that a more
complete image of social processes in neighborhoods is obtained. This idea is a part
of Sutherland's (1939) rich legacy and has several times been reformulated by

Matsueda (2006), who convivially argued that organization against and toward crime is multi-faceted. While the breakdown in informal control initiates the invasion of areas and micro-places with criminal activities, we feel that it would be naïve to ignore the potential influence of the presence of counter-narratives in areas.

We adopt a micro-place perspective as we consider micro-places to be a more appropriate ecological setting that genuinely reflects a behavioral setting, compared to the fuzzy concept of 'neighborhoods,' which is vague and difficult to define and geographically demarcate. A behavioral setting is a setting that one can view and experience with one's own senses (Wikström, 2010). A micro-setting is a useful reconceptualization of neighborhoods, which are primarily seen as too heterogeneous to be able to operate as a developmental context, in which one is exposed to different levels of informal control and different moral contexts.

While our integrated model puts a lot of emphasis on control (social support and monitoring, self-control, control orientation, micro-place control), we do not just see our integrated model as a pure control model. We submitted earlier that some assumptions made in the classic control models do not fit reality; i.e. it is wrong to assume that motivation is a constant and that only control varies, and it is wrong to assume that the image of human nature in control theories (rational choice) is correct. Therefore, we feel we should relax all these strict and binding assumptions about human nature and social order that are outdated, i.e. no longer in congruence with contemporary knowledge from the life sciences. Thus, in order to avoid misunderstandings of the model outlined, we stress that we are not supportive of the idea that individuals are merely guided by the principles of free will who commit offenses when the perceived benefits exceed the perceived costs. We just accept the idea of bounded cognitive rationality and assume that individuals possess the ability to deliberate, and by that, we do not mean that individuals engage in lengthy deliberations when performing behaviors. Using theory-laden concepts such as rational choice usually leads to misunderstandings and criticisms that are to a large extent a consequence of some individuals' tendency to equate all choice processes with a narrow and pure economic vision of rational choice, in which no place is made for other incentives or preferences than cost-benefit analyses (see Opp, 1999) for a discussion on the many misconceptions of rational choice). That may be so for some behaviors, but need not be so and probably is not so for most behaviors as individuals are rule-guided animals; i.e. they are inclined to follow some rules and are quite easy in taking on habits. We distinguish between setting control, locus of control (control orientation or subjective powerlessness), moral beliefs about rule breaking (legal cynicism or 'dérèglement' in Durkheim's conception and moral disengagement in Bandura's (1991) conception), social bonds, and the ability to exercise self-control as separate mechanisms that each in its own sense and for different reasons affects individuals' deliberations to act (i.e. the perception-choice process in situational action theory; see Wikström et al., 2012) or to join a problematic youth group. Contrary to that, we stress that controls are important inhibitors of street-oriented and risky lifestyles, and we view a risky lifestyle as major thriving force that instigates the process by which the individual further drifts away from society's conventional influential hemispheres and pushes individuals into the hemisphere of the problematic youth group. The adaptation of a risky lifestyle is a major indicator of exposure to situational inducements and is seen as a process that is able to provide gradual situational reinforcement (Osgood et al., 1996). Thus, we acknowledge that learning processes play a role, especially when the risky lifestyle turns into a habit, but also with regard to the way micro-place control and organization in favor of crime may operate. We recognize that learning processes include reinforcement, cognitive learning, and imitation. In our view, learning theories and control theories are conceptually complementary as have also been noticed by learning theorists (Akers, 1998; Bandura, 2001). The fact that social control theories and social learning theories have had a history of mutually exclusive visions of human nature can no longer be a reason not to consider the benefits of such a theoretical integration. We neither believe the man is a blank slate when being born nor do we believe that men are purely rational. In fact, we are unwilling to partake in fruitless discussions about nature and nurture. When we look back on theories that were developed in the 20th century, we cannot but come to the conclusion that those theories shared outdated visions on human nature. We strongly believe in the importance of both nature and nurture and especially the interactions between both.

Micro-places differ in terms of their level of social control and the moral orientation of the context: just like scholars in the classic model of disorganization have argued, disorganized communities are characterized by low social controls and a moral context that is primitive of the idea that not-abiding by the law pays off: a context of social disorder represented by the presence of unsupervised youth groups (as a consequence of low informal control) is of major relevance in the integrated model of problematic youth group involvement. The presence of unsupervised youth groups is indicative for the existence of a delinquent counter-narrative. While control theorists such as Kornhauser (1978) were not willing to recognize the causal importance of counter-narratives, we stress that these counter-narratives are of crucial importance for one's personal belief system. Therefore, we believe that Sutherland's redefinition of social disorganization as differential social organization is a better description of the ecological state, which is a fact in some settings.

We recognize the importance of the breakdown of controls as a key mechanism in explaining why some neighborhoods become vulnerable to the invasion of counter-narratives (e.g. by the ongoing presence of unsupervised youth groups and visible criminal activities such as dealing in public, public violence), but we submit that in a model of problematic youth group involvement, both controls and counter-narratives are important as they jointly contribute to the cues that exist in some communities. It is important to stress that we adopt a very dynamic view on micro-places. Each micro-place is in constant development over time: some micro-places are experiencing a spiral of decline and other micro-places are on their way up, due to changes in composition, social control, external crime prevention initiatives, etcetera.

2.1   The role of micro-setting differential social organization

Growing up in differentially organized micro-settings may have consequences for one's personal control orientation. Building on Mirowsky and Ross (2003) we argue that

> (1) the presence of social disorder in micro-settings may promote the view that people are by nature rapacious, untrustworthy, and unhelpful, and that life is essentially chaotic, alienating, and beyond personal control and (2) that the presence of counter-narratives may promote the view that law-abiding is futile and law enforcement is low.

Such arguments about the detrimental effects of micro-settings conditions are not new but can also be found in Sampson et al. (1997) and Wilson (1987). Graffiti, noise, vandalism, dirty streets, public drinking, violence, and run-down buildings are cues. These cues tell residents about themselves and the world they live in. They indicate the breakdown of social control and order. Exposure to such unfavorable micro-place social conditions contributes through the principles of social learning (reinforcement) to the installation of an external locus of control and the adaptation of the normative belief that low moral beliefs reign.

Micro-place disorder as a residential context virtually promotes the installation of external locus of control in youths as it signals the potential for harm, which youths hardly can avoid through guided action, while *micro-place disorder together with unstructured routines and deviant counter-narratives* shapes beliefs that deterrence is low and a risky lifestyle is the norm. These micro-place conditions challenge the socialization of youths through the key socialization agents such as the school and the family. Unfavorable micro-place conditions are extremely demanding and stressful for family management and parental controls.

2.2   The role of control orientation

Control orientation can be internal or external. Once installed, an external locus of control has indirect consequences for problematic youth group involvement. The belief or sense of being in control provides individuals with a belief that they have a grip on one's own life. Individuals with an internal locus of control believe that they have agency and can steer their life. Individuals with an external locus of control believe that they do not have a grip of their life: the belief in destiny and fate is fostered. This general belief in destiny and fate, or put in other words, this pessimistic or fatalistic view, has been suggested by early gang theorists as a typical characteristic of street corner groups. This notion of fatalism has, for example, been stressed by Miller (1958), Cloward and Ohlin (1960), Shaw and Scott (1991), and Colvin (2000). The development of a pessimistic belief not to be in charge of one's own life should be considered as a an additional mechanism that may have consequences for problematic youth group involvement in several ways: (1) external locus of control challenges youths to personally invest in conventional moral standards, which are of less use in a world that is experienced as driven by fate. Living by conventional moral standards pays off in the long run, but that makes less sense to individuals low in personal control, as they are not guided by a belief that they can control the outcome of their action and thus their future; (2) external locus of control is a belief that challenges the establishment and maintenance of self-control as it promotes an orientation toward present instead of delayed gratification. Individuals who share the belief that they are not in control of the future instead concentrate on the present, on one-self, and put less efforts in controlling one's temper. An external locus of control makes one less resistant to withstand thrill-seeking behavior. Shaw and Scott (1991) related parenting to control orientation.

The concept of control orientation is a key concept that binds sociology to psychology, just as Walter Reckless (1961) meant to do with his containment theory: bridging between external controls (social ties) and internal controls (e.g. norm retention, the self, moral beliefs). In Colvin's coercion theory, external locus of control is one of the negative outcomes of coercion, leading to alienation. Control orientation was quintessential in early alienation theories, as we mentioned in previous chapter. We were directly influenced by these theories. Instead of focusing on coercive family relations, we argue that the absence of social bonds is sufficient to install feelings of external locus of control. We thereby do not say that coercion is not important; it is a concept that deserves study of its own, but we merely think that alienation, conceptualized as control orientation, can be produced by a lack of social cohesion in diverse domains (schools and the family). By linking control orientation to social support and monitoring, we incorporate elements of recent attempts to reformulate control theories.

2.3   *The role of low social integration as differential social support/control*

We conceive social integration as a cumulative process that encompasses both social support (see Cullen, 1994) and social control. An accumulation of low social ties in diverse domains has many times been reported to be related to delinquency and problematic youth group involvement (Sampson & Laub, 2003). We stress the importance of a cumulative effect of low social integration: weak social bonds with parents and with the school, as well as poor parental monitoring. While we acknowledge (and previously have shown, see Pauwels, Hardyns & van de Velde, 2010) that each of these bonds that ties the individual to society has independent effects on offending and problematic youth group involvement, we study the effect of low social integration of the individual in conventional society in this study in terms of an accumulative effect on low moral beliefs, self-control (see Gottfredson & Hirschi, 1990), and lifestyle risk.

2.4   *The role of low moral beliefs*

External control orientation and cumulative low social integration are the key mechanisms through which micro-place disorder affects a personal state of low moral beliefs. This state of low moral beliefs is not an irreversible state but a temporary condition of personal breakdown of the moral attachment to society's rules of the game. We believe that there is only consensus at the societal level on some 'basic rules of the game.' We argue that these basic rules of the game can be considered as synonymous for the collective conscience: Durkheim's concept of the "conscience collective," "the totality of beliefs and sentiments common to the average citizens of the same society," which Durkheim (2014) then endowed with quite distinctive characteristics: it forms a determinate system with its own life; it is 'diffuse' in each society and lacks a 'specific organ'; it is independent of the particular conditions in which individuals find themselves; it is the same in different locations, classes, and occupations; it connects successive generations rather than changing from one to another; and it is different from individual consciences, despite the fact that it can be realized only through them.

Different views on conflict and consensus have generally produced many strong debates among scholars in the field of criminology (Agnew, 2011), and we personally feel that this discussion has not always made a giant contribution to the development of crime causation theories.[1] The main point made here is that differences exist between and within groups and that these differences have causes and consequences for the involvement in a problematic youth group.

We propose the concept of low moral beliefs as an individual-level counterpart of social disorganization as originally defined by Thomas and Znaniecky (1920) in their study of the Polish Peasant: the term disorganization refers primarily to a process rather than to a state or condition and was defined as a decrease of the influence of existing social rules of behavior upon the individual members of the group. In a personal state of low moral beliefs, general beliefs about the acceptance of the rule of law become fuzzy; i.e. the boundaries between conformity and deviance become blurring. This state of low moral beliefs is comparable to the state of personal anomia (or political powerlessness), as earlier described by the sociologist Srole (1956) and Seeman (1959) in studies of institutional distrust and political violence (Gurr, 1970). *Low moral beliefs* refers to the personal cognitive evaluation of norms that ties the individual to society. In our interpretation, the state of low moral beliefs is a state of temporal loosening of the bond between society's general rules We conceptualize this sense of low moral beliefs in the same sense as Durkheim did in his influential classic writings. It is this temporarily weakened state that makes the individual at such moments more tolerant toward the rule breaking and susceptible to the adaptation of the street corner lifestyle. Individuals who experience a high level of low moral beliefs will be less hindered by their moral beliefs to resist an upcoming urge to strive for immediate gratification and will finally feel less moral resistance to indulge in a risky lifestyle.

---

1. That statement should not be interpreted as a statement that disregards the importance of this discussion. We only submit the thesis that the discussion about social order should take place elsewhere and not within the field of action theories of crime causation. It is clear that there is both conflict and consensus (see Agnew, 2011; Bunge, 1999).

2.5   *The role of the ability to exercise self-control*

Gottfredson and Hirschi (1990) utilize the concept of self-control as a latent trait leading to criminal or conformist behaviors. Individuals who share a low ability to exercise self-control are more likely to become involved in criminal, deviant, and
accidental behaviors than those who have a strong ability to exercise self-control.
Gottfredson and Hirschi (1990) consider gang membership as an additional outcome
variable in their general theory as they point to criminal and analogous behavior.
However, it is stated that the simple level of self-control is not, in and of itself, the only
necessary condition leading to criminality. As they state:

> lack of self-control does not require crime and can be counteracted by situational condi-
> tions…, {but} high self-control effectively reduces the possibility of crime–that is, those pos-
> sessing it will be substantially less likely at all periods of life to engage in criminal acts.
> (Gottfredson & Hirschi, 1990: 89)

Individuals who lack self-control, according to Gottfredson and Hirschi (1990: 90), tend to
be "impulsive, insensitive, physical (as opposed to mental), risk-taking, shortsighted, and
nonverbal." Criminal and deviant behaviors tend to provide only short-term benefit and
require little planning or skill, often resulting in pain or discomfort to the victim, while providing thrill and/or excitement for the perpetrator (Gottfredson & Hirschi, 1990). Since
offending typically involves risk and immediate gratification, individuals who participate
in a problematic youth group are motivated by these stimuli, according to this theory.
Wikström and Treiber (2007) have proposed to make a distinction between the individual traits that might influence an individual's ability to exercise self-control and the
exercising of self-control itself.[2] They suggested a new conceptualization of self-control:
it is "the successful inhibition of perceived action alternatives, or interruption of a
course of action, that conflicts with an individual's morality." If a person is willing
to exercise self-control, that person should recognize a conflict that has emerged
between personal motivation and his or her personal moral rules and successfully
inhibits the commitment of an offense in the context of moral judgment. It is unclear
whether people recognize such conflicts, given the fact that much crime is decided
in minutes, not in months. Personally, we prefer the definitions that are given by contemporary theorists of self-control, like Vohs and Baumeister (2011) and Wikström and
Treiber (2007). The consequence of the position taken here is that self-control no longer
should be seen as a six-dimensional construct. The ability to exert self-control is reflected by impulse control, thrill-seeking behavior, and anger management.

---

2. To say that individuals who exercise self-control 'have high self-control' and individuals who do
    not 'have low self-control' obscures this distinction. An individual will apply different degrees of
    self-control in different situations. What one 'possesses' is the ability to exercise self-control. Wikström
    and Treiber (2007) that individual differences in the ability to exercise self-control arise from individual
    differences in executive capability.

Table 3   Overview of key concepts and explanation of the causal mechanisms at work

Concept	Effect on …	How does it work?
Accumulation of low collective efficacy and exposure to micro-place disorder and delinquent youth	External locus of control	Differential reinforcement of the perception that life is out of control and guided by fate; reinforcement of the perception that nobody cares and law breaking goes unpunished
	Moral beliefs about rule breaking	Weakening of the normative tie to society through the signaling function that rule breaking is tolerated and inhabitants do not care, stimulated the acceptance of alternative normative systems
	Low social integration	Harsh micro-place conditions weaken informal controls: under harsh conditions it is more difficult to maintain as counter-narratives are present
Low social integration	External locus of control	Weak integration may install the learned belief of external locus of control. External locus of control is not seen as a trait but as a learned belief.
	Moral beliefs about rule breaking	Impedes the neutralization societal norms and justification of the breaking of societal norms and the joining of problematic youth groups
	Lifestyle risk (situational criminogenic exposure)	Releases the individual from constraints to indulge in a street corner-oriented lifestyle
External locus of control	Moral beliefs about rule breaking	External locus of control weakens the preparedness to invest in conventional norms or to live by conventional moral beliefs
	Ability to self-control	External locus of control weakens the ability to control immediate gratification and volatile temper
Low ability to self-control	Moral beliefs about rule breaking	Low self-control pulls individuals toward adopting unconventional moral beliefs
	Lifestyle risk (exposure)	A low ability to self-control pulls individuals toward unstructured socializing with delinquent youths
Moral beliefs on rule-breaking	Lifestyle risk Problematic youth group involvement and offending	Deviant moral beliefs make people see offending as an action alternative, and a problematic youth group involvement as a viable option.
Lifestyle risk (situational exposure)	Offending and problematic youth group involvement	Brings potential offenders in contact with perceived opportunities (temptation and provocation), reinforcement, imitation, and identification with informal groups that engage in risky behavior

Wikström and Treiber (2007) argue that individual differences in the ability to exercise self-control arise from individual differences in executive capability. In the present study, we will consistently talk about the capability to exercise self-control.

2.6   *The role of lifestyle risk or criminogenic exposure*

Routine activities theory (Osgood et al., 1996; Osgood & Anderson, 2004) argues that adolescent offending results, in part, from spending time in situations that offer appealing opportunities for that behavior. This perspective finds support in evidence that many problem behaviors are associated with spending time in unstructured and unsupervised socializing with peers (e.g. Osgood et al., 1996; Osgood & Anderson, 2004; Vazsonyi et al., 2002). When the individual becomes habituated to the street corner lifestyle, the chances of becoming affiliated with problematic youth groups are further increased. The street corner lifestyle is characterized by unstructured socializing with peers that one considers to be similar than oneself, living on the edge, being involved in exciting unstructured routine activities day by day, unhindered by feelings of future responsibilities, which have primarily been being neutralized by lowered levels of personal control, weak social bonds, and perceived low moral beliefs. The development of a risky lifestyle can be viewed as a next step in the process of drifting away toward a problematic youth group.

In Table 3 we present an overview of the key concepts and how each concept influences the other concepts in the model.

6 | A MULTI-METHOD APPROACH IN THE CITY OF ANTWERP

Antwerp is the biggest city/municipality of Belgium and has approximately 510.000 inhabitants. Around 55.2% of the inhabitants have a fully native Belgian background, i.e. of Belgian descent (background of parents taken into account), 9.3% are newest Belgians (background of parents taken into account), 15.3% are new Belgians, and 20% are non-Belgians in Antwerp. These data are based on descent and not just on having the Belgian nationality (as many individuals who are born in Antwerp do not have an Antwerp descent). These data refer to the situation in 2014. Antwerp is a city that has a well-known international harbor and can probably best be compared to the city of Rotterdam in the Netherlands.

This chapter briefly discusses the multiple sources that were used to conduct this study of correlates of problematic youth group involvement. Additionally, attention is paid to the aggregation levels used in the present study. The level of aggregation still remains a huge problem for studies that are interested in the ecological context of problematic youth group involvement. Boundaries may be arbitrary, and the aggregation of data may suffer validity problems if the chosen (or available) level of aggregation is flawed. We therefore carefully explain how the city of Antwerp is divided into administrative neighborhoods (i.e. neighborhoods that have administrative boundaries) and neighborhood clusters (which are aggregates of adjacent administrative neighborhoods) in order to be able to study the neighborhood context of PYG and offending. The smallest geographical unit of analysis at which structural data are systematically gathered is the level of the census tract (in Dutch, 'statistische sector'), and at this level, information from both police records and administrative data on social structure is available. This level allows for very detailed analyses, but often contains too few inhabitants in the theoretical population of juveniles to perform contextual analyses of neighborhood context on PYG involvement and offending in early adolescence.

Problematic youth group involvement, the key dependent variable in the present study, was measured in a questionnaire through a classroom paper-and-pencil-survey approach. In order to be able to study the neighborhood structural context of problematic youth group involvement, it was vital to obtain information that could be geo coded. Although information was gathered on the respondents' home addresses, information to fully allocate addresses to census tracts was impossible due to missing data.[1] Antwerp's 312 census tracts have been clustered into 42 neighborhood clusters, using an official area classification system that is also used by social workers as working areas of neighborhoods in Antwerp. These 42 neighborhood clusters can be seen as functional units, providing in everyday economic and social needs, and are clusters of geographically adjacent census tracts. In short, structural data were gathered at the census tract level and then aggregated into neighborhood clusters.

2   THE ANTWERP YOUTH SURVEY

The Antwerp youth survey is a school-based paper-and-pencil survey among 2.486 young adolescents clustered in 23 schools and 42 neighborhood clusters (effective sample size) in the first grade of the Belgian secondary school system in the city of Antwerp.[2] The Antwerp Youth Survey is a large-scale Belgian study among youths in early adolescence that was initially set up to test theories of crime causation. The survey is unique because it covers a wide array of theoretical variables and covers youths from all neighborhood clusters in Antwerp. Antwerp is the largest city in Belgium. As many books and articles have been published using data from the Antwerp Youth Survey, we will only briefly cover the basics here. Details can be found elsewhere (Pauwels, 2007; Pauwels, Hardyns & van de Velde, 2010).

The Antwerp sample respondents were on average 13 years old when entering the first grade and 14 years when leaving the first grade. Information on unit nonresponse is restricted to noncooperation of students. The level of noncooperation was 7.5% of the Antwerp students in the participating schools. Thus, 92.5% of the questionnaires turned in by the students were suitable for further analysis. The Antwerp survey consisted of 49.4% boys and 50.6% girls; 44.2% of the respondents had a fully native background (both parents from Belgian descent), 10.4% of the respondents had one parent with immigration background, while 45.5% of the respondents had an immigrant background (both parents). This overrepresentation is due to a higher participation of schools in inner-city areas, although the population of schools was asked for permission to conduct the survey. The oversampling of youths in inner-city areas serves the purpose of the study very well, as problematic youth group involvement is statistically rare and problematic groups are overrepresented in inner-city areas. 73.9% of the respondents were aged 12-14 years, while 26.2% of the respondents were aged

---

1. Especially house numbers were missing on the 'address question'; against our expectations, the young adolescents were willing to provide their addresses, at least the street they lived in.
2. As countries have differing educational systems, we should point out the following about the Belgian school system: the first grade of the Belgian secondary school system is meant to be a preparation for future study. The secondary school system in Belgium consists of three grades: each grade is of 2 years' duration. People enter the secondary school system after 6 years of education in an elementary school.

15-17 years. Around 15% of the respondents lived in a single-parent/caretaker family and 85% of the respondents lived with two parents or caretakers.

3   COMMUNITY EXPERT SURVEY OF KEY INFORMANTS TO MEASURE
         COLLECTIVE EFFICACY AND DISORDER

The most commonly used method to capture social processes is to survey residents of ecological settings through representative samples. However, one can argue that residents are not necessarily aware of social situations in their residential areas, as many employees, students, etc. commute and therefore do not have a clear idea of what is really going on in their neighborhoods. Using only residents as subjects may therefore lead to measurement error and bias. For this reason, it is important to develop alternative ways of measuring social processes. Oberwittler and Wikström (2009) recently demonstrated that smaller units of analysis generate more reliable ecological measures. Earlier, Raudenbush and Sampson (1999) suggested that 20 to 30 respondents (residents) are sufficient to reliably measure neighborhood social processes. They also found that more than 40 respondents provide little incremental improvement of ecological reliability. Raudenbush and Sampson used combined census tracts as their operational measure of local communities. It is therefore not possible to generalize their findings to other units of analysis that also refer to small areas. One can assume that the higher the level of analysis, the more heterogeneous the area. It is also reasonable to assume that more residents are necessary to obtain reliable measures of community processes at the higher level (e.g. postal code areas). However, survey costs may rise dramatically if the unit of analysis is at a higher level, such as the postal code level, since postal code areas consist of several census tracts.

One interesting and useful alternative to a survey of residents is the use of systematic social observation, a technique that has successfully been used when trying to measure disorder (social and physical disorder – see Raudenbush & Sampson, 1999). Systematic social observation avoids bias in respondents' lack of knowledge on disorder and directly measures visible aspects of community organizational processes, such as alcohol consumption on streets, the presence of litter, graffiti, etc. The high cost of this method is one reason why it has never (as far as we know) been used within European empirical research on area variation in crime and disorder. The method of systematic social observation may be accurate when studying disorder, but it may not capture social cohesive processes.

One other method for measuring social processes in local areas such as neighborhoods is the expert survey or key informant analysis. Pauwels (2006; 2007) and Pauwels and Hardyns (2009) have extensively explored this technique in different Belgian criminological studies on urban crime and disorder in small areas. These studies demonstrated that the technique of 'key informant analysis' could be used to create ecologically reliable and valid measures of neighborhood organizational processes, referring to social cohesion/social trust and disorder. One major question that arises then is "what kinds of people should be considered as the *optimal* key informants?" Key informants are defined as persons who have a *privileged* position that enables them to provide detailed information on local area processes. Thus, in studies of community organizational processes, key informants are expected to have in-depth knowledge of issues such as social trust and disorder. Therefore, fewer informants are required to get reliable measures of ecological processes. Some people can, through their jobs, provide more meaningful and less-biased information on matters such as social trust and disorder. One major task is to select such key informants.

Key informants who meet this criterion of above-average knowledge of local area processes have been identified as being employed in certain types of jobs such as social workers, local police officers, local shop keepers (e.g. grocery stores, newspaper kiosks, etc.), local bartenders, and people who work with local policies. The methodology is similar to the kind used when conducting a survey of neighborhood residents: the key informants are given self-completion questionnaires. However, the selection procedure is one area in which there are major differences between surveys among residents and profession-based key informants. While random selection is the criterion used in resident surveys, professional key informants are chosen on the basis of their knowledge about community organizational processes. Key informants are thus field experts. The importance of this principle has been underscored by Campbell (1955: 340), who stated "if the use of informants as a social science research tool is to be developed, it seems likely that principles of optimal selection will have to be developed." The principle of optimal selection should ensure that the knowledge of professional key informants exceeds the knowledge of ordinary residents. The key informants were used to create measures of neighborhood-level social disorganization, social trust, and crime and disorder.

4   ADMINISTRATIVE CENSUS TRACT LEVEL DATA AND POLICE REGISTER
         DATA

The objective measures of neighborhood-level risk factors that are used in the present study to evaluate the effects of structural characteristics and problematic youth group involvement are mainly derived from official sources, mainly the Antwerp department of local statistics, the municipality's study service working for the municipal government, and the Mayor, and were obtained at the smallest level of aggregation, which is the census tract level. The main concern during the present study was to gather as good measures as possible with regard to neighborhood structural disadvantage. Administrative data are available at the smallest level at which data are systematically gathered, the census tract, and annual updates of these data are conducted through the Antwerp's department of local statistics. Police data on neighborhood crime levels, adult offender rates, and juvenile delinquency rates were more difficult to obtain, and it took more time than expected to get access to the data, which enabled us to create measures of the offender rate and juvenile delinquency rate. At the time the data collection of this study began, the Belgian Local Police has just changed software and the data processing system of crime registration. The 'Integrated System of the Local Police' (ISLP), the Belgian data processing system of the Local Police, was fully operational, but it took a very long time to translate the original police records of adult and minor suspects into meaningful numbers at the smallest unit of analysis. Data on neighborhood crime rates, i.e. where crimes were committed, were more easily obtained, and it was less difficult to create neighborhood crime rates. The policy makers' view with regard to their preparedness to share data and present data that can be consulted readily on the internet has increased. Nowadays, the Local Police of Antwerp display official crime statistics at local levels (neighborhood clusters) to demonstrate transparency, i.e. the willingness of the local government to be as open as possible toward the public opinion with regard to crime levels and local criminal and prevention policy.

5   AGGREGATION OF CENSUS DATA TO THE NEIGHBORHOOD CLUSTER
       LEVEL

The neighborhood cluster level is the geographical level that will be used in this study of the structural correlates of problematic youth group involvement. Neighborhood clusters had on average 10.331 inhabitants in 2005 (at the moment of data collection) and contained on average three census tracts. The Antwerp Youth Survey contained three questions with regard to the area of residence: the address (street), a question on the official neighborhood clusters, and postal code, the full range of neighborhood clusters. It was carefully checked what impact the aggregation of census data to the neighborhood cluster had on the relationship between structural variables. The impact on the correlations between area characteristics was negligible. Therefore, the data obtained at the neighborhood cluster level could be used to check the ecological validity of the youth survey: the youth survey contained a series of questions on the demographic background of the respondents, such as poverty and immigrant background. In Table 4, we present the correlation matrix of neighborhood cluster-

Table 4   Ecological correlations between social structural characteristics of respondents in the Antwerp Youth Survey (AYS) and neighborhood disadvantage (as aggregated from the census data)

	(1)	(2)	(3)	(4)
Neighborhood disadvantage (1)	1			
% non-Western inhabitants (2)	0.83***	1		
% youths in family disadvantage (AYS) (3)	0.58***	0.39*	1	
% non-EU immigrant background (AYS) (4)	0.80***	0.82***	0.47***	1

*Correlation is significant at the 0.05 level (2-tailed).
***Correlation is significant at the 0.001 level (2-tailed).

aggregated structural background characteristics derived from the youth survey and administrative data on disadvantage.

The bivariate correlation matrix between social structural neighborhood character-istics reveals some very interesting results concerning ecological validity between the administrative data at the neighborhood cluster level and the aggregate survey responses on social demographics. Although measured differently, our sample measure of ethnic segregation (% having parents with a descent outside the EU) and administrative measure of ethnic segregation (% of Moroccan and Turkish inhabitants) are correlated very high at the neighborhood cluster level (0.82). The administrative measure of unemployment and our measure of deprivation are also correlated rather strong, although both variables are not the same, strictly speaking (0.58). But, it can be seen that deprivation from the perspective of youth responses and unemployment in administrative data cluster geographically. The correlation between the administrative measure of deprivation and the administrative measure of ethnic segregation is almost as high as the correlation of the administrative meas-ure of deprivation and the sample measure of ethnic segregation (respectively, 0.83 and 0.80).

When looking at the relation between the sample measure of deprivation and the sample measure of ethnic segregation on the one side and, on the other side, the cor-relation between the sample measure of deprivation and the administrative measure of ethnic segregation, these are also very similar (0.39 and 0.47). It is clear that these correlations cannot be expected to be perfect, both because of different ways of meas-uring and different sources of error going in to the data, which can never be controlled by the researcher (such as lying about background or exaggerating and overstating offending in the survey), but despite these differences, the geographical clustering is more than acceptable. These correlations actually lead us to conclude that we may have confidence in the data. From an ecological point of view, they are a relative good reflection of 'true' neighborhood composition.

6   BASIC SOCIO-DEMOGRAPHIC STATISTICS AND THE RELATIVE
         STABILITY OF NEIGHBORHOOD DISADVANTAGE AND DISORDER

Let us first describe the variation between the 42 neighborhood clusters. At the moment of data collection, Antwerp could be divided into 42 neighborhood clusters. The offender rate varies between 0% and 7.55%. The offender rate is based on the number of inhabitants (adults) who were suspected by the local police because of a crime divided by the number of inhabitants (adults). The juvenile delinquency rate is based on the number of juveniles (11-17) who were suspected by the police of a crime. These data are highly skewed, as can be seen from the huge difference between the mean score and the maximum score. The same goes for the proportion of youths who report to be involved in a problematic youth group: percentages range from 0% to 12% percent at the neighborhood cluster level. Official data are also very skewed, with unemployment varying between 3.54% and 20.83%, and the percent of non-Western immigrants ranging from 0%% cent to 12.64%. These data refer to 2005, the moment of data collection. In order to get an insight into the relative stability of neighborhoods, we report some important correlations, which can be interpreted as stability coefficients (Table 5).

At the level of the census tract, the geographical disparity becomes even clearer. We just discuss some of the variables that are presented in their original metric, like the percent of owner-occupied dwellings (ranging from 0.62% to 94.81%), the juvenile delinquency rate (from 0% to 35.00%), and the percent of unemployed (from 0.5% to 24.52%) (Table 6). The percent of non-Belgians (from 0.75% to 38.33%). Again, these data refer to 2005. How stable are these structural characteristics of places? At the moment of data collection, we had only a limited view based on census data

Table 5   Some basic descriptives of Antwerp neighborhood clusters at the moment of data collection (2005)

	N	Minimum	Maximum	Mean	Standard deviation
Offender rate	42	0.00	7.55	2.40	1.64
Juvenile delinquency rate	42	0.00	14.47	5.79	4.05
Violent crime rate	42	0.00	393.44	68.18	86.89
Proportion involved in a problematic youth group	42	0.00	0.12	0.04	0.04
% unemployed	42	3.54	20.83	8.79	4.28
% non-Western immigrants	42	0.00	12.64	2.76	3.03
Population density	42	1137.49	17,599.80	6900.38	4048.82
% home owners	42	19.54	95.45	48.77	17.34
% of stable households (>5 years)	42	43.48	75.00	60.41	7.92
Valid N (listwise)	42				

Table 6   Some basic descriptives of Antwerp census tracts at the moment of data collection

	Minimum	Maximum	Mean	Standard deviation
Disadvantage	−2.23	3.63	0.00	1.00
Nonprofit housing	0.00	103.50	8.41	17.61
Owner-occupied dwellings	0.62	94.81	49.45	19.76
Social disorganization	−0.95	1.54	0.10	0.58
Juvenile offender rate	0.00	35.00	6.38	6.94
% empty dwellings	0.00	20.89	1.72	2.60
Median income (Euro)	10,507.00	33,544.00	17,717.44	3316.59
% unemployed	0.45	24.52	7.98	5.03
% non-Belgians	0.75	38.33	11.93	9.14
Population density	215.58	22,457.24	8790.32	4779.56

N = 210 census tracts; omitted: tracts <200 inhabitants. **Correlation is significant at the 0.01 level (2-tailed).

Note: Disadvantage is based on an exploratory factor analysis of % unemployed, median income, % empty dwellings, and % non-Belgians.

Table 7   Stability coefficients of immigrant concentrations

	% Non-Belgian citizens 1990	% Non-Belgian citizens 2001	% Non-Belgian citizens 2012
% non-Belgian citizens 1990	1		
% non-Belgian citizens 2001	0.896**	1	
% non-Belgian citizens 2012	0.736**	0.862**	1

**Correlation is significant at the 0.01 level (2-tailed).

Table 8   Stability coefficients of unemployment rate

	Unemployment rate 1990	Unemployment rate 2001	Unemployment rate 2012
Unemployment rate 1990	1		
Unemployment rate 2001	0.886**	1	
Unemployment rate 2012	0.800**	0.867**	1

**Correlation is significant at the 0.01 level (2-tailed).

Table 9   Stability coefficient of disorder

	Log disorder 2002
Log disorder 2010	0.77***

***Correlation is significant at the 0.001 level (2-tailed).

(1990 and 2001). Today, we can look back and give some additional image of the stability of neighborhood characteristics (Tables 7-9).

Neighborhood structural characteristics are relatively stable over time. We were able to collect additional data within the framework of this research project and present the ecological correlations between key structural characteristics that are of relevance from the point of view of social ecological theories.

Attention is paid to the stability in ethnic heterogeneity, disadvantage, and disorder, key theoretical variables that were measured at the neighborhood level. All stability coefficients are approximately 0.80, which is extremely high.

7   DEFINITION OF PROBLEMATIC YOUTH GROUP INVOLVEMENT

In this paragraph, we explain how we conceived problematic youth group involvement. Despite the increasing number of studies, there still is little consensus among social scientists as to the meaning of the term 'gang.' Part of the problem stems from the fact that many definitions can be extremely general and inclusive. The main problem inherent in defining what constitutes a gang lies in the changing dynamics of what represents gangs (or any group) over time. Several prominent researchers have proposed definitions for gang, which are widely used in gang literature. Perhaps, the most cited definition is that which is operationalized by Klein (1971), distinguishing a gang as any identifiable group of youngsters who are generally perceived as a distinct aggregation by others in their neighborhood; recognize themselves as a denotable group (often with a group name); and have been involved in a sufficient number of delinquent incidents to elicit a negative response from neighborhood residents and/or law enforcement agencies. Klein's definition, although not perfect, has the advantage of capturing the essence of the word 'gang' while speaking to the dynamics of gang formation and interaction as well as external reaction to gangs.

Differences in definitions impede the comparability of cross-national findings, and this is one major reason for developing a standard definition in cross-national research, to a large extent stimulated by the Eurogang network. Klein, Weerman, and Thornberry (2006: 418) defined involvement in troublesome youth groups as follows: "A street gang (or a troublesome youth group corresponding to a street gang elsewhere) is any durable, street-oriented youth group whose own identity includes involvement in illegal activity." Thus, such a group is characterized by a certain degree of duration, independent of shifts in individual membership, group identity, and involvement in illegal (criminal) activities. In the present study, we are restricted to the questionnaire used by the research team.

The questions used to measure PYG involvement are partially inspired by an early version of the measurement instrument currently developed by the Eurogang working group (for a contemporary version, see Weerman et al., 2009), but also by a study of Heitmeyer et al. (1995). We need to point out that there are considerable differences between both instruments. The data collection of the Antwerp Youth Survey dates from 2005, and the questionnaire was developed between 2003 and 2004, thus some years before the publishing of some influential Eurogang publications. The current version of the Eurogang measurement instrument includes questions concerning the durable character of the group, which has not been taken into account in the present study. We therefore need to stress that our measurement instrument is somewhat different. Analogous to the Eurogang instrument that measures troublesome youth group involvement, we have made use of definers, i.e. elements that are absolutely necessary to define the group as a problematic youth group. Problematic youth group definers are those elements that are absolutely necessary to characterize the group as a problematic group (Esbensen & Maxson, 2011). Thus, we still argue that our instrument may provide insight into the phenomenon, albeit in a slightly restricted way. Similar to the Eurogang instrument, our instrument refers to the street (or neighborhood) orientation of the group, the approval of violence, and engagement in violent activities. To avoid any misleading interpretation, we use the term problematic youth group involvement instead of troublesome youth group involvement.

PYG involvement was measured using a funneling technique; i.e. we combined answers to one filter question and four follow-up questions to measure self-reported

Table 10   Questions measuring problematic youth group involvement

Problematic youth group involvement definers	Answer categories
Do you consider yourself to be a member of a group of friends (no organization or association) that frequently meets and considers itself as a group?	Yes No
1. Does your group quarrel with other young people?	Never/sometimes/often/very often
2. Do members of your group need to be prepared to do exciting and dangerous things?	
3. Does your group act and does not talk if the image of the group is in danger?	
4. Does your group have fights with juveniles from other areas than your area?	
5. Is the group engaged in illegal behavior?	

PYG involvement. As shown in Table 10, the leading question was "Some adolescents have a steady group of friends to do things together, or to hang around outside. Do you consider yourself to be a member of a group of friends (no organization or association) that frequently meets and considers itself as a group?" (1 = yes, 0 = no). The four follow-up questions were as follows: (1) "Does your group quarrel with other young people?" (2) "Do members of your group need to be prepared to do exciting and dangerous things?" (3) "Does your group act and does not talk if the image of the group is in danger?" (4) "Does your group have fights with juveniles from other areas than your area?" (5) "Is the group engaged in illegal behavior?" These follow-up questions were originally polytomous (answering categories on a four-point scale: never-sometimes-often-very often), but were dichotomized (1 = sometimes or more; 0 = never). Respondents were categorized as involved in a PYG if they answered affirmatively to the leading question as well as to the five follow-up questions. The important element here is that illegal activities are part of the group definition.

The measure of PYG involvement was created by recoding all respondents who positively answered the filter question and positively answered the aforementioned follow-up questions. 8.1% of the youths who participated in the survey are defined as being involved in a problematic youth group. If we apply a stricter criterion and count as a member of a problematic youth group those who have reported 'often or more' on all these follow-up questions, the percent decreases from 8.1% to 4.9%. While we did not notice any significant effect on the correlates of problematic youth group involvement, which are to be discussed in the subsequent chapters, we identified one potential threat, namely the inability to carefully dissect the tests of the integrated model in subsamples by gender and immigrant background.

8   PREVIOUS STUDIES ON THE SOCIAL ECOLOGY OF CRIME AND DELINQUENCY IN ANTWERP

The city of Antwerp is one of the most segregated in the Flemish part of Belgium. Poor neighborhoods are situated around the city center. Contemporary problems in urban areas usually have historical roots. This is not different in Antwerp. The 'poverty belt' is actually a series of neighborhoods where the 19th-century working class was living. It is in these areas where newly arrived migrants came to live when they first entered Antwerp.

Previous studies of the social ecology of crime can be divided into two groups of studies: studies of the social ecology of crime and the role of social trust (collective efficacy) and studies of the social ecology of juvenile delinquency (Table 11).

With regard to the spatial distribution of offender rates, previous studies showed that neighborhood stability, neighborhood disadvantage, and ethnic heterogeneity were strong predictors of the juvenile arrest rate. The effect of neighborhood structural characteristics was partially mediated by social disorganization, as measured by professional key informants. The number of male arrestees aged 11-17 could be predicted from the key structural characteristics of social disorganization (Pauwels, 2007). The effect of neighborhood structural characteristics on neighborhood crime levels was additionally tested in a comparative study (Mellgren, Pauwels & Torstensson, 2010). It was found that neighborhood social trust mediated the effect of neighborhood

Table 11   Regression estimates of effects of community structure on crime in Antwerp neighborhoods

Dependent: crime	Model 1 (A) Beta	Model 2 (A) Beta	Model 3 (A) Beta
Population density	0.376***	0.078 ns	−0.004 ns
Disadvantage	–	0.560***	0.429***
Disorder	–	–	0.318***
Model evaluation			
Rsq adj.	0.137	0.360	0.424
F-change	34.04***	73.03***	23.79***

N = 210, ***p < 0.001, ns: not significant.
Source: Table adapted from Mellgren, Pauwels and Torstensson (2010).

Table 12   Path coefficients of neighborhood characteristics on the juvenile delinquency rate in Antwerp neighborhoods

Dependent → ↓ Independent	Juvenile delinquency rate	Disorganization	Disadvantage	Owner-occupied dwellings
Disorganization	0.21			
Disadvantage	0.46	0.20		
Owner-occupied dwellings	–	–	−0.57	
Nonprofit housing	–	–	–	−0.50
Density	–	0.39	0.30	−0.31
R square	0.33	0.27	0.55	0.39

Note: Standardized coefficient presented. Global model fit indices: RMSEA: 0.025 RMR: 0.022 AGFI: 0.96.
Source: Adapted from (Pauwels, 2007).

disadvantage in Antwerp and Malmö neighborhoods in a very similar way. The indirect effect went through collective efficacy (social trust), which in turn affected disorganization and disorder (Table 12).

Concluding, Antwerp is a highly segregated city on both the census tract level and neighborhood cluster level. The stability coefficients of structural characteristics are very high. This study of problematic youth group involvement will benefit from all the efforts that were done in the first decade of the 21st century to understand neighborhood differences in problematic youth group involvement. These patterns will be fleshed out in the following chapters, that will each on their own pays in detail attention to the family social position, the community context (chapter eight), individual characteristics, and lifestyle-related characteristics and their relationship with problematic youth group involvement and offending.

1   INTRODUCTION AND GOALS

The objective of crime pattern analysis is to describe criminal phenomena in a particular area. This chapter aims to contribute to the literature on crime pattern analysis by describing the involvement in delinquent behavior of young adolescents (grade 7 and 8 in the US school system) attending school in the city of Antwerp during the school year 2004-2005.

The structure of this chapter is as follows:

* First, we present the proportions of youths who have engaged in a series of offenses as well as problematic youth group involvement. Results are presented for the sample as a whole and for immigrant and nonimmigrant boys and girls. This is innovative as few studies consist of sufficient high sample size to be able to conduct analyses in these subgroups.
* Second, we present the PYG-to-non-PYG involvement odds ratios (OR's) to get insight into the relationship between problematic youth group involvement and offending. The analyses are presented separately for males and females and for immigrants and nonimmigrants.
* Third, we present the number of offenses committed by members of a problematic youth group and youths who are not involved in a problematic youth group.

2   SELF-REPORTED DELINQUENCY PER ITEM AND BY GENDER AND IMMIGRANT BACKGROUND

Self-reported offending was surveyed using a series of delinquency-related items very similar to the questioning method used by the international self-report study (Junger-Tas, Haen-Marshall & Ribeaud, 2003). Nine offenses form the basis of this descriptive study. These nine offenses all fall under the concept of so-called 'commonplace offending.' These are violence toward persons or goods and various types of property offenses. Specifically, the delinquency items referred to are damaging public goods and vehicles; graffiti; fencing; shoplifting; stealing goods with a value over 25 euro; threatened and robbed someone in group (UK slang: steaming); hitting someone to hurt; fighting outside school; and burglary (breaking and entering of houses or

Table 13 **Proportions of youths who engaged in crime and used substances during the past 12 months**

	N	Proportions of total sample	Proportions of immigrant females	Proportions of Belgian females	Proportions of immigrant males	Proportions of Belgian males
Committed more than 4 different acts of crime	2439	0.13	0.08	0.07	0.24	0.12
Vandalism	2442	0.12	0.06	0.07	0.22	0.14
Graffiti	2440	0.15	0.14	0.15	0.17	0.13
Fencing	2439	0.07	0.03	0.02	0.18	0.05
Shoplifting	2443	0.16	0.10	0.19	0.18	0.20
Theft (>25 euro)	2436	0.05	0.02	0.02	0.11	0.05
Threatening and robbery in group	2439	0.09	0.07	0.04	0.16	0.08
Hitting someone on purpose	2447	0.30	0.23	0.20	0.44	0.30
Fighting outside school	2442	0.20	0.15	0.07	0.39	0.18
Being drunk	2442	0.14	0.10	0.18	0.11	0.19
Smoking cannabis	2438	0.06	0.03	0.05	0.09	0.05
Burglary	2436	0.02	0.01	0.00	0.05	0.02
Reported no offense	2437	0.32	0.43	0.40	0.18	0.27
Mean variety scale	2437	1.84	1.41	1.33	2.66	1.86
PYG	2476	0.08	0.07	0.04	0.14	0.06
Valid N (listwise)	2427		N = 678	N = 553	N = 657	N = 529

vehicles). Furthermore, two types of substance use were included in the questionnaire: being drunk and smoking cannabis. An initial filter question inquired whether the youths had ever committed one of these offenses. Filter questions were always followed by follow-up questions. These follow-up questions concerned the age of onset and the number of times each specific offense was committed in the 12-month period prior to the survey. Based on the respondents' replies to the filter questions and follow-up questions, the prevalence per offense was calculated.

Table 13 shows the proportions of youths who engaged in these nine offenses, together with substance use, during the past 12 months. Proportions are shown for the total sample and for immigrant and nonimmigrant boys and girls.

3   OFFENDING BY PROBLEMATIC YOUTH GROUP PARTICIPATION

Table 14 shows the PYG to non-PYG involvement ORs. These are interesting because they show the relationship between members in problematic youth groups and

Table 14   PYG-to-non-PYG odds ratios for delinquency and substance use in the past 12 months

	Total sample	Males	Females	Belgian	Non-Belgian
Vandalism	13.77	9.99	20.43	26.17	10.01
Graffiti	6.19	5.13	8.87	10.71	4.88
Buying stolen goods	7.98	6.86	7.45	11.32	6.10
Shoplifting	5.00	4.27	5.05	10.47	4.37
Theft of goods (>25 euro)	10.15	9.33	8.02	20.91	6.98
Mobbing	7.79	6.29	9.23	10.18	6.33
Hitting on purpose	3.66	2.81	4.51	3.67	3.41
Fighting in public	7.36	6.04	8.39	14.94	4.88
Being drunk	4.26	3.15	7.06	8.37	4.09
Cannabis use	9.65	8.91	9.40	16.55	7.33
Burglary	10.46	9.58	6.03	22.17	7.22

offending: for all offenses that are shown in the table, problematic youth group involvement increases the odds of having committed the offenses and types of substance use that are presented in the table. The effect sizes vary by the type of crime but are large, especially for serious offending, vandalism, and violent offending.

4   AGE OF ONSET AND PROBLEMATIC YOUTH GROUP PARTICIPATION

Age of onset is a well-studied aspect of criminal career research. Criminal career research shows that adolescents who start offending at an early age tend to commit a wider variety and more serious offenses. On average, they keep offending for a longer time compared to youngsters with a later age of onset (Blumstein et al., 1986; Farrington & Loeber, 2000). In the questionnaire used in the present study, we inquired at what age the respondents reported offending for the first time. This research question is of relevance for the study of problematic youth group participation as well. From our analysis, it seems that respondents who participate in a problematic youth group do not report an earlier age of onset.

The Table 15 shows their responses according to age group. We consider the category 'younger than 10' to be particularly interesting from an empirical perspective because it can provide us with some insights into the question how early respondents start offending. The category aged between 10 and 12 refers to grade 5 and 6, which are the highest level of primary compulsory education in the Belgian educational system. Those youths who reported that they started offending at age 12 or older were already in grade 7 or 8 (the start of the secondary compulsory education in the Belgian educational system) at the time the research was conducted.

The self-reported modal age-of-onset category is 'between 10 and 12 years.' Only for 'having bought something you knew was stolen' the modal age of onset is 'older than 12.' Age of onset for youngsters in grade 7 and 8 is different for each offense.

Table 15   Age of onset of youths involved in a problematic youth group

Type of offense	% <10 years of age (N)	% 10-12 years of age (N)	% >12 years of age (N)	% total (N)
Vandalism	20.4 (115)	54.5 (307)	25.1 (142)	100 (564)
Spraying graffiti	16.0 (102)	53.3 (339)	30.7 (196)	100 (637)
Having bought something you knew was stolen	12.6 (39)	42.7 (132)	44.7 (138)	100 (309)
Shoplifting	32.2 (332)	50.2 (517)	17.6 (180)	100 (1029)
Theft >5 euro	20.3 (53)	49.5 (129)	30.2 (79)	100 (261)
Harassing people in the streets	11.5 (38)	46.9 (155)	41.6 (138)	100 (331)
Deliberately hitting somebody	26.6 (317)	49.4 (588)	24.0 (286)	100 (1191)
Get into a fight after school	9.7 (75)	48.4 (374)	41.9 (324)	100 (773)
Burglary	19.4 (21)	40.7 (44)	39.9 (43)	100 (108)

Note: Differences in age of onset between those involved and youths not involved in a problematic youth group were not statistically significant. Therefore, no separate tables are given.

However, it is striking that a relatively large percentage of respondents report having committed their first offense before the age of 10. The percentages vary between 9.7% and 32.2% of the total sample. However, the higher percentages are found for the less severe offenses such as shoplifting, deliberately hitting someone, and vandalism.

5   PREVALENCE OF OFFENDING BY PROBLEMATIC YOUTH GROUP PARTICIPATION

If one compares the prevalence per number of times committed, i.e. the percentage among those youths who reported an offense, per number of times they reported the offense, one can get an overview of the intensity of crime involvement. For eight out of nine offenses, the youths who participate in a problematic youth group are situated at the high end of the distribution. The results can be read in Table 16. Let us give some illustrations. 27.5% of the youths involved in a problematic youth group report to have committed vandalism more than 10 times. That is 23.9% for graffiti, 18.8% for having bought stolen goods, 21% for shoplifting, 30.9% for theft >5 euro, 18.9% for harassing people in the streets, 37.4% for deliberately hitting someone, and 24.0% for getting into fights. There is only one exception: burglary.

This is highly suggestive for the idea that offending intensifies among problematic youth group participants, a case we cannot prove because that would require panel data, but nevertheless, we validated this finding by looking at the relationship between problematic youth group participation and being a serious offender and

Table 16 Prevalence of offending in the past 12 months in problematic youth group participants and non-participants

		Prevalence per number of times committed**							Blumstein's Lambda***
		1 time	2 times	3 times	4 times	5 times	6 to 10 times	7 to more than 10 times	
Vandalism***	NO PYG	40.2	21.1	16.1	7.5	4.0	6.5	4.5	2.51
	PYG	14.0	14.0	14.0	4.4	12.3	14.0	27.5	4.37
Graffiti***	NO PYG	37.0	23.5	12.6	6.1	9.4	4.3	6.1	2.36
	PYG	17.4	20.7	18.5	8.7	6.5	4.3	23.9	3.75
Fencing***	NO PYG	43.3	15.0	17.3	6.3	7.1	4.7	6.3	2.58
	PYG	23.4	25.0	10.9	7.8	3.1	10.9	18.8	3.50
Shoplifting***	NO PYG	42.0	21.9	11.0	4.7	6.3	6.9	7.2	2.60
	PYG	17.8	16.7	11.1	11.1	17.8	4.4	21.1	3.92
Theft > 5 euro***	NO PYG	39.0	22.0	13.4	7.3	4.9	7.3	6.1	2.63
	PYG	25.5	16.4	9.1	3.6	5.5	9.1	30.9	3.98
Harassing people in the streets***	NO PYG	35.6	22.5	10.0	7.5	8.1	5.6	10.6	2.89
	PYG	20.3	12.2	17.6	9.5	10.8	10.8	18.9	3.86
Deliberately hitting somebody***	NO PYG	24.7	23.2	15.2	7.4	8.5	8.1	12.9	3.27
	PYG	8.7	16.5	9.6	7.0	9.6	11.3	37.4	4.75
Get into a fight after school***	NO PYG	36.2	23.1	13.9	7.7	6.9	5.4	6.7	2.68
	PYG	15.7	14.9	19.0	8.3	7.4	10.7	24.0	4.04
Burglary***	NO PYG	22.9	22.9	14.3	5.7	11.4	2.9	20.0	3.48
	PYG	39.3	7.1	14.3	14.3	7.1	3.6	14.3	3.10

Percent of youths who have reported the offense one time, two times, etc. all percentages are based on the number of respondents who reported an offense at least once. The example was taken from Boxford (2006). Blumsteins lambda was calculated as the total number of acts reported by those that reported the act. The reference period is the past twelve months. Thus, if hundred adolescents together have committed 200 acts (as an aggregate), Blumsteins lambda is 200 divided by 100 and equals 2.
**Correlation is significant at the 0.01 level (2-tailed).
***Correlation is significant at the 0.001 level (2-tailed).

high-frequency offender.[1] An additional analysis revealed that the odds of youths involved in a problematic youth group belonging to the category 'high-frequency offenders' is 13.2 as high as the odds that youths not involved in a problematic youth group falls into the category of high-frequency offenders. The odds of youngsters participating in a problematic youth group belonging to the group serious offenders is 13.27 times as high as the odds of a youth who is not involved in a problematic youth group belonging to the group high-frequency offenders.

---

1. These are of very theory-laden concepts. High frequency offender is defined as an individual who reported four different offenses (or more in the past twelve months). A serious offender is a respondent who reported burglary, buying stolen goods and theft >5 euro. This is only a small percentage of the sample.

6   CONCLUSION

This descriptive chapter revealed patterns of offending in problematic youth group participants and youths who do not report problematic youth group participation. In general, the less serious offenses are reported more than the serious ones, this finding is fully in line with findings from international self-report studies. The descriptive results revealed differences in crime involvement between those involved and those not involve in a problematic youth group. The odds ratios of offending versus not offending in participants and nonparticipants of problematic youth groups are striking. We conclude that these results are in line with findings from previous studies of the Eurogang working group (Esbensen & Maxson, 2011). These descriptive results add to the existing knowledge by demonstrating the patterns of offending in subsamples by gender and immigrant background. From the next chapter on, we will examine the relationship between different characteristics and problematic youth group involvement. We start by examining the relationship between structural background characteristics and problematic youth group participation.

FAMILY SOCIAL POSITION AND PROBLEMATIC YOUTH GROUP INVOLVEMENT

1 INTRODUCTION

The objectives of this chapter are to contribute to the knowledge on problematic youth group involvement by presenting descriptive findings regarding the family social position of individuals who have reported to be affiliated with a problematic youth group. Furthermore, we describe and compare patterns of offending of youths who are involved in problematic youth groups in comparison with those not involved in problematic youth groups.

The structure of this chapter is as follows:

- First, we study the relationships between different measures of family social position and problematic youth group involvement. We make a distinction between family structure (one-parent family or being brought up in a traditional two-parent family) and family social position (poverty or disadvantage). We additionally study this relationship by gender and immigrant background and study the cumulative effect of family position risk scores.
- Second, we make a distinction between objective and subjective measures of disadvantage, i.e. disadvantage measured using objective indicators and perceived dissatisfaction with one's life standard as a measure of relative deprivation.
- Third, we focus on the relation between immigrant background and problematic youth group involvement by paying attention to different operationalizations of immigrant background and by looking for gender differences.
- Fourth, we pay attention to the relation between repeating a class and problematic youth group involvement. The reason we pay attention to repeating a class and problematic youth group involvement in this chapter is because repeating a class is a characteristic that has traditionally been linked to the social structure of the family.

2 FAMILY SOCIAL POSITION

The question of whether an individual's social position affects his or her involvement in a problematic youth group is one of the classic criminological questions. The issue has been raised by many of the famous gang theorists of the previous century. Wikström and Butterworth (2006) argue that, in the media and general debate, it is sometimes taken for granted that the social position of an individual is the key factor in explanation of gang membership and offending. The results of criminological research show more fuzzy results. In this descriptive chapter, we will take a look into the relationship between self-reported problematic youth group involvement and socio-demographic background variables. The relationship between family disadvantage and crime is still the subject of debate and a controversial issue in criminology as self-report studies continue to find modest to absent relationships between measures of disadvantage and offending. The use of school samples, as in the Antwerp Youth Study, is a possible reason for the lack of a larger class-gang relationship in self-report studies. However, the results should be interpreted within a life course dynamic framework: the absence of a relationship merely means that there is no relationship at this point in the life course. Often, a relationship is found between structural disadvantage and problematic youth group involvement at later stages of the life course, and we can observe an accumulation of disadvantage during different developmental stages.

We are aware of the fact that classifying family disadvantage on the basis of the child's information about his or her parents work may suffer severe problems. Therefore, we have only asked the adolescents about a subjective indicator (the financial situation at home) and an objective indicator (do they have a car at home). Although one may question the fact that this is an accurate way of measuring disadvantage, the measure was aggregated at the neighborhood level and strongly correlated with the unemployment rate ($r = 0.58$; $p < 0.01$).

2.1   Family structure

Another major characteristic of youths' social position that often figures in discussions of potential causes of problematic youth group involvement is the family composition or family structure. In particular, the role of living in a split family, either with a single parent or with a step-parent, has been highlighted in previous research as a risk factor for gang membership. In this study, we asked whether the respondents lived with their parents, either one or both, or with somebody else. The measure of family structure was created based on the responses of the respondents with regard to their family composition. The question in the questionnaire consisted of a range of answer categories of possible family members who lived together under one roof. Based on the answers, we created a dummy variable that refers to the classic two-parent family structure versus the situations in which the child lives with only one parent (or one parent and a step-parent). Previously, we found family structure to be indirectly related to self-reported offending in young adolescents (Pauwels, Hardyns & Van de Velde, 2010): the effect disappears once measures of social control theory (especially parental monitoring and the school social bond) are taken into account. This is suggestive of the fact that if family structure is to be a triggering event, its mechanism is the weakening of control.

From Table 17, we can read that there are no statistically significant effects of family structure on PYG. 7.7% of the respondents involved in a problematic youth group

Table 17   **PYG involvement by family structure**

| | **Family structure** | | **Overall** |
	No split family	Split family	
NO PYG	92.3% (1942)	89.8% (334)	91.9% (2276)
PYG	**7.7% (162)**	**10.2% (38)**	**8.1% (200)**
Total	100.0% (2104)	100.0% (372)	100.0% (2476)

Chi square = 2.69, df = 1, p = 0.101.

Table 18   **PYG involvement by co-parenthood**

| | **Moving between parents** | | | **Total** |
	No co-parenthood	Co-parenthood (50-50)	Instable intervals co-parenthood	
NO PYG	92.5% (1919)	87.4% (111)	89.6% (240)	91.9% (2270)
PYG	**7.5% (156)**	**12.6% (16)**	**10.4% (28)**	**8.1% (200)**
Total	100.0% (2075)	100.0% (127)	100.0% (268)	100.0% (2470)

Chi square = 6.38, df = 2, p = 0.040.

come from an intact family and 10.2% come from a split family. The difference is small and contradicts statements from structural strain theories.

Another way of looking into family disruption is by looking at the stability of the adolescent's family situation. Some adolescents have a stable situation and live together with their parents or caretakers at one place, while others move between parents in co-parenting. From the analysis presented in Table 18, we can see that there is a significant effect of moving between parents: youths who move between parents have a greater chance of being in a PYG. While the effect is there, it is rather small.

2.2   *Family structural risk*

Family disadvantage and family structure were used to create an overall family structural risk score. Family ethnicity was not included in the index, because ethnicity does not per definition means structural disadvantage, although a correlation exists at the individual level. As only two measures were used, the family structural risk score ranges from zero to two.

From Table 19, there seems to be a statistical significant relation between family structural risk and PYG involvement: the percentage of youths reporting PYG involvement increases with the structural risk score; however, the effect is rather small.

If we look at the relationship between family structural risk and problematic youth group involvement by gender in Table 20, a small interaction effect pops up. The relationship is not significant for females but is significant for males. This effect is clearly nonlinear: while 9.9% of the youths that are involved in a problematic youth group experiences no family structural risk (based on the structural risk score), 13.1% experiences structural risk on one dimension and 23.1% on both dimensions of family structural risk. The effect of family structural risk on PYG involvement also varies by immigrant status. From the analysis presented in Table 21, we can see that there is an effect only for youths who have a fully native background. This finding is very interesting. How can it be explained that there is no relationship among immigrant youths? The overall

Table 19   PYG involvement by family structural risk

	Family structural risk			Total
	No risk factors	One risk factor	Two risk factors	
NO PYG	92.6% (1799)	89.7% (393)	87.0% (80)	91.9% (2272)
PYG	7.4% (143)	10.3% (45)	13.0% (12)	8.1% (200)
Total	100.0% (1942)	100.0% (438)	100.0% (92)	100.0% (2472)

Chi square = 7.22, df = 2, p = 0.027.

Table 20   PYG involvement by family structural risk and gender

		Family structural risk			Total
		No risk factors	One risk factor	Two risk factors	
Females	**NO PYG**	95.3% (907)	91.9% (227)	94.3% (50)	94.6% (1184)
	PYG	4.7% (45)	8.1% (20)	5.7% (3)	5.4% (68)
	Total	100.0% (952)	100.0% (247)	100.0% (53)	100.0% (1252)
Males	**NO PYG**	90.1% (891)	86.9% (166)	76.9% (30)	89.2% (1087)
	PYG	9.9% (98)	13.1% (25)	23.1% (9)	10.8% (132)
	Total	100.0% (989)	100.0% (191)	100.0% (39)	100.0% (1219)

Chi square = 4.34, df = 2, p = 0.110 (females).
Chi square = 7.93, df = 2, p = 0.019 (males).

Table 21   PYG involvement by family structural risk and immigrant status

		Family structural risk			Total
		No risk factors	One risk factor	Two risk factors	
Immigrant background parents	**NO PYG**	89.6% (926)	88.6% (234)	90.1% (64)	89.5% (1224)
	PYG	10.4% (107)	11.4% (30)	9.9% (7)	10.5% (144)
	Total	100.0% (1033)	100.0% (264)	100.0% (71)	100.0% (1368)
Belgian background both parents	**NO PYG**	96.0% (867)	91.9% (158)	80.0% (16)	95.1% (1041)
	PYG	4.0% (36)	8.1% (14)	20.0% (4)	4.9% (54)
	Total	100.0% (903)	100.0% (172)	100.0% (20)	100.0% (1095)

Chi square = 0.26, df = 2, p = 0.878 (immigrant background).
Chi square = 15.18, df = 2, p = 0.001 (Belgian background).

percentage of youths who are involved in a problematic youth group is much higher for immigrant youth than for nonimmigrant youth. What mechanisms are responsible for the higher levels of involvement and the lack of a relationship with structural risk? It is clear that this table does not provide an answer, but the question should be posed, as it remains important to question the effects of disadvantage. A possible explanation is that immigrant youth react differently toward the experience of disadvantage than nonimmigrant youth. However, the rather small absolute numbers, in Belgian youth, the effect is striking: the percentage is highest in those youths who are at risk on both structural risk factors (disadvantage and family structure).

3   PERCEIVED RELATIVE DEPRIVATION AND PYG INVOLVEMENT

So far, objective measures of family social position have taught us, that there is only a small effect on PYG involvement. Some scholars have argued that relative deprivation, rather than deprivation as measured by objective criteria, may foster delinquency and PYG. One example of that idea can be found in the general theory of strain by Agnew (2011). The questionnaire contained a scale that measures satisfaction with one's own life standard. The scale was adopted from a study conducted by Rovers (1997) in the Netherlands and consisted of three items that tap into satisfaction with the life standard. The psychometric qualities of the scales can be found in Appendix.
The results in Table 22 indicate that relative satisfaction with one's own life standard is not significantly related to PYG. This is interpreted as a lack of effect of relative deprivation regarding economic resources. Other resources, such as social capital, may be of importance. Relative deprivation theories have not fared well in empirical studies.

4   IMMIGRANT BACKGROUND VERSUS BELGIAN NATIVE BACKGROUND

Immigrant background is still one of the most controversial topics in the media and public debate on crime. In Belgium, the controversy is to a high degree caused by the anti-immigrant policies of the extreme right-wing party ('Vlaams Belang' which translates into 'Flemish Interest'). Previous studies have demonstrated the

Table 22   PYG involvement by perceived deprivation

	Perceived deprivation				Total
	Very low	Low	High	Very high	
NO PYG	90.2% (313)	92.5% (720)	92.9% (819)	90.3% (352)	91.9% (2204)
PYG	9.8% (34)	7.5% (58)	7.1% (63)	9.7% (38)	8.1% (193)
Total	100.0% (347)	100.0% (778)	100.0% (882)	100.0% (390)	100.0% (2397)

Chi square = 4.29, df = 3, p = 0.231 (cut-off points at mean and one standard deviation).

overrepresentation of immigrant groups in prisons, but also studies that rely on self-report methodologies reveal differences between ethnic groups. Most studies of ethnicity and gang membership have been focusing more on the establishment of the relationship between ethnic background and gang membership, than on the search for the causal mechanisms that may account for the observed differences. Already in the early studies of the Chicago School, Shaw and McKay showed that neighborhood offending rates were disproportionally high in areas of immigrant concentration and, also in Belgium, the ecological relationship between immigrant concentration and levels of crime is an established one, as is established elsewhere in this book. Ecological studies do not allow for interpretation at the individual level, and the existence of an ecological correlation may be spurious. Therefore, it is of importance to measure the relationship at the individual level. The present study measured the respondent's background (not nationality) and additionally asked for the country of origin of the mother and father. We were able to create different measures that reflect immigrant background: a general measure that distinguishes between Belgian and non-Belgian immigrant background. Non-Belgian is defined as having at least one parent who does not have a Belgian background. Another measure that we have created is based on the country of origin: Western Europe versus non-Western European background. Two of the largest represented non-Western immigrant communities are the Moroccan and the Turkish population in Antwerp. These groups have a long history of migration in Belgium that goes back to the 1960s. As in many other European countries, new groups of immigrants are coming from former Eastern European countries and African countries. Finally, a measure of immigrant status was created. This measure distinguishes respondents based on their immigrant status: no immigrant status, newly arrived, versus second generation (or higher). It is an important issue as theories of cohesion and integration point to social disintegration in newly arrived immigrants. Newly arrived immigrants experience higher levels of acclimatization problems. Their problems of adjustment may be related to the strains that are linked to the fact that one is in the beginning of a process of integration in a new society. The results in Table 23 clearly indicate that there is a significant relationship between immigrant background and PYG involvement: 10.5% of the youths with an immigrant background are involved in a problematic youth group while 4.9% of the Belgian youths are involved in a problematic youth group.

Table 23   PYG involvement by immigrant background

	Immigrant background		Total
	Immigrant background	Belgian background	
NO PYG	89.5% (1228)	95.1% (1041)	92.0% (2269)
PYG	**10.5%** (144)	**4.9%** (54)	**8.0%** (198)
Total	100.0% (1372)	100.0% (1095)	100.0% (2467)

Chi square: 25.54, df = 1, p = 0.000.

Many immigrants come from countries outside the EU and these are often economic refugees. We have to make an important remark here about the definition on EU. The data come from a survey conducted in 2005, and this means that respondents from many Eastern European countries are not defined as members of EU. Therefore, we recoded the immigrant background variable in another way, measuring the country of origin (as being outside the EU or not). When taking into account the region of descent in regard to the EU, we find an even more striking difference than when only taking into account the fact that the youths come from a family with an immigrant background. As shown in Table 24, there is a clear interaction between immigrant background, gender, and problematic youth group involvement: the relationship between gender and immigrant background is very strong among youth with an immigrant background outside the EU and is highest among the youths who have both parents outside EU: 15.2% of boys who have both parents outside EU are involved in a problematic youth group.

Table 25 shows that the relationship between PYG involvement and immigrant status is significant. The highest proportion is found in the group that was defined as the first-generation immigrants (thus, not born in Belgium and parents who come from

Table 24   PYG involvement by gender and immigrant background

		Gender		Total
		Females	Males	
Both parents Belgian descent	**NO PYG**	95.1% (615)	92.6% (589)	93.8% (1204)
	PYG	**4.9% (32)**	**7.4% (47)**	**6.2% (79)**
	Total	100.0% (647)	100.0% (636)	100.0% (1283)
One parent non-EU	**NO PYG**	91.2% (93)	89.4% (84)	90.3% (177)
	PYG	**8.8% (9)**	**10.6% (10)**	**9.7% (19)**
	Total	100.0% (102)	100.0% (94)	100.0% (196)
Both parents non-EU	**NO PYG**	94.7% (467)	84.8 % (406)	89.8% (873)
	PYG	**5.3% (26)**	**15.2% (73)**	**10.2% (99)**
	Total	100.0% (493)	100.0% (479)	100.0% (972)

Chi square = 3.21, df = 1, p = 0.06 (both parents Belgian).
Chi square = 0.18, df = 1, p = 0.668 (one parent non-EU).
Chi square = 26.37, df = 1, p = 0.000 (both parents non-EU).

Table 25   PYG involvement by immigrant status

	Immigration status			Total
	Native Belgians	**First-generation immigrants**	**Second-generation immigrants**	
NO PYG	95.1% (1041)	87.6% (333)	90.2% (893)	92.0% (2267)
PYG	**4.9% (54)**	**12.4% (47)**	**9.8% (97)**	**8.0% (198)**
Total	100.0% (1095)	100.0% (380)	100.0% (990)	100.0% (2465)

Chi square = 28.10, df = 2, p = 0.000.

Table 26   **PYG involvement by immigrant status and gender**

		Immigration status			Total
		Native Belgians	**First-generation immigrants**	**Second-generation immigrants**	
Girl	**NO PYG**	96.4% (541)	91.5% (183)	93.8% (457)	94.6% (1181)
	PYG	3.6% (20)	8.5% (17)	6.2% (30)	5.4% (67)
	Total	100.0% (561)	100.0% (200)	100.0% (487)	100.0% (1248)
Boy	**NO PYG**	93.6% (500)	83.3% (150)	86.7% (435)	89.2% (1085)
	PYG	6.4% (34)	16.7% (30)	13.3% (67)	10.8% (131)
	Total	100.0% (534)	100.0% (180)	100.0% (502)	100.0% (1216)

Chi square = 28.1, df = 2, p = 0.000 (males) and not significant for females.

a different country than Belgium). Among the second (and higher) generation of immigrants, the proportion of PYG is still higher than among the fully Belgian youths, but still lower than among the first-generation group. This may be a reflection of the fact that the newest immigrant groups still face more structural problems of adaptation/integration into the Belgian culture.

We analyzed the association between immigrant status and PYG involvement separately for males and females and found that the relationship does not exist for females, but only for males (Table 26).

5   REPEATING A CLASS, DISADVANTAGE, AND PROBLEMATIC YOUTH GROUP INVOLVEMENT

In the present paragraph, we analyze the relationship between repeating a class (failure to successfully pass an academic year as an indicator of school failure) and PYG involvement. Repeating a class is in itself not an indicator of *family social position*. For a long time, sociology of education focused on the relation between the economical capital of the family and the success in schooling. Additionally, to the traditional understanding of capital as economical capital, Bourdieu (1986) extended the concept of capital by cultural and social capital. Cultural capital describes educational resources and social capital is defined as "the aggregate of the actual or potential resources which are linked to the possession of a durable network of more or less institutionalized relationships of mutual acquaintance and recognition" (Bourdieu, 1986: 190). Repeating a class may thus be indirectly seen as an indicator of low cultural capital, which is affected by low family SES. Albert Cohen stressed that status frustration is the mechanism that explains why youths from disadvantaged strata drop-out school and become involved in informal cliques. Therefore, we decided to treat school failure, as measured by repeating class more than once, under the chapter of family social position characteristics as an additional indicator of low SES. School failure is measured by asking the respondents how many times they had to repeat a school year. School failure is a well-established covariate of adolescent offending and has also been established in previous studies of problematic youth groups as an important risk factor. However, we must stress that there are several other ways of explaining the relationship between previous school failure and PYG involvement and offending. One would be that school failure is a negative event that may foster strain feelings of frustration and anger in line with Agnew's strain theory. Another explanation is that school failure is a consequence of IQ. In fact, many psychologists have demonstrated a relationship between IQ and school failure. In the present study, we did not measure IQ directly, but we asked the respondents about their school achievements. Farrington and Welsh (2006) argue that the key explanatory factor underlying the link between intelligence and delinquency may be the ability to manipulate abstract concepts. People who are poor at this tend to do badly in intelligence tests and in school achievement, and they also tend to commit offenses, probably because of their poor ability to foresee the consequences of their offending and to appreciate the feelings of victims (i.e. their low empathy).

As can be seen in Table 27, the overall relationship between repeating a class and PYG is statistically significant, with a higher proportion of youths who have experienced school failure two times or more, who are involved in a problematic youth group. We have conducted some additional analyses to find out if the relationship between school failure is conditional on other background variables, such as family disadvantage (Table 28).

When the relationship between repeating a class and PYG involvement is further explored, it is found that the relationship only holds for youths who do *not* live in a disadvantaged family. This finding contradicts the earlier cultural and social capital view that measures of school failure are related to family disadvantage. For youths who live in a disadvantaged family, the relationship is not statistically significant. We did an additional analysis with regard to possible interactions between background characteristics. The relationship between repeating a class and PYG involvement is more or less identical for both immigrant and Belgian youth, but for reasons of parsimony, we decided not to add this table. The relationship between repeating a class and PYG exists only for boys and not for girls. The finding that the relationship between repeating a class is significantly related to problematic youth group involvement in youth who does not come from a disadvantaged background is a finding that

Table 27   PYG involvement by having repeated a class

| | School failure | | Total |
	No	Yes	
NO PYG	94.0% (1492)	88.5% (772)	92.1% (2264)
PYG	**6.0% (95)**	**11.5% (100)**	**7.9% (195)**
Total	100.0% (1587)	100.0% (872)	100.0% (2459)

Chi square = 23.16, df = 1, p = 0.000.

is inconsistent with Cohen's subcultural model. It is impossible to explain this contradiction based on our data, but we can formulate a hypothesis that is worth investigating in future inquiries of problematic youth group involvement: it may be that parents in non-disadvantaged families are more demanding regarding to academic achievement than parents in disadvantaged families and that they react differently (i.e. in a more negative way) toward failures of their children. If parents in non-disadvantaged families react in a harsher or more inconsistent way, it might be that it actually is such a triggering effect that is responsible for the association.

6   MULTIPLE REGRESSION ANALYSES OF PROBLEMATIC YOUTH GROUP
         INVOLVEMENT BY FAMILY STRUCTURAL BACKGROUND
         CHARACTERISTICS

The analyses of family structural variables, gender, and immigrant background reveal that gender, school failure, and immigrant background are related to PYG involvement in the multiple logistic regression model that is shown in Table 29, while

Table 28   PYG involvement by repeating a class and family disadvantage

		Having repeated a class		Total
		No	Yes	
No family disadvantage	NO PYG	94.4% (1381)	88.7% (659)	92.5% (2040)
	PYG	5.6% (82)	11.3% (84)	7.5% (166)
	Total	100.0% (1463)	100.0% (743)	100.0% (2206)
Family disadvantage	NO PYG	89.2% (107)	87.6% (113)	88.4% (220)
	PYG	10.8% (13)	12.4% (16)	11.6% (29)
	Total	100.0% (120)	100.0% (129)	100.0% (249)

Chi square = 23.01, df = 2, p = 0.000 (no family disadvantage).
Chi square = 0.15, df = 1, p = 0.844 (family disadvantage).

Table 29   Logistic regression of PYG involvement on background variables

	B	S.E.	Wald	df	Sig.	Exp(B)
Being male	0.77	0.16	23.62	1	0.00	2.17
Split family	0.23	0.20	1.29	1	0.25	1.26
Disadvantage	0.24	0.23	1.08	1	0.29	1.27
School failure	0.50	0.15	10.38	1	0.00	1.65
Immigrant background	0.63	0.17	13.63	1	0.00	1.89
Constant	−3.58	0.186	372.63	1	0.000	0.028

Nagelkerke pseudo-R square: 0.06.
Percent correct predictions PYG: 0.0%.
Percent overall correct predictions: 92.1%.

the key measures of family social position are not related to PYG involvement. Besides that, there is only a very small impact of these background variables on problematic youth group involvement. If we look at the model fit parameters ('explanatory power' and 'classification plots'), we see that little is to be learned from the inclusion of family structural variables. As many other studies have concluded before this one, it is very hard to actually *predict* PYG involvement from family social position variables. While prediction does say nothing on causation, the existence of a causal relationship requires that at least a substantial part of the variability in problematic youth group involvement should be explained by the variables in the model. To disentangle the difficult issue of social class and family position regarding offending and problematic youth group involvement, a prospective panel study is required to see how lower- and higher-class groups evolve.

9 | THE COMMUNITY CONTEXT OF PROBLEMATIC YOUTH GROUP INVOLVEMENT

1   INTRODUCTION

The idea that the characteristics of a context, i.e. collective structures, influence the behavior and attitudes of individuals through process of socialization is rooted deep in classical sociological writing. From a historical point of view, criminologists have paid most attention to the ways in which neighborhoods as collective structures can influence socialization and offending (Oberwittler, 2004; Peeples & Loeber, 1994; Rovers, 1997; Tolan, Gorman-Smith & Henry, 2003). The contemporary collective efficacy perspective (Sampson, 2012) emphasizes the role of social trust and informal control as key mechanisms that explain ecological differences in the presence of problematic youth groups.

Wikström and Sampson (2003) have argued that there are two ways in which the community context may influence offending behavior. Firstly, the community may be a situational context of offending, providing clues to the offender that offending can take place unpunished (i.e. low levels of deterrence). In other words, communities may influence offending by providing contexts of action, i.e. contexts in which action takes place. This hypothesis cannot be tested in the present study as we have no information on where the acts of crime that the youngsters have reported are committed. Therefore, it is not from that point of view that communities will be dealt with in this chapter. In this chapter, we will look for evidence of the 'breeding ground hypothesis.' Communities may be an important context of development that contributes to shaping and forming youth during their development. In that case, the community context is a context of development. Wikström and Butterworth (2006) already stressed that this hypothesis is extremely difficult to test in a cross-sectional study like this one, as a cross-sectional study only includes one measurement in time and cannot be used to address the question of development. On the other hand, if problematic youth group involvement would be a consequence of developmental processes in local areas, it may be expected that a statistical association is found, even in a cross-sectional survey.

In this chapter, we answer following research questions:

- What is the relationship between neighborhood structural characteristics, social processes, and problematic youth group involvement?

- Is the relationship between neighborhood characteristics and problematic youth group involvement comparable to the ecological relationship between the juvenile arrest rate and the adult offender rate?
- Is the relationship between neighborhood density, disadvantage, and problematic youth group involvement mediated by disorganizational processes at the neighborhood cluster level?
- How do we have to interpret neighborhood cluster level differences in problematic youth group involvement: do these differences reflect genuine ecological (contextual effects), or do they reflect the demographic compositions of youths that are differentially segregated into different neighborhood clusters? In that case, there is no genuine contextual effect but a compositional effect.
- What is the relationship between neighborhood cluster level cumulative risk and street-level cumulative risk?
- What are the relative effects (net odds ratios) of neighborhood cluster level- and street-level-based measures on problematic youth group involvement?

2   THE ECOLOGICAL DISTRIBUTION OF PROBLEMATIC YOUTH GROUP
         INVOLVEMENT

Research on the neighborhood context and problematic youth group involvement is still scarce in Belgium. However, previous research conducted in Belgian cities has shown that the neighborhood level distribution of juvenile delinquents is strongly correlated to ecological measures of disadvantage (Pauwels, 2007; 2012). Table 30

Table 30   Neighborhood cluster level covariates of the percentage of youth involved in a PYG, offender rates, and the violent crime rate (N = 42)

	Percent PYG	Adult offender rate	Juvenile offender rate	Violent crime rate
Adult offender rate	0.44**	1	–	–
Juvenile arrest rate	0.53**	0.79**	1	–
Violent crime rate	0.15	0.71**	0.44**	1
Disorganization (key informant survey)	0.18	0.46**	0.63**	0.35*
Collective efficacy (key informant survey)	−0.02	−0.34*	−0.45**	−0.34*
% Welfare recipients	0.42**	0.88**	0.72**	0.59**
% Unemployed	0.53**	0.90**	0.78**	0.55**
Population density	0.39*	0.53**	0.48**	0.62**
Home ownership	−0.37*	−0.71**	−0.54**	−0.51**
Residential stability	−0.40**	−0.83**	−0.58**	−0.64**
Disorder (key informant survey)	0.19	0.64**	0.62**	0.50**
Disorder (youth survey)	0.62**	0.78**	0.74**	0.52**
Mean parental control (youth survey)	−0.53**	−0.34*	−0.36*	0.06

**p < 0.01, *p < 0.05 (2-tailed).

shows the ecological correlates of problematic youth group involvement. In order to get an insight into the similarity of effects of neighborhood characteristics and problematic youth group involvement, we additionally present the neighborhood level correlates of the adult offender rate, the juvenile delinquency rate, and the problematic crime rate.

The percentage of youths involved in a problematic youth group is strongly correlated to the adult offender rate and the juvenile arrest rate, but not with the problematic crime rate. The percentage of youths involved in a problematic youth group is strongly related to the usual suspects, i.e. the percentage of welfare recipients, the percentage of unemployed, population density, home ownership, and residential stability. The percentage of youths involved in a problematic youth group is not related to our measures of social disorganization and collective efficacy that were drawn from our independent survey of key informants, but is very strongly related to our youth survey measures of disorder and the mean level of parental control. That may seem to be a contradictory finding, but we submit that there is a logical explanation: the measures derived from the youth survey reflect the respondents' evaluation of the area in the immediate surroundings of the respondents' residence, i.e. the street segment. The key informant survey reflects the evaluation of key informants, but refers to a much larger area, namely the neighborhood cluster.

3   THE MEDIATING ROLE OF DISORGANIZATIONAL PROCESSES

Next, we investigate whether neighborhood disorganization mediates the relationship between neighborhood cluster level population density, disadvantage, the percentage of adolescents engaged in a problematic youth group, and the juvenile arrest rate. This is a classic assumption of social disorganization theory (Shaw & McKay, 1969 [1942]), while contemporary neighborhood level theories stress that mechanisms of informal control mediate the effects of social structural neighborhood characteristics (Kornhauser, 1978; Morenoff et al., 2001; Oberwittler, 2004; Sampson & Groves, 1989; Wikström, 1991). To investigate direct and indirect effects, a path analysis was conducted. Social disorganization was measured using an independent sample of key informants (see Pauwels & Hardyns, 2009; Pauwels, Hardyns & Van de Velde, 2010).[1]

Figure 1 shows that social disorganization fully mediates the relation between economic disadvantage and youth group involvement and partly mediates the relation between economic disadvantage and juvenile arrest rate at the neighborhood cluster level.

From Figure 1, it can be seen that there is a strong positive effect of population density on disadvantage (β = 0.60). R-square is 0.37. There is a strong direct effect of

---

1. In appendix, information about the measurement on disorganization and the key informant analysis can be found.

Figure 1   Explaining neighborhood cluster differences in PYG involvement and juvenile arrest rates

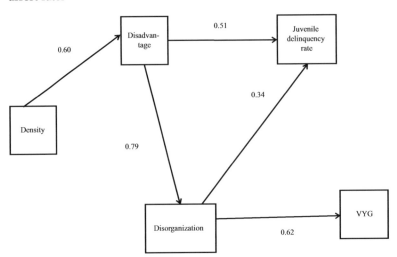

disadvantage on social disorganization ($\beta = 0.79$). R-square is 0.62. The juvenile delin-quency rate can be explained by social disorganization ($\beta = 0.34$) and disadvantage ($\beta = 0.51$). R-square is 0.65. The percent of adolescents who participate in a problem-atic youth group can be explained exclusively by disorganization ($\beta = 0.62$). Contrary to the explanation of neighborhood differences in the juvenile delinquency rate, the effect of disadvantage on the spatial concentration of youths who are involved in a problematic youth group is not direct at all. The results suggest that the bivariate cor-relation between the juvenile delinquency rate and the percent of youths involved in a problematic youth group has a common cause, namely social disorganization. This finding is reminiscent of Kornhausers (1978) these.

4   CONTEXT OR COMPOSITION?

At the ecological level, there is empirical evidence of the moderating effect of social mechanisms. But as been documented many times before, ecological analyses should be interpreted with care due to inferential problems, such as the ecological fallacy (Robinson, 1950). In fact, Byrne and Sampson (1986) and Wikström (1991) pointed out conflicting explanations: either the ecological correlation is due to the presence of genuine contextual effects or the ecological correlation is due to population com-position effects.

As ecological research in the traditional field of sociology has been plagued for a long time by inferential problems, multilevel modeling will be used to understand the nature of the ecological correlation between neighborhood deprivation and neighborhood level concentrations of problematic youth group involvement. Some exploratory analyses can provide insights into the existence of the so-called contextual effects. The analyses are conducted with HLM6.0 (Raudenbush, Bryk & Congdon, 2004). Table 31 shows the ecological variation, statistically controlling for compositional effects of background characteristics of individuals. In the previous paragraph, it became clear that problematic youth group involvement is unequally distributed among homogeneous and adjacent neighborhood clusters. However, while ecological correlations are highly suggestive for the existence of contextual effects, this remains an assumption that needs to be empirically tested. These results are discussed here. Since we have performed multilevel logistic modeling, it is not appropriate to calculate intra-class correlation coefficients (ICCs) using the same method as OLS regression models for continuous dependent variables (see Oberwittler, 2004 for a discussion). We therefore present variance components as well as the lambda value. The empty model (random intercept model without covariates) already shows that there is no statistically significant variation at the neighborhood cluster level. This also means that it is not useful to do any further multilevel modeling of problematic youth group involvement *at this level*, but because of the fact that we can interpret the significance level as being 'borderline' significant (p < 0.10), we also conducted a conditional model controlling for gender, low SES, single-parent family, and immigrant background. Previously, we have observed a similar result for adolescent offending. None of the different measures that we constructed (general delinquency scale, violent offending, and serious offending subscales) exhibited significant variation at the neighborhood cluster level (Pauwels, 2007). We reach a similar conclusion when problematic youth group participation is the dependent variable. The results (not reported here) are not altered when analyses are conducted in subsamples based on gender and immigrant background or when analyses are run in subsamples based on length of residence. Thus, contrary to the findings of Oberwittler (2004), no contextual effects at the neighborhood cluster level are found. This null finding may be explained by the fact that small ecological levels are much more important than higher-level aggregates. This will become clear when present the results of the micro-place context.

Table 31   Variance components and lambda values in the total sample

Random effects	Variance component	Df	Chi square	P value	Lambda
Empty model	0.06	13	19.98	0.095	0.358
Neighborhood level	0.97				
Level 1 R					
Conditional model	0.00	13	6.95	>0.500	0.001
Neighborhood level	1.03				
Level 1 R					

Note: Conditional model: controlling for gender, low SES, single-parent family and immigrant background; binomial model (over-dispersed because of extreme skewness of the dependent variable).

5   NEIGHBORHOOD CLUSTER VERSUS STREET-LEVEL INDICATORS
           OF NEIGHBORHOOD CHARACTERISTICS

In the remaining paragraphs, neighborhood characteristics will be compared to street-level characteristics to get an insight into the magnitude of the differences in effects on problematic youth group involvement. Ideally, such an analysis would be conducted from a multilevel perspective, where individuals are nested into street segments and street segments into neighborhood clusters, but as there are not enough respondents per street segment, this is not possible. The main idea is that it is interesting to compare the relationship between official measures of structural disadvantage and (lack of) collective efficacy on the one hand and the respondents' own observations of (lack of) collective efficacy, disorganization/disorder on the other hand.

Additionally, the questionnaire contained a range of questions with regard to collective efficacy and observed crime and disorder, as observed by the youths themselves. In the questionnaire, we asked the respondents to think of the street where they lived. If the youth lived at multiple places (which occurred), it was asked to reflect on the place where one resides the most. Thus, these questions refer to the micro-ecological context. The questions regarding social trust and informal control were in a similar way given a very local character, as we asked the respondents to think of their neighbors. Neighbors were defined as the residents who live next to the respondent, i.e. in the surrounding dwellings. In the questionnaire, we asked the respondents to consider as neighbors, the people who lived in the houses or apartments next to the place where the respondent lived.

5.1   *Neighborhood cluster cumulative risk score*

The neighborhood cluster cumulative risk score that is used in the present chapter was calculated based on the risk end of the distribution of four constructs: neighborhood disadvantage, neighborhood disorder, neighborhood social trust (dimension of collective efficacy as obtained from an independent survey of key informants), and the neighborhood crime rate, based on police records of violent crimes (robbery, car theft, assault and aggravated assault, theft from vehicles, and burglary). The risk ends of the distribution of the original measures were then summed as to create an overall measure of neighborhood cluster level cumulative risk. Next, all youths were assigned a neighborhood cumulative risk score, based on their official area of residence. The sample of Antwerp youths is somewhat skewed with regard to neighborhood disadvantage: 36.32% of the research participants lived at the moment of the survey in a neighborhood cluster that had a high score on the four risk variables. This overrepresentation is due to a disproportional number of schools in poor areas that were willing to participate in the survey (see Figure 2). Table 32 shows that respondents who live in a neighborhood cluster with a high risk score are significantly more involved in a problematic youth group.

Figure 2   Distribution of respondents by neighborhood risk score

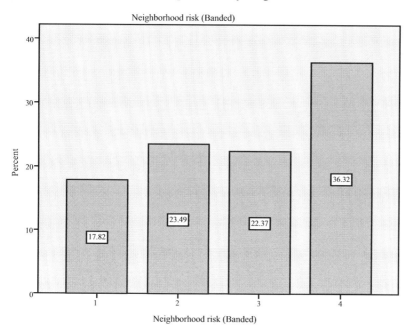

Table 32   PYG involvement by neighborhood cumulative risk score

	Neighborhood cumulative risk score				
	1	**2**	**3**	**4**	**Overall**
Not involved	95.5% (426)	92.8% (540)	91.5% (506)	89.9% (807)	91.9% (2276)
Involved	4.5% (20)	7.2% (42)	8.5% (47)	10.1% (91)	8.1% (200)
Total	100.0% (443)	100.0% (582)	100.0% (553)	100.0% (898)	100.0% (2476)

Chi square: 13.40 3, p = 0.004.

5.2   *Observations of collective efficacy and disorder*

Additionally, observational measures of (dis)organizational processes at the micro-place (street-level) were created based on the youth questionnaire, which contained a series of questions that tapped into observations during the last 12 months of crime and disorder, social cohesion between neighborhood inhabitants, and informal control, e.g. (neighbors knowing the names of the adolescent). In fact, the social cohesion/ trust scale was borrowed from the well-known collective efficacy study by Sampson and colleagues (1997). To measure informal control viewed through the lens of adolescents, the questions were adjusted so that they could be answered from the respondents' eye of the beholder.

From Table 33, it becomes obvious that there is a relationship between neighborhood classifications based on police-recorded crime and youths' observations of disorder. The percentage of youths observing disorder varies with the level of the neighborhood crime rate, resulting in higher proportions of youths observing disorder in the high-crime areas, yet this relationship is far from perfect. The neighborhood crime rates are based on the police records that refer to the year of 2004, the year preceding the youth survey.

From Table 34, it becomes obvious that there is a relationship between neighborhood classifications based on the expert survey of crime and disorder and youths' observations of disorder. The expert survey was conducted between October and November of 2004, i.e. just a couple of months prior to the administration of the self-report survey.

To further assess the impact of the neighborhood cluster structure on youths, observations of disorder, and unsupervised youths, key concepts in social disorganization theory, we performed some multilevel analyses. Multilevel analyses provide a basic insight into the nature of the observed neighborhood cluster variation in observations made by youths. If the observations made by youths are truly related to area

Table 33   Micro-place observations of disorder by neighborhood cluster level crime rates

| | | Neighborhood cluster crime rate | | | Overall |
		Low	Medium	High	
Micro-place observed disorder	Very low	17.7% (338)	11.3% (48)	7.1% (8)	16.1% (394)
	Low	45.2% (862)	40.9% (174)	26.8% (30)	43.6% (1066)
	High	21.4% (408)	27.1% (115)	33.9% (38)	23.0% (561)
	Very high	15.6% (298)	20.7% (88)	32.1% (36)	17.3% (422)
	Total	100.0% (1906)	100.0% (425)	100.0% (112)	100.0% (2443)

Chi square: 55.08, df = 6, p = 0.000.

Table 34   Micro-place observations of disorder by neighborhood disorder (key informant survey)

| | | Neighborhood cluster disorder (key informant survey) | | | | Overall |
		Low	Medium	High	Very high	
Observed disorder	Very low	33.3% (96)	16.2% (203)	13.4% (85)	3.7% (10)	16.1% (394)
	Low	51.4% (148)	47.6% (595)	37.7% (239)	31.1% (84)	43.6% (1066)
	High	11.8% (34)	22.1% (277)	26.2% (166)	31.1% (84)	23.0% (561)
	Very high	3.5% (10)	14.1% (176)	22.7% (144)	34.1% (92)	17.3% (422)
	Total	100.0% (288)	100.0% (1251)	100.0% (634)	100.0% (270)	100.0% (2443)

Chi square = 225.66, df = 9, p = 0.000.

Table 35   Hierarchical regression of neighborhood disadvantage on micro-place observations of street-level disorder

Dependent variable: observed street-level crime and disorder	Model 1 B	Model 2 B
Constant	5.18	5.07
Control variables level 1		
Gender	1.19***	1.17***
Length of residence	0.10	0.09
Belgian background	0.41*	0.55*
One-parent family	0.87**	0.84**
Family disadvantage	1.32**	1.25**
Age	0.62***	0.64***
Level 2		
Neighborhood cluster disadvantage		0.34***
Intercept variation	2.66***	0.68***
Level 1 variation	25.01	25.00

***p < 0.001, **p < 0.01, *p < 0.05 (2-tailed).

differences at the level of aggregation (i.e. the neighborhood cluster level), independent of the characteristics of the respondents that may affect differential perceptions, then an effect should be there. Table 35 presents such an analysis, where neighborhood disadvantage was used to predict individual differences in observations, and the results clearly indicate that there is a significant effect.

Table 36 presents an analysis of youths' observations of perceived unsupervised youths, and the results indicate that there is a strong relationship between the neighborhood cluster level disadvantage and youths' observations of unsupervised youths. Finally, we have run multilevel models to assess the relationship between youth's self-reported social ties with neighbors and youths' self-reports of social cohesion, and there seems to be no indication that there is variation at the neighborhood cluster. That is an important finding that suggests that the neighborhood cluster level might be too heterogeneous to act as a context.

5.3   *Problematic youth group involvement and street segment conditions (youths' observations)*

The relationship between PYG involvement and youths' observation of disorder is much stronger than the relationship between neighborhood cluster crime and disorder and PYG. Virtually, no youths who live in a place where no observations of disorder are reported report being in a PYG, while that is the case for 23.8% of the youths who live in a place where high levels of crime and disorder are reported (see Table 37). We can observe the same result for the relationship between PYG involvement and youths' street segment observation of unsupervised youths: virtually no youths who live in a place where no unsupervised youth activities are reported report being in a PYG, while that is the case for 22.4% of the youths who live in a place where high levels of unsupervised youth activities are reported (see Table 38).

Table 36   Hierarchical regression of neighborhood disadvantage on youths' observations of unsupervised youths

Dependent variable: observed street-level unsupervised youth	Model 1 B	Model 2 B
Constant	9.84	9.84
Control variables level 1		
Gender	0.94***	0.94***
Length of residence	−0.04	−0.04
Belgian background	0.24(*)	0.35(*)
One-parent family	0.15	0.13
Family disadvantage	0.93(0.31)**	0.90(0.31) **
Age	0.47(0.10)	0.44(0.10)***
Level 2		
Neighborhood cluster disadvantage		0.17***
Intercept variation	1.12***	0.69***
Level 1 variation	19.50	19.54

***p < 0.001, **p < 0.01, *p < 0.05 (2-tailed).

Table 37   PYG involvement by levels of observed street segment disorder

	Youths' observations of crime and disorder				Overall
	1	2	3	4	
NO PYG	98.0% (385)	96.2% (1021)	91.6% (512)	76.2% (320)	92.0% (2238)
PYG	2.0% (8)	3.8% (40)	8.4% (47)	23.8% (100)	8.0% (195)
Total	100.0% (393)	100.0% (1061)	100.0% (559)	100.0% (420)	100.0% (2443)

Chi square = 187.23, df = 3, p = 0.000.

Table 38   PYG involvement by levels of observed street segment unsupervised youth groups

	Levels of observed street segment unsupervised youth groups				Overall
	1	2	3	4	
NO PYG	98.3% (532)	96.3% (618)	92.2% (746)	77.6% (353)	91.9% (2249)
PYG	1.7% (9)	3.7% (24)	7.8% (63)	22.4% (102)	8.1% (198)
Total	100.0% (541)	100.0% (642)	100.0% (809)	100.0% (455)	100.0% (2447)

Chi square = 172.08, df = 3, p = 0.000.

Table 39   **PYG involvement by levels of observed street segment informal control**

	Youths' observations of informal control				Overall
	Very high	**High**	**Low**	**Very low**	
NO PYG	94.3% (312)	94.1% (965)	92.5% (606)	84.5% (366)	92.0% (2249)
PYG	**5.7%** (19)	**5.9%** (60)	**7.5%** (49)	**15.5%** (67)	**8.0%** (195)
Total	100.0% (331)	100.0% (1025)	100.0% (655)	100.0% (433)	100.0% (2444)

Chi square: 41.91, df = 3, p = 0.000.

Table 40   **PYG involvement by levels of observed social cohesion with neighbors**

	Youths' reports of cohesion with neighbors			Overall
	Very low	**Low**	**High**	
NO PYG	89.2% (321)	89.8% (397)	93.2% (1541)	92.0% (2259)
PYG	**10.8%** (39)	**10.2%** (45)	**6.8%** (112)	**8.0%** (196)
Total	100.0% (360)	100.0% (442)	100.0% (1653)	100.0% (2455)

Chi square = 10.16, df = 2, p = 0.006.

The relationship between PYG involvement and youths' observation of informal control is also stronger than the relationship between neighborhood cluster crime and disorder and PYG. Only 5.7% who live in a place where high levels of informal control are reported report being in a PYG, while that is the case for 15.4% of the youths who live in a place where very low levels of informal control youth activities are reported (see Table 39). The relationship between PYG involvement and youths' reports of social cohesion with neighbors is rather modest. While the statistical relation exists, it is not extremely strong as can be derived from the small differences in percentage points (see Table 40).

5.4   *Street segment cumulative risk score*

Previous studies have pointed out the fact that there often is a threshold effect when studying the impact of neighborhoods. Such studies often take the 'upper 10%' or 'upper quartiles' of the distribution of neighborhood disadvantage and crime indicators. From the above-presented tables, it could be seen that some measures of organizational and disorganizational processes have an effect on PYG. In order to get insight in the cumulative nature of that effect, we have created a cumulative street segment indicator, which sums the risk ends of the distribution. We argue that such a cumulative street segment level measure fits the idea of the developmental processes that undermine the self-regulatory capacity of a small community to neighborhood breakdown of informal control: neighborhoods that have a risk score of four (out of four indicators) are probably in another state than neighborhoods that only have a score of one out of four indicators. The cumulative approach allows for a more complete measure of exposure: exposure to criminogenic moral settings does not only depend on the length of the exposure but also on the intensity of the setting one is exposed to. The forces that undermine social order probably operate together: neighborhoods do not affect peoples' lives as variables but as a whole, consisting of a series of characteristics that, when combined, may exercise some influence on those who are exposed to it. Thus, the cumulative combined approach reflects the process of social emergence, which deserves more attention in criminological research.

Figure 3 shows the cumulative distribution of street segment risk scores. The distribution is much more skewed than the distribution of objective risk. As can be seen from the histogram, only a marginal number of youths live in a neighborhood that is extremely at risk.

From Table 41, we can observe that higher street segment risk scores are exponentially associated with problematic youth group involvement.

Figure 3   Distribution of respondents by street segment risk score

Street segment risk (low efficacy, unsupervised youth and disorder)

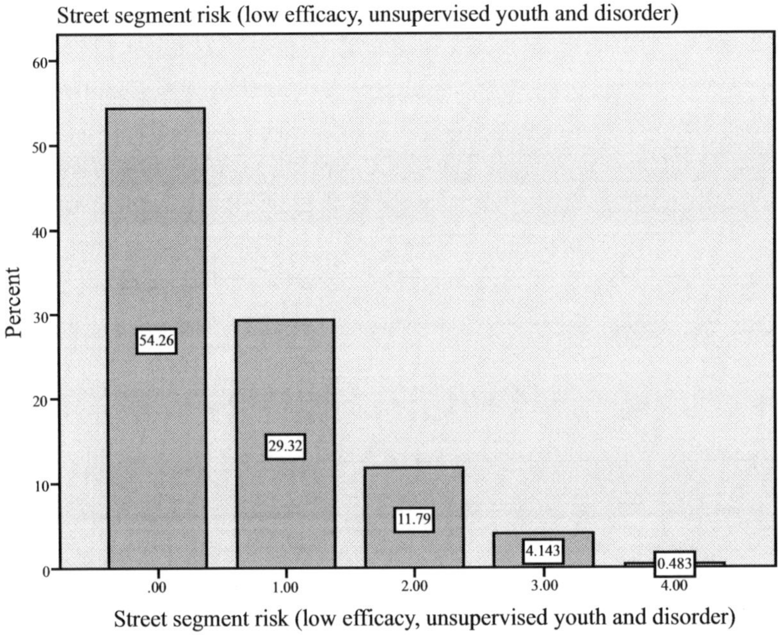

Table 41   PYG involvement and street segment cumulative risk score

	Street segment cumulative risk score					Total
	0.00	1.00	2.00	3.00	4.00	
NO PYG	97.5% (1308)	90.6% (659)	79.5% (232)	68.9% (71)	50.0% (6)	91.9% (2276)
PYG	**2.5%** (34)	**9.4%** (68)	**20.5%** (60)	**31.1%** (32)	**50.0%** (6)	**8.1%** (200)
Total	100.0% (1342)	100.0% (727)	100.0% (292)	100.0% (103)	100.0% (12)	100.0% (2476)

Chi square: 220.028, df = 4, p = 0.000.

6   MULTIPLE LOGISTIC REGRESSION ANALYSES OF PYG ON OBJECTIVE
AND SUBJECTIVE MEASURES OF COMMUNITY DISADVANTAGE

In this paragraph, we take a closer look at the effects of measures at the neighborhood cluster level and measures at the street segment level. This gives us some important insight in the relative importance of variables at both levels.

Table 42 shows the result of a block-wise regression analysis that starts by presenting the effect of neighborhood cluster level disadvantage. All variables are standardized before entering the equation. The odds ratio is significant but rather small (OR: 1.22). When street segment-level social mechanisms are added, the effect of neighborhood cluster disadvantage diminishes and subsequently vanishes when street segment unsupervised youths and crime and disorder are added. The odds ratios of these variables are much higher.

In Table 43, the effect of the neighborhood cluster level cumulative risk and the street segment cumulative risk (low efficacy, high disorder and crime, high level of unsupervised youth) is compared, and the results are quite clear: the effects of the same cumulative construct but measured at the smallest unit of analysis is much stronger.

Table 42   **Logistic regression of PYG on neighborhood cluster disadvantage and street-level social processes**

	Model 1 OR	Model OR	Model 3 OR	Model 4 OR
Neighborhood cluster disadvantage	1.22***	1.21**	1.04	0.94
Street segment cohesion		0.762**	0.81*	0.86
Street segment unsupervised youth			2.73***	1.94***
Street segment crime and disorder				1.94***
Nagelkerke R-square	0.008	0.015	0.146	0.185

***p < 0.001, **p < 0.01, *p < 0.05 (2-tailed).

Table 43   **Logistic regression of PYG on neighborhood objective and street level cumulative risk**

	Model 1 OR	Model OR
Nhood objective cumulative risk (crime and social processes)	1.22***	1.02
Street segment cumulative risk (crime and social process)		2.29***
Nagelkerke R–square	0.008	0.185

***p < 0.001 (2-tailed).

1   INTRODUCTION

In the present chapter, we will investigate the relationship between problematic youth group involvement, social bonds, and individual cognitions and traits. The basic idea is that those who are poorly integrated in conventional society are more likely to be engaged in a problematic youth group, partly because poorly integrated individuals experience less constraints when joining problematic groups. Free from controls, it is much easier to select peers who have a risky lifestyle or who are involved in any kind of gang-related activity. Thus, the school social bond, the family bond, parental monitoring, and integration in the class one attends are hypothesized to be inversely related to problematic youth group involvement.

This chapter studies a broad range of risk factors that are headed under the denominator 'individual characteristics.' A clear distinction is made between variables derived from social bonding theory, which are social–psychological in nature and individual psychological characteristics, i.e. internal mechanisms. While social bonds are related to the relationships of the individual with significant others, we will also take a look at individual cognitions such as moral beliefs (legal cynicism), the ability to exert self-control, and subjective powerlessness (lack of personal control). Poor moral beliefs and the lack of the ability to exert self-control are the main dimensions that determine one's crime propensity or the preparedness to see crime as an action alternative, as outlined in situational action theory. We will start this chapter by describing the relationship between each of these constructs separately and problematic youth group involvement, then move beyond the bivariate descriptive analyses, and finally describe some basic multivariate analyses that give us an insight in which of the mechanisms in each cluster (social bonds and cognitions/traits) are independently related to problematic youth group involvement.

2   SOCIAL BONDS AND PROBLEMATIC YOUTH GROUP INVOLVEMENT

The constructs for family bonds and school bonds were created by adding responses to selected questions regarding the adolescent's family and school situation, parental monitoring, and integration of the pupil within the class. The constructs were created in a way that a high score indicates the protective end of the distribution, thus a strong social bond. We refer to Appendix for details on the measurement level (reliabilities and factor scores). Finally a cumulative 'social bonds' scale was created, based on the upper risk ends (quartiles) of the distribution of each construct. Social bonds have numerously been identified as important protective factors in delinquency and gang research. The social bonds variables are correlated, suggesting that the scales perform well.

2.1   *Family social bonds*

Due to the skewness of the scale, we divided the original social bonds scale in three categories based on the tertiles (lower tertile, medium tertile, and upper tertile). From Table 44, it can be seen that the percentage of youths who were identified as involved in a problematic youth group varies by the attachment to parents. Youths who are weakly tied to their parents are disproportionally involved in a problematic youth group. The relationship between the family bond and problematic youth group involvement is statistically significant.

2.2   *Parental monitoring*

Next, we present the relationship between parental monitoring and problematic youth group involvement.

Youths were then categorized into four categories based on their deviation from the mean. 'Very low' refers to a position below one standard deviation below the sample mean; 'low' refers to the category that has a value between one standard deviation and the mean; 'high' refers to a value that lies between the mean and one standard deviation, while finally 'very high' refers to the scores that are higher than one standard deviation from the mean. The results in Table 45 show that parental monitoring is negatively associated with PYG involvement. The percentage involved decreases drastically as the level of parental monitoring increases and ranges from 18.9% in the lowest group to 2.2% in the highest group. This relationship is statistically significant.

2.3   *School social bond*

The school social bond refers to the academic interest of the students. The questionnaire thus taps into the academic orientation of students.

Table 44   PYG involvement by family social bonds

	Family social bonds			Overall
	Lower tertile	Medium tertile	Upper tertile	
No PYG	86.3% (679)	92.3% (552)	95.8% (1039)	91.9% (2270)
PYG	13.7% (108)	7.7% (46)	4.2% (45)	8.1% (199)
Total	100.0% (787)	100.0% (598)	100.0% (1084)	100.0% (2469)

Chi square = 56.51, df = 2, p < 0.000.

Table 45   PYG involvement by parental monitoring

	Parental monitoring				Overall
	Very low	Low	High	Very high	
NO PYG	81.1% (559)	94.0% (719)	97.7% (473)	97.8% (497)	91.9% (2248)
PYG	18.9% (130)	6.0% (46)	2.3% (11)	2.2% (11)	8.1% (198)
Total	100.0% (689)	100.0% (765)	100.0% (484)	100.0% (508)	100.0% (2446)

Chi square = 158.00, df = 3, p < 0.000.

Table 46   PYG involvement by school social bond

	School social bond				Total
	Very low	Low	High	Very high	
NO PYG	86.1% (630)	92.4% (620)	94.5% (496)	97.1% (501)	91.9% (2247)
PYG	13.9% (102)	7.6% (51)	5.5% (29)	2.9% (15)	8.1% (197)
Total	100.0% (732)	100.0% (671)	100.0% (525)	100.0% (516)	100.0% (2444)

Chi square = 57.32, df = 3, p < 0.000.

Youths were categorized into four categories based on their deviation from the mean. 'Very low' refers to a position below one standard deviation below the sample mean, 'low' refers to the category that has a value between one standard deviation and the mean, 'high' refers to a value that lies between the mean and one standard deviation, while finally 'very high' refers to the scores that are higher than one standard deviation from the mean. This table looks rather similar to the table that presents the relationship between parental monitoring and PYG involvement. We find a rather strong negative association (see Table 46): the percentage of youngsters involved in a PYG decreases by the level of the school social bond and ranges from 13.9% in the lowest category to 2.9% in the highest category. The relationship is statistically significant.

2.4   *Class integration*

Class integration refers to the level of social integration of the student in the class and is less studied in relationship to PYG involvement than the previous dimensions of social bonds. Class integration is highly skewed in the sample: large proportions of students report high levels of integration.
The class integration scale was categorized into three groups based on +/− one standard deviation, and the results indicate that the association between classroom integration and PYG involvement is much less pronounced. As one can see in Table 47,

Table 47   **PYG involvement by class integration**

	Class integration			Total
	Low	**Medium**	**High**	
NO PYG	89.1% (293)	91.1% (514)	92.9% (1441)	92.0% (2248)
PYG	**10.9% (36)**	**8.9% (50)**	**7.1% (110)**	**8.0% (196)**
Total	100.0% (329)	100.0% (564)	100.0% (1551)	100.0% (2444)

Chi square = 6.16, df = 3, p < 0.05.

10.9% of the respondents who are engaged in a problematic youth group are poorly integrated in their class, while still 7.1% of the youths who are highly integrated in the class report being involved in a PYG. The relationship is weak but still statistically significant.

2.5   *Social bonds risk score*

We have finally created one measure which we call the 'social bonds risk measure' and which categorized each scale in three groups, scored –1 for respondents who scored below one standard deviation from the mean, scored 0 for those between –1 std and +1 std, and scored 1 for respondents who scored above one standard deviation above the mean. From Figure 4, we can see that the cumulative risk score is rather normally distributed. The cumulative risk score is strongly related to PYG involvement, as the mean risk score strongly differs by whether or not youths are involved in a PYG (see Table 48).

The mean risk score is much higher in youths who are involved in a problematic youth group compared to youths who are not involved in a problematic youth group. Table 49 presents a multiple logistic regression analysis of PYG involvement on social bond variables. When all four variables of the social bond are analyzed simultaneously, it is found that only parental monitoring and the school social bond are statistically significantly inversely related to PYG involvement. The classification table (not shown) demonstrates that the overall percentage correct classification is 91.9%, but the percentage correct prediction in the category PYG is only 6.7%. Nagelkerke R-square is 19.7%.

3   COGNITIONS AND INDIVIDUAL TRAITS

In this paragraph, the relationship between individual cognitions and PYG involvement is examined through a series of bivariate and multivariate analyses. First we discuss the measurement of the constructs or subscales that we rescaled into normlessness (legal cynicism), low self-control, and perceived lack of personal control (subjective powerlessness). Low self-control was measured using a scale that consists of

Figure 4   **Distribution of sample by social bonds risk score**

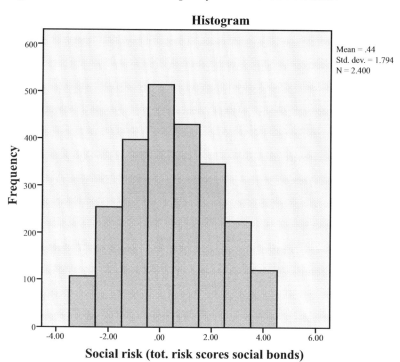

Histogram

Mean = .44
Std. dev. = 1.794
N = 2.400

Social risk (tot. risk scores social bonds)

Table 48   **Mean risk score by PYG involvement**

PYG involvement	Mean risk score	N	Standard deviation
No PYG	0.28	2199	1.73
PYG	2.27	194	1.44
Total	0.44	2393	1.79

F = 243.61, df = 1, p < 0.000.

Table 49   **Multivariate analysis of PYG on social bonds**

Social bond variables	B	Sig.	Exp(B)
Class integration	−0.08	0.28	0.92
Family bonds	0.02	0.75	10.02
Parental monitoring	−0.80	**0.00**	**0.43**
School bond	−0.34	**0.00**	**0.70**
Constant	−208.00	**0.00**	**0.05**

items that refer to impulsiveness or immediate gratification and volatile temper. The low self-control scale fell apart into two subscales: volatile temper and impulsiveness/ risk taking. The two subdimensions were then combined into one overall low self-control scale to more adequately present a measure of low self-control. Sampson and Bartusch's (1998) legal cynicism scale served as inspiration to measure attitudes toward rule breaking. While legal cynicism is a broader concept, one dimensions uses items that refer to how morally wrong it is to break laws (e.g. it is okay to break the law, as long as you are not caught, or if I cannot obtain something legally, it is okay to use illegitimate ways, ...). Finally, lack of personal control was measured by a scale that was designed to measure lack of personal control in adolescents. The scale was developed and validated in sociological inquiries of school effects (Brutsaert, 2001). That scale is not well known in the field of criminology and consists of items that measure the perception of how much control a person has over his or her life.

3.1   Control orientation

External locus of control was categorized into four groups using the mean and one standard deviation as criteria. Table 50 reveals that external locus of control is related to PYG involvement. The percentage of respondents who are involved in a problematic youth group increases by the level of external locus of control and ranges from 2.3% to 19.3% in the group that has a very high score on external locus of control. The relationship is statistically significant.

3.2   Low moral beliefs

The low moral beliefs scale was categorized based on the means and one standard deviation from the mean principle, resulting in three categories that were labeled 'low', 'medium,' and 'high'. In Table 51, we can see a very strong relationship between moral beliefs and PYG involvement. Almost no youngsters who are in the category of PYG involvement report low or medium levels of legal cynicism, while 24.2% of the youngster who are in a PYG have high scores on the low moral beliefs scale. The relationship is strong and highly significant.

Table 50   **PYG involvement and external locus of control**

	External locus of control				Overall
	Very low	**Low**	**High**	**Very high**	
NO PYG	97.7% (470)	95.6% (736)	90.4% (689)	80.7% (305)	92.0% (2200)
PYG	**2.3% (11)**	**4.4% (34)**	**9.6% (73)**	**19.3% (73)**	**8.0% (191)**
Total	100.0% (481)	100.0% (770)	100.0% (762)	100.0% (378)	100.0% (2391)

Chi square = 103.21, df = 3, p < 0.000.

3.3   Poor ability to exercise self-control

While the term self-control is used, the reader should bear in mind that we refer to the ability and follow the definition given by contemporary scholars who study self-control, such as Baumeister, Wikström and Treiber (2007). The scale is approximately normally distributed and combines low impulse control and anger management (volatile temper).

The low self-control scale was categorized based on the means and one standard deviation from the mean principle, resulting in three categories that were labeled 'low', 'medium,' and 'high'. Table 52 shows that the percentage of youngsters who are involved in a PYG increases with the level of low self-control; thus, as self-control decreases the chance of PYG involvement increases. The relationship is very pronounced and statistically significant.

3.4   Propensity to offend as overall construct

The scale is the combination of the legal cynicism scale and the low self-control scale. Both scales are strongly correlated ($r = 0.45$, $p < 0.000$). The concept of propensity is derived from Wikström and Butterworth (2006) and is considered in Wikström's situational action theory (Wikström et al., 2012) as the most important individual characteristic that guides people in their willingness to see crime as an alternative.

Table 51   PYG involvement by low moral beliefs

	Low moral beliefs			Overall
	Low	Medium	High	
NO PYG	99.1% (668)	95.6% (1158)	75.8% (430)	92.0% (2256)
PYG	0.9% (6)	4.4% (53)	24.2% (137)	8.0% (196)
Total	100.0% (674)	100.0% (1211)	100.0% (567)	100.0% (2452)

Chi square = 269.32, df = 2, p < 0.000.

Table 52   PYG involvement by low ability to exercise self-control

	Low ability to exercise self-control			Total
	Low	Medium	High	
NO PYG	99.1% (667)	93.1% (1102)	79.8% (407)	91.9% (2176)
PYG	0.9% (6)	6.9% (82)	20.2% (103)	8.1% (191)
Total	100.0% (673)	100.0% (1184)	100.0% (510)	100.0% (2367)

Chi square = 1490.93, df = 2, p < 0.000.

Applying this logic to the study of problematic youth group involvement, it may be expected that it is a strong predictor of getting involved in a problematic youth group. The relationship between the overall propensity scale and problematic youth group involvement is very strong, with the proportion of PYG involvement increasing as the propensity to offend increases. The relationship is highly statistically significant (Table 53).

Next, we present a multiple logistic regression analysis of PYG involvement on low self-control and low moral beliefs to compare the net effects of each construct. In order to compare the magnitude of the regression weights, the scale constructs were standardized before entering them into the equation. This means that we have z-transformed the independent variables.

The logistic regression analysis reveals that both aspects of propensity are relevant as predictors of PYG involvement, but still we can see from Table 54 that low moral beliefs have a stronger effect, i.e. its effect is larger than the effect of a low ability to exercise self-control. The classification table (not shown for reasons of parsimony) shows that 80.5% of all observed PYG involved cases were classified correctly. The overall classification percentage correct was 99.5%. Nagelkerke R-square was 28.2%. The bivariate relationship between propensity to offend as a general measure and PYG involvement is really huge (see Table 55): the odds ratio is 4.28 for a one standard deviation increase in propensity to offend.

Table 53   PYG involvement by individual propensity

| | Propensity | | | Overall |
	Low	Medium	High	
NO PYG	99.8% (639)	94.6% (1096)	77.5% (426)	92.0% (2161)
PYG	0.2% (1)	5.4% (63)	22.5% (124)	8.0% (188)
Total	100.0% (640)	100.0% (1159)	100.0% (550)	100.0% (2349)

Chi square = 2210.87, df = 2, p < 0.000.

Table 54   The effect of low self-control and low moral beliefs on PYG involvement

	B	Sig.	Odds ratio
Low ability to exercise self-control	0.54	0.00	1.72
Low moral beliefs	1.09	0.00	2.98

Table 55   The effect of propensity to offend on PYG involvement

	B	Sig.	Odds ratio
Propensity to offend	1.45	0.00	4.28

4   EXPLORING THE INTERACTIONS BETWEEN CONTROL ORIENTATION
        AND INDIVIDUAL CHARACTERISTICS

The nature of interaction effects are notoriously difficult to grasp from numeric coefficients (Svensson & Oberwittler, 2010). We therefore illustrate the effect of the interaction by plotting the predicted values for the effect of external locus of control and
social bonds, moral beliefs, and low self-control. This paragraph is restricted to the
study of interactions between control orientation and other individual characteristics
for one major reason: we know not much is known about the additive or multiplica-
tive nature of the relationship between control orientation and problematic youth
group involvement. The existence of interaction effects between control orientation
and problematic youth group involvement may shed some new light on previous null
findings of the effect of control orientation.

All interaction effects were studied by plotting the predicted odds of being involved in a
problematic youth group in logistic regression models that were full factorial in nature,
meaning that both the main effects and the interaction term were included. In order to
properly visualize the interaction term, control orientation was always entered into the
equation as a scale variable, while the other independent variable was categorized
(above and below the median value) to be able to visually display the effect (Figure 5).

Figure 5   External locus of control by parental attachment

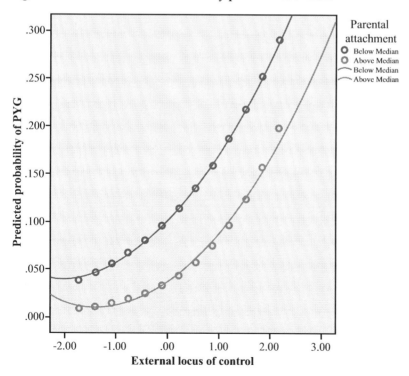

There is no statistical interaction between locus of control and parental attachment. The odds ratios (not reported here) are similar in both groups (Figure 6).

The odds of being involved in a problematic youth group is positively related to control orientation, but the relationship is exacerbated when parental monitoring is low (Figure 7).

The odds of being involved in a problematic youth group is positively related to control orientation, and the relationship is stronger for youths who have a low social bond than for youths who have a high social bond (Figure 8).

The odds of being involved in a problematic youth group is positively related to control orientation, and the relationship is stronger for youths who have low moral beliefs than for youths who have high moral beliefs (Figure 9).

The odds of being involved in a problematic youth group is positively related to control orientation, and the relationship is stronger for youths who have a low ability to exercise self-control than for youths who have a high ability to exercise self-control (Figure 10).

Finally, there is an interaction between propensity (low moral beliefs and low self-control) and locus of control. For those youths who have high scores on propensity, external locus of control is strongly related to the likelihood of problematic youth group involvement. For youths who have a low score on crime propensity, the effect

Figure 6   External locus of control and parental monitoring

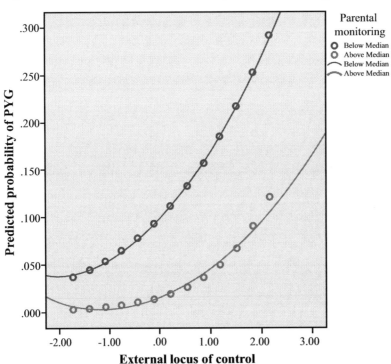

Figure 7   External locus of control and the school social bond

Figure 8   External locus of control and low moral beliefs

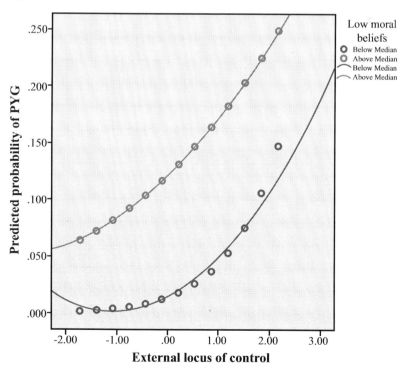

Figure 9 **External locus of control and low ability to exercise self-control**

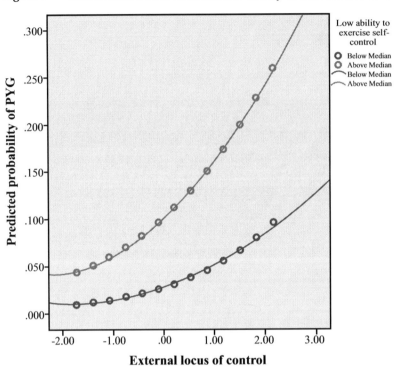

Figure 10 **External locus of control and propensity to offend**

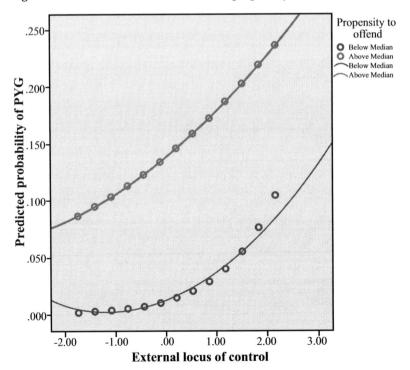

of external locus of control seems to be postponed, and there seems to be a threshold effect. Only when one reaches a score that is one standard deviation from the mean, the effect of propensity on problematic youth group involvement increases. These findings shed new light on previous studies of external locus of control. As we have seen, previous studies have yielded inconsistent results and that might be because previous studied failed to take into account possible interactions.

11 | SITUATIONAL EXPOSURE AND PROBLEMATIC YOUTH GROUP INVOLVEMENT

1   INTRODUCTION

In this chapter, we will introduce situational exposure using the multidimensional concept of lifestyle risk as an important explanatory factor of PYG involvement. We will analyze how lifestyle risk is related to individual differences in PYG involvement. The concept of lifestyles was introduced in victimization research in the 1970s (Hindelang, Gottfredson & Garofalo, 1978) and has been successfully used in victimization research. Since some influential studies of Osgood and recently the publication of Wikström and Butterworth (2006), more research has focused on the role of situational exposures to criminogenic moral settings/lifestyles in the explanation of offending.

We will focus on different dimensions of lifestyles, being (1) unstructured routines; (2) peer delinquency; and (3) the use of alcohol and hash/cannabis. The main assumed effect of lifestyles is that people with different lifestyles are differentially exposed to risky situations (i.e. situations that contain temptations and provocations) that may trigger offending and the process whereby young individuals see gang membership as a viable alternative.

The focus of this chapter will be on lifestyles as represented by the youths' self-reported frequency of time spent in high-risk public environments (city center public spaces, on the streets, street corners, etcetera), the extent of their friends' involvement in crime, and their usage of alcohol (being drunk) and drugs. The assumption is that youths who spend a lot of time in high-risk public environments, with high-risk friends, and who use alcohol and drugs will have a much higher risk of being involved in a problematic youth group. We will start this chapter by exploring the relationship between problematic youth group involvement and the three components that make up the composite measure.

2   UNSTRUCTURED ROUTINES

Some type of environments are more likely than others to entail the risk of creating situations conducive to offending (and risk of victimization). Wikström and Butterworth (2006: 176) argued that it may be assumed that spending more time in public space reflects a lifestyle in which a person is more often confronted with opportunities to offend.

The concept of routine risk was measured using five variables from the questionnaire that measured how much of the respondents free time was spent, without parental supervision, in high-risk public environments (time spent in public space parks, time spent hanging around in the streets, at street corners, time spent in the city center, time spent in the absence from parents).

In the following tables, we highlight a few items of the routine risk index. Table 56 shows the relationship between leisure time spent in public parks and PYG involvement, which is significant. The percentage of youngsters involved in a PYG increases by the time spent in parks. Table 57 presents the relationship between leisure time at street corners and on the streets with PYG involvement. The results are statistically significant: the proportion of youths reporting PYG involvement increases as the amount of time spent on the street increases.

Table 56   PYG involvement by leisure time in public parks

	Leisure time at public parks			Overall
	Low	Medium	High	
Not involved	94.2% (393)	93.5% (1606)	81.3% (247)	92.1% (2246)
Involved in a problematic youth group	5.8% (24)	6.5% (112)	18.8% (57)	7.9% (193)
Total	100.0% (417)	100.0% (1718)	100.0% (304)	100.0% (193)

Chi square = 56.23, df = 2, p < 0.000.

Table 57   PYG involvement by leisure time at street corners or on the streets

	Leisure time on street corners/on the streets			Overall
	Low	Medium	High	
Not involved	96.0% (811)	92.6% (1297)	68.0% (121)	92.0% (2229)
Involved in a problematic youth group	4.0% (34)	7.4% (103)	32.0% (57)	8.0% (194)
Total	100.0% (845)	100.0% (845)	100.0% (178)	100.0% (2423)

Chi square = 158.38, df = 2, p < 0.000.

3   PEER DELINQUENCY

Three variables from the questionnaire were chosen to measure the extent to which the youths had friends who were more seriously engaged in offending. The subjects were asked for each of the three different types of crime how many of their friends they knew had committed any of the three mentioned types of rule breaking.

Table 58 presents PYG involvement by categories of peer delinquency. The peer delinquency scale was categorized into three groups based on the already-mentioned principle of mean and standard deviation as guideline. The proportion of youngsters who are involved in a PYG is a function of peer delinquency: the proportion dramatically increases by category of peer delinquency. The relationship is highly significant.

Table 58   PYG involvement by peer delinquency

	Peer delinquency			Overall
	Low	Medium	High	
Not involved	1469	469	329	2267
	97.5%	94.0%	71.5%	92,0%
Involved in a problematic youth group	37	30	131	198
	2.5%	6.0%	28.5%	8.0%
Total	1506	499	460	2465
	100.0%	100.0%	100.0%	100.0%

Chi square: 326.43, df = 2, p < 0.000

4   SUBSTANCE USE

The relationship between substance use and problematic youth group involvement is assessed here. In the questionnaire, two types of substance use were questioned: alcohol use (being drunk) and cannabis use. The response categories for these measures were originally detailed ordinal questions that were posed on a seven-point scale and then recoded for analysis (using the same criterion of +/− 1 standard deviation). Table 59 presents the relationship between the frequency of alcohol use (being drunk as an indicator of a certain lifestyle) and involvement in a problematic youth group. The results show that 34.6% of those involved in a problematic youth group have been drunk a lot in the past twelve months. The relationship is statistically significant.

Table 59   PYG involvement by alcohol use (being drunk)

	Alcohol use (being drunk)			Overall
	Low	Medium	High	
Not involved	1951	179	106	2236
	94.1%	89.9%	65.4%	91.9%
Involved in a problematic youth group	122	20	56	198
	5.9%	10.1%	34.6%	8.1%
Total	2073	199	162	2434
	100.0%	100.0%	100.0%	100.0%

Chi square = 166.48, df = 2, p < 0.000.

Table 60 presents the relationship between the frequency of cannabis use (smoking weed as an indicator of a certain lifestyle) and involvement in a problematic youth group. The results show that 40.7% of those involved in a problematic youth group report having smoked weed many times in the past twelve months. The relationship is statistically significant.

Table 60   PYG involvement by cannabis use

	Low	Medium	High	Total
Not involved	2138	40	54	2232
	93.9%	64.5%	59.3%	91.9%
Involved in a problematic youth group	139	22	37	198
	6.1%	35.5%	40.7%	8.1%
Total	2277	62	91	2430
	100.0%	100.0%	100.0%	100.0%

Chi square = 203.15, df = 2, p < 0.000.

Table 61 presents the relationship between PYG involvement and overall substance use, which is the combination of alcohol use and cannabis use. There is a very large effect of substance use on PYG involvement. Nearly half of the youths reporting problematic youth group involvement are at the highest category of the combined alcohol and cannabis composite risk measure.

Table 61   PYG involvement by substance use (alcohol and cannabis)

	Substance use (alcohol and cannabis)					Total
	Very low	Low	Medium	High	Very high	
Not involved	1924	162	93	25	28	2232
	94.6%	89.5%	78.2%	62.5%	50.0%	91.9%
Involved in a problematic youth group	110	19	26	15	28	198
	5.4%	10.5%	21.8%	37.5%	50.0%	8.1%
Total	2034	181	119	40	56	2430
	100.0%	100.0%	100.0%	100.0%	100.0%	100.0%

Chi square = 228, df = 4, p < 0.000.

5   THE OVERALL LIFESTYLE RISK SCORE

The overall lifestyle risk measure is a composite measure based on the measures of youths' unstructured routines, peer delinquency, and substance use (alcohol). This measure taps overall exposure to criminogenic moral settings. For each of the three measures, the lowest quartile of the scores were re-coded to the value of −1, the second and third quartile were coded zero, and they represent being 'averaged,' and the highest quartile were re-coded to the value of -1. The recoded scores were then added for the three separate measures to give a final measure of lifestyle risk that could vary between -3 and $+3$. Having a score of 3 means that the youth has a score in the highest quartile of all three aspects of lifestyle risk. Having a score of -3 means that the youth has a score in the lowest quartile of all three aspects of lifestyle risk.

Table 62   PYG by overall lifestyle risk score

	Lifestyle risk			Total
	Low	Medium	High	
Not involved	1377	421	386	2184
	98.2%	92.5%	74.5%	92.0%
Involved in a problematic youth group	25	34	132	191
	1.8%	**7.5%**	**25.5%**	**8.0%**
Total	1402	455	518	2375
	100.0%	100.0%	100.0%	100.0%

Chi square = 287.52, df = 2, p < 0.000.

Table 62 presents the relationship between the overall lifestyle construct and PYG involvement. The results indicate that among the youths who have a low score on the overall lifestyle construct, the percentage of being involved in a PYG is extremely low: only 1.8%. The percentage further increases by category of the lifestyle risk score. The relationship is highly significant.

Table 63   Multiple logistic regression of PYG on lifestyle measures

	B	OR
Independent variables		
Unstructured routines (combined risk)	0.67***	1.96***
Substance use (combined risk)	0.49***	1.63***
Peer delinquency scale	0.79***	2.2***

Nagelkerke pseudo R-square: 0.32.
Percent correct PYG: 24.1.
Overall percent correct: 98.9.
***p < 0.001 (2-tailed).

Table 63 presents the multiple logistic regression analysis of PYG involvement on the separate lifestyle indicators. We can observe significant effects of all lifestyle indicators, with a Nagelkerke R-square of 32%.

6   EXPLORING THE INTERACTIONS BETWEEN SITUATIONAL MECHANISMS

In the present paragraph, we study the interactions between different indicators of lifestyle risk and pay special attention to the interactions between peers and routine risk (see Table 64), as earlier outlined by Bernburg and Thorlindsson (2001). In their article, they demonstrated that the effect of unstructured routines is strongly conditional on the social context. Additionally, we take a look at the interaction between substance use and the peer effect (see Table 65).

Table 64   **PYG involvement by routine risk and peer delinquency**

		Routine risk index				Total
		Very low	**Low**	**High**	**Very high**	
Peer delinquency low	**Not involved**	418	455	387	167	1427
		98.8%	98.5%	96.5%	96.0%	97.7%
	Involved in a problematic youth group	5	7	14	7	33
		1.2%	**1.5%**	**3.5%**	**4.0%**	**2.3%**
	Total	423	462	401	174	1460
		100.0%	100.0%	100.0%	100.0%	100.0%
Peer delinquency medium	**Not involved**	79	125	173	82	459
		95.2%	94.7%	94.5%	91.1%	94.1%
	Involved in a problematic youth group	4	7	10	8	29
		4.8%	**5.3%**	**5.5%**	**8.9%**	**5.9%**
	Total	83	132	183	90	488
		100.0%	100.0%	100.0%	100.0%	100.0%
Peer delinquency high	**Not involved**	44	69	122	82	317
		84.6%	82.1%	73.9%	56.9%	71.2%
	Involved in a problematic youth group	8	15	43	62	128
		15.4%	**17.9%**	**26.1%**	**43.1%**	**28.8%**
	Total	52	84	165	144	445
		100.0%	100.0%	100.0%	100.0%	100.0%

Chi square = 8.59, df = 3, p < 0.030 (low).
Chi square = 1.75, df = 3, p < 0.620 (medium).
Chi square = 24.36, df = 3, p < 0.000 (high).

Further analysis of the interaction effect shows that there is indeed a strong effect of unstructured socializing, especially when peer delinquency is high (Weerman et al., 2013). Recent research has found that the effect of unstructured socializing on offending also depends on its location (Hoeben & Weerman, 2014). This may be an interesting research area for studies of problematic youth group involvement (see Figure 11 beneath).

Figure 11   The interaction between peer delinquency and unstructured routines

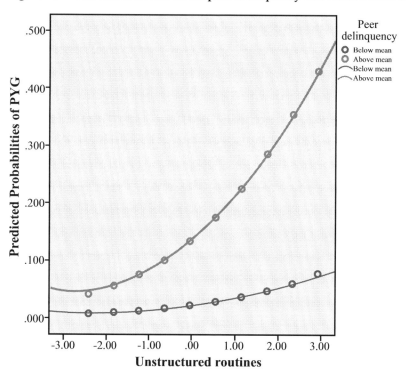

Table 65   **PYG involvement by peer delinquency and substance use risk**

		Peer delinquency			Total
		Low	Medium	High	
Low risk on substance use scale	Not involved	1297	371	247	1915
		98.2%	95.1%	78.9%	94.6%
	Involved in a problematic	24	19	66	109
	youth group	1.8%	4.9%	21.1%	5.4%
	Total	1321	390	313	2024
		100.0%	100.0%	100.0%	100.0%
Medium risk on substance use scale	Not involved	86	47	29	162
		92.5%	94.0%	76.3%	89.5%
	Involved in a problematic	7	3	9	19
	youth group	7.5%	6.0%	23.7%	10.5%
	Total	93	50	38	181
		100.0%	100.0%	100.0%	100.0%
High risk on substance use scale	Not involved	54	44	48	146
		91.5%	84.6%	46.6%	68.2%
	Involved in a problematic	5	8	55	68
	youth group	8.5%	15.4%	53.4%	31.8%
Overall	Total	59	52	103	214
		100.0%	100.0%	100.0%	100.0%

Chi square = 21.25, df = 2, p < 0.000 (low).

Chi square = 8.85, df = 2, p < 0.010 (medium).

Chi square = 40.09, p < 0.000 (high).

From Table 66, it can be seen that the relationship between PYG involvement and peer delinquency becomes more pronounced for youths who are frequently engaged in substance use. Substance use has an amplification effect: it amplifies the relationship between peer delinquency and problematic youth group involvement. However, further analysis of the interaction effect shows that the effect of substance use on problematic youth group involvement differs by levels of peer delinquency (see Figure 12 below).

Figure 12   The interaction between peer delinquency and substance use

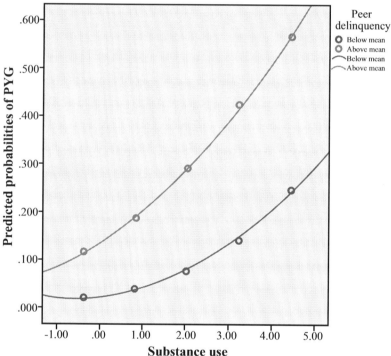

Table 66   PYG involvement by routine risk and substance use

		Routine risk index				Total
		Very low	Low	High	Very high	
Low risk on substance use	No involvement	485	570	565	251	1871
		97.4%	96.8%	94.0%	87.8%	94.8%
	Involved in a problematic youth group	13	19	36	35	103
		2.6%	3.2%	6.0%	12.2%	5.2%
	Total	498	589	601	286	1974
		100.0%	100.0%	100.0%	100.0%	100.0%
Medium risk on substance use	No involvement	31	47	56	27	161
		91.2%	94.0%	91.8%	77.1%	89.4%
	Involved in a problematic youth group	3	3	5	8	19
		8.8%	6.0%	8.2%	22.9%	10.6%
	Total	34	50	61	35	180
		100.0%	100.0%	100.0%	100.0%	100.0%
High risk on substance use	No involvement	16	20	51	51	138
		94.1%	74.1%	67.1%	60.0%	67.3%
	Involved in a problematic youth group	1	7	25	34	67
		5.9%	25.9%	32.9%	40.0%	32.7%
	Total	17	27	76	85	205
		100.0%	100.0%	100.0%	100.0%	100.0%

Chi square = 40.79, df = 3, p = 0.000 (low).
Chi square = 7.18, df = 3, p = 0.06 (high).
Chi square = 8.18, df = 3, p = 0.000 (very high).

From Table 66, it can be seen that the relationship between PYG involvement and unstructured routines becomes more pronounced for youths who are frequently engaged in substance use. Substance use has an amplification effect: it amplifies the relationship between unstructured routines and problematic youth group involvement (see also Figure 13).

Figure 13   The interaction between substance use and unstructured routines

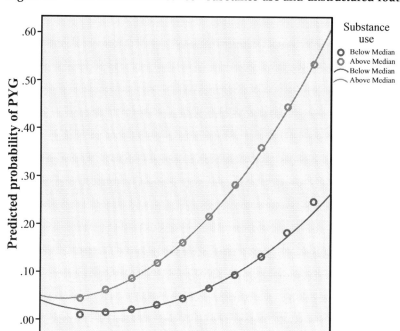

7   EXPLORING THE INTERACTIONS BETWEEN PROPENSITY
           AND EXPOSURE

Table 67   PYG involvement by overall lifestyle risk/exposure and propensity to offend

		Lifestyle risk/exposure			Total
		Low	Medium	High	
Low propensity	No involvement	527	61	25	613
		99.8%	100.0%	100.0%	99.8%
	Involvement in a problematic youth group	1	0	0	1
		0.2%	0.0%	0.0%	0.2%
	Total	528	61	25	614
		100.0%	100.0%	100.0%	100.0%
Medium propensity	No involvement	632	235	200	1067
		98.0%	95.5%	84.4%	94.6%
	Involvement in a problematic youth group	13	11	37	61
		2.0%	**4.5%**	**15.6%**	**5.4%**
	Total	645	246	237	1128
		100.0%	100.0%	100.0%	100.0%
High propensity	No involvement	152	106	151	409
		94.4%	84.1%	62.1%	77.2%
	Involvement in a problematic youth group	9	20	92	121
		5.6%	**15.9%**	**37.9%**	**22.8%**
	Total	161	126	243	530
		100.0%	100.0%	100.0%	100.0%

Chi square = 0.163, df = 2, p = 0.92.
Chi square = 63.17, df = 2, p =0.000.
Chi square = 61.78, df = 2, p = 0.000.

A final interaction effect that is taken into consideration is the interaction between life-style risk (overall situational exposure) and propensity. The interaction effect has deserved attention in recent years in empirical studies that intended to test key hypotheses that were derived from situational action theory (Svensson, Pauwels & Weerman, 2010; Wikström & Butterworth, 2006; Wikström et al., 2012). In situational action theory, this interaction effect is called the PEA interaction, i.e. the person-environ-ronment action interaction. The analysis shows that virtually all self-reported prob-lematic youth group members are situated in the upper categories for the variables lifestyle risk and propensity (see Table 67). The effect of lifestyle risk is less pronounced in adolescents who have low levels of propensity to offend (see Figure 14). This is a very important finding, as this suggests that the key interaction that explains offending as action can also be applied to the explanation of problematic youth group involvement. We have modeled the odds of problematic youth group participation and exposure.

Figure 14   Interaction between lifestyle risk and propensity to offend

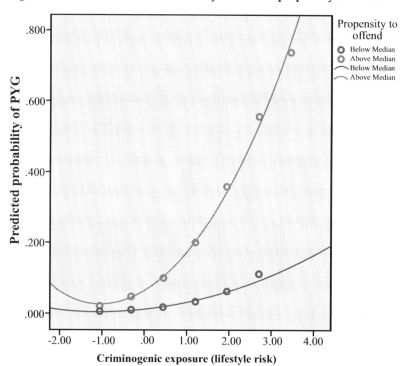

This analysis is actually very interesting, as it is the first time the interaction between propensity and criminogenic exposure (measured by lifestyle risk) is demonstrated when problematic youth group involvement is the dependent variable. A risky lifestyle seriously increases the odds of problematic youth group participation, but especially for youths who have an above mean on propensity. Low-propensity youths seem to be hardly affected (although there still is an increase in the likelihood of being involved in a problematic youth group, the effect is rather small).

8   SURPRISING THREE-WAY INTERACTIONS: PROPENSITY, EXPOSURE, AND SOCIAL INTEGRATION

Three-way interactions are less commonly studied in studies of crime causation. This is due to the high demands on the data. First, large samples are needed as it is difficult to find stable interaction patterns in small samples. Second, three-way interactions are more difficult to interpret than two-way interactions.

Having established empirical evidence for person-environment interactions, we now challenge the person-environment interaction and scrutinize whether an amplification affect can be observed when cumulative social integration (the overall social integration scale) is taken into account. The results can be seen from the figures below. A separate figure is presented for each group of youths based on their overall social integration scale.

Figure 15   Interaction between lifestyle risk and propensity to offend (low social integration)

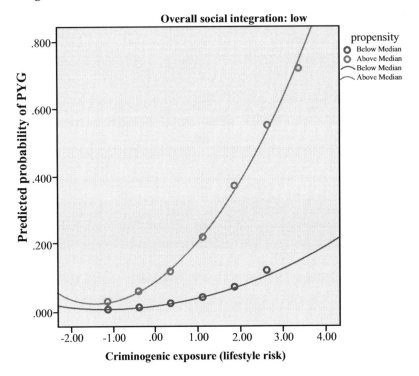

Among the youths who have the lowest score of social integration, the interaction effect is clearly present, and still a small effect of exposure can be observed in low-propensity youths.

Figure 16 **Interaction between lifestyle risk and propensity to offend (medium social integration)**

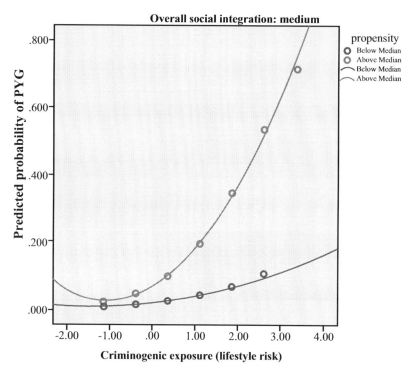

The same goes for the youths who have a medium score on social integration. There is a strong effect of exposure among high-propensity youths while the effect of exposure in the medium still exists, but has slightly diminished.

Figure 17   Interaction between lifestyle risk and propensity to offend (high social integration)

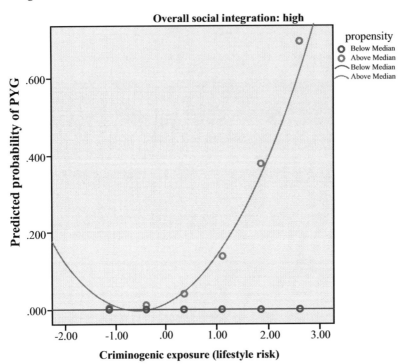

Finally, the interaction effect between propensity and exposure is studied among youths who are highly integrated. Interestingly, there is no effect at all of exposure among low-propensity youths. The effect of exposure remains strong among high-propensity youths.

9   PYG INVOLVEMENT AND CUMULATIVE RISK FACTORS

In this paragraph, we study the cumulative effect of risk factors in the different theoretical domains that we studied up to now. An overall evaluation is made of problematic youth group involvement by the total amount of risk factors and by domain-specific risk factors (Figure 18).

Figure 18   Distribution of risk factors among the sample

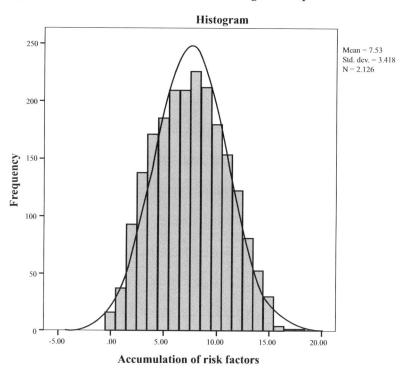

Histogram

Mean = 7.53
Std. dev. = 3.418
N = 2.126

Accumulation of risk factors

The figure above shows the overall distribution of risk factors of separate character-istics (objective neighborhood cluster characteristics, micro-place characteristics, fam-ily structural risk factors, social bonds risk factors, risk factors of individual characteristics (low self-control, low morality, external locus of control), and lifestyle risk factors (peers, substance use, and unstructured routines). This allows for testing whether the effect of risk factors is cumulative (Table 68).

Table 68   PYG by overall number of risk factors

	B	S.E.	Wald	df	Sig.	Exp(B)
First quartile (ref.)	–	–	150.439	3	0.000	–
Second quartile	1.330	0.566	5.528	1	0.019	**3.780**
Third quartile	2.779	0.531	27.364	1	0.000	16.099
Fourth quartile	3.998	0.513	60.705	1	0.000	**54.511**
Constant	−5.067	0.502	102.068	1	0.000	0.006

Analogous to the findings made by Thornberry et al. (2003), the number of risk factors is strongly related to problematic youth group involvement. Respondents who were classified in the second quartile have an increased likelihood of being in a problematic youth group (OR: 3.78). The odds of being in a problematic youth group versus not being in a problematic youth group is 16.09 times higher for those respondents in the third quartile of the overall risk score and 54.51 times higher for those respondents in the fourth quartile of the overall risk score than the odds of being in a problematic youth group for the respondents in the lowest quartile.

10 PROBLEMATIC YOUTH GROUP INVOLVEMENT AND RISK FACTORS BY DOMAIN

Table 69   Logistic regression of PYG involvement on cumulative risk factors by domain[1]

Independent variables	B	S.E.	Sig.	Odds Ratio
Being male	0.338	0.205	0.099	1.40
Age (15-16)	−0.0348	0.211	0.099	0.70
Belgian background	−0.684	0.226	**0.002**	**0.504**
Cumulative family structural risk			0.377	
One risk factor	0.325	0.233	0.163	1.34
Two risk factors	0.043	0.448	0.923	1.04
Cumulative social bonds risk			**0.022**	
One risk factor	0.141	0.497	0.776	1.15
Two risk factors	0.706	0.470	0.133	2.02
Three risk factors	0.922	0.468	**0.049**	**2.51**
Cumulative street-level disorganization			**0.008**	
One risk factor	0.891	0.372	**0.016**	**2.43**
Two risk factors	1.089	0.351	**0.002**	**2.97**
Cumulative objective neighborhood risk			0.781	
One risk factor	0.235	0.335	0.484	1.26
Two risk factors	0.077	0.223	0.731	1.08
Cumulative lifestyle risk			**0.000**	
One risk factor	0.978	0.259	**0.000**	**2.66**
Two risk factors	2.280	0.332	**0.000**	**9.77**
Cumulative alienation risk			**0.006**	
One risk factor	1.378	0.623	**0.027**	**3.96**

Continued

---

1. Cumulative family structural risk consists of family structure and family low SES; cumulative social bonds risk consists of the summation of the social bonding scales; cumulative objective neighborhood risk consists of neighborhood disadvantage and the neighborhood crime rate; street-level cumulative risk consists of observed disorder and the presence of delinquent youths. The cumulative lifestyle risk scale consists of peer delinquency and unstructured routines. The cumulative alienation risk score consists of external locus of control and legal cynicism. The cumulative low self-control risk scale consists of volatile temper and impulsiveness. Finally, a substance use risk scale was created based on the frequency of cannabis use and alcohol use. The scale combines use and the frequency of use and is therefore as detailed as possible. The scale was divided in sextiles.

Table 69—continued

Independent variables	B	S.E.	Sig.	Odds Ratio
Two risk factors	1.787	0.621	**0.004**	**5.97**
Cumulative self-control risk			**0.048**	
One risk factor	0.775	0.416	0.063	2.17
Two risk factors	0.980	0.404	**0.015**	**2.66**
Previous arrest	0.352	0.209	0.093	1.42
Substance use risk score			**0.000**	
Low	0.602	0.321	0.061	1.82
Medium	0.986	0.297	**0.001**	**2.68**
High	1.476	0.429	**0.001**	**4.37**
Very high	1.728	0.363	**0.000**	**5.62**
Constant	−7.277	0.817	**0.000**	**0.001**

%correct: no PYG: 99.0

%correct PYG: 23.4

Overall %correct: 93.0

Nagelkerke pseudo R-square: 39.2 – 2loglikelihood: 793.05

Table 69 shows the results of a logistic regression analysis that presents the cumulative effects of domain-specific risk factors, controlling for gender, age, and nonimmigrant status.

Cumulative risk scales were created for social bonds, street-level social processes, neighborhood cluster structural characteristics, lifestyle, alienation (external locus of control and legal cynicism), self-control (volatile temper and impulsiveness), substance use, and previous arrest. These risk scales are simply the summation of the 'above-median' value, the risk end of the distribution per variable within each domain and then we counted the number of risk factors per domain. This method allows for a detection of cumulative risk effects and a comparison of cumulative risk effects per domain. The multivariate analysis allows us to identify significant cumulative effects within each domain while controlling for all other domains. This type of analysis is interesting because it is suggestive of direct effect. The existence of cumulative risk effects is actually a very straightforward way of identifying interactions between variables within domains and is a neat way of modeling nonlinear effects by treating each risk factor as categorical covariate. Let us now turn to the discussion of the research findings.

Once risk factors are taken into account, gender and age are no longer significantly related to problematic youth group involvement. The effect of nonimmigrant background remains.

There are no direct cumulative risk effects for family structural characteristics and for objective neighborhood cluster characteristics. Observed street-level characteristics have a cumulative direct effect on problematic youth group involvement. The ORs are 2.42 and 2.97. Lifestyle risk has the strongest direct cumulative effect on problematic youth group involvement, i.e. controlling for all other risk factors. Alienation also has a direct cumulative effect on (the ORs are 2.66 and 5.97). This means that a person who has an above-median value for legal cynicism and subjective powerlessness has a higher likelihood of being in a problematic youth group than someone who has no above-median value on those scales. Self-control has a similar cumulative effect. Previous arrest has no direct effect when control is held for all other variables in the model. Finally, we observe a direct and cumulative effect of substance use. Recall that substance use is excluded from the lifestyle measure as there are plenty of reasons of studying independent effects of substance use. Although one can see substance use as an indicator of a risky lifestyle, substance use may affect youths' involvement in a problematic youth group through other mechanisms, substance use is often a subcultural aspect of many gangs and problematic youth groups, so a selection effect may be at work : youths who score high on substance use may be drawn through groups where substance use is tolerated.

To detect similarities and differences, the same analysis is conducted with the versatility offending scale as a dependent variable. The versatility scale is simply the sum of the different crimes that were probed. The scale is based on the questions that refer to the past twelve months (1 = reported versus 0 = not reported). Additional scale information is found in Appendix. We additionally control for the effect of problematic youth group participation.

Table 70   Negative binomial regression of versatility scale on cumulative risk factors

Parameter	B	Std. error	Exp(B)
(Intercept)	−1.764	0.13	0.17
Being male	0.356	0.06	**1.42**
Age (15-16)	−0.003	0.07	0.99
Belgian background	−0.224	0.07	0.79
Cumulative family structural risk (CFSR)			
One risk factor	−0.01	0.08	0.98
Two risk factors	−0.03	0.16	0.97
Cumulative social bonds risk (CSBR)			
Three risk factors	0.49	0.11	**1.64**
Two risk factors	0.41	0.11	**1.50**
One risk factor	0.31	0.11	**1.37**
Cumulative street-level disorganization			
Two risk factors	0.27	0.04	**1.31**
One risk factor	0.10	0.08	1.11
Cumulative objective neighborhood risk			
Two risk factors	−0.07	0.07	0.92
One risk factor	−0.00	0.11	0.99
Cumulative lifestyle risk			
Two risk factors	0.62	0.14	**1.87**
One risk factor	0.45	0.0738	**1.57**

Continued

Table 70—continued

Parameter	B	Std. error	Exp(B)
Cumulative alienation risk			
Two risk factors	0.56	0.10	1.76
One risk factor	0.28	0.10	1.32
Cumulative self-control risk			
Two risk factors	0.61	0.09	1.84
One risk factor	0.36	0.09	1.44
Problematic youth group involvement	0.29	0.10	1.33
Previous arrest	0.36	0.08	1.43
Substance use risk			
Very high	1.191	0.16	3.28
High	1.242	0.19	3.46
Medium	0.953	0.12	2.59
Low	1.092	0.10	2.98

As the versatility scale is a count variable, negative binomial regression is used to detect the main effects of the independent variables on self-reported offending. The versatility scale is a count variable that represents how many of the different offenses the respondents had reported. This scale ranges from zero to nine (see Appendix). The results presented in this table are very similar to the results in the previous table. This reaffirms the strong overlap between problematic youth group involvement and offending. Significant effects have been found for cumulative street-level disorganization, cumulative lifestyle risk, cumulative alienation risk, cumulative self-control risk, previous arrest, and substance use risk (Table 70).

It is striking that the strongest direct effects are found of lifestyle variables, the specific combination of legal cynicism and external locus of control (subjective alienation), and low self-control. It is important to notice that the effects of theory-driven mechanisms remain unaltered, even when control is held for previous self-reported arrest. Previous arrest has an independent effect of its own, which is definitely worth further analyzing in panel studies. Problematic youth group remains significantly related to offending, but caution is warranted as stronger designs are necessary to discuss the relationship between both constructs. A provisional conclusion is that risk factors in many domains are related to both problematic youth group involvement and offending. Of the background variables, only being male and Belgian background remain statistically significant, when controlling for risk factors in the subsequent domains. Objective neighborhood level conditions are not directly related to problematic youth group involvement and offending, while a small direct effect exists when looking at micro-place conditions. The cumulative effects of social bonds remain significant even under statistical control of individual-level mechanisms. In the next chapter, we will assess direct and indirect effects among the key constructs derived from the integrative theoretical model.

1   INTRODUCTION

The present chapter summarizes the results of the multivariate analyses that were conducted to test the indirect and direct effects that were stipulated in the general integrative conditions-controls-exposure model, an integrate framework that incorporated elements from lifestyle/routine activities theories, social bonding, and social disorganization theory and at the same time applied the logic of situational action theory to the study of problematic youth group participation. The analyses presented here will highlight direct effects (proximate causes) and indirect effects (distal causes) of offending and problematic youth group involvement. In the previous chapters we have found strong empirical evidence of the relationship between micro-place disorganization, social bonds, and internal mechanisms such as external locus of control, low morality (moral beliefs), low ability to exercise self-control, and exposure to criminogenic moral settings, as measured by an overall lifestyle risk score and problematic youth group involvement.

There are several ways one can proceed if one is willing to apply the logic of an integrative version of a theory to empirical data. One can proceed data driven and one can proceed strictly theory based. As this study is aimed at getting insight into the empirical validity of an integrative model, we proceed theory based when formulating the hypotheses. We confront the data with the empirical results and for reasons of parsimony when present the best fitting model, f that is in line with the logical structure. Although the analyses are based on cross-sectional data, there is a developmental touch at least in the social development model that explains the causes of the causes: by studying the cumulative effects of micro-place disorganization (the accumulation of low social trust, low informal control, micro-place disorder, and the presence of delinquent youth), we hope to capture at least some of the logic of developmental theories. The same goes for social bonds: while each element of the social bond can be said to have independent effects on problematic youth group involvement (see Pauwels & Svensson, 2014) and offending, it is especially relevant to also study the cumulative effects of social bonds as an indicator of how integrated the youths 'have become.' Those who have undergone a rather prosocial development can be expected to be socially integrated on a larger number of domains than those who have undergone a less prosocial development.

The hypotheses refer to a strong version of the theory, i.e. where full mediation of the effects of micro-place conditions is assumed. In the path models, the effect of micro-place conditions is measured the way it has been described in the descriptive part of this study. Our overall measure of micro-place conditions takes into account absence of collective efficacy and presence of disorder.

H1: The effect of observed micro-place disorganization (low collective efficacy, high levels of unsupervised youths, and high levels of disorder) on PYG involvement and offending is positive but fully indirect. Observed micro-place cumulative risk is positively related to low social integration and positively related to external locus of control and low moral beliefs. The rationale for these relationships has been given in the chapter on the integrative model. We have especially drawn upon collective efficacy theory and previously discussed empirical findings to justify these hypotheses.

H2: External locus of control is positively related to low moral beliefs and positively related to the lack of an ability to exercise self-control and as such indirectly related to problematic youth group involvement. We draw on Mirowsky and Ross' alienation theory to justify the hypotheses. Hypothesis 2 is crucial as a test of our extension of our general conditions-controls-exposure model. If this hypothesis fails the test, then control orientation should be abandoned as an explanatory mechanism in a causal chain toward offending and problematic youth group involvement in early adolescence.

H3: Low social integration is negatively related to external locus of control, low moral beliefs, low self-control, and lifestyle risk. Justification is provided by referring to alienation theory, social bonding theory, lifestyle theories, and self-control theory.

H4: Low moral beliefs is positively related to low self-control, lifestyle risk, offending, and problematic youth group involvement. These hypotheses are drawn from social bonding theory, social cognitive learning theory, and lifestyle theories.

H5: Low self-control is positively related to lifestyle risk and problematic youth group involvement. We draw on situational action theory to justify the hypothesized relations.

H6: Lifestyle risk is positively related to problematic youth group involvement and offending. We draw on the routine activities theory of general deviance and situational action theory .

H7: Offending is directly related to problematic youth group involvement, independent of all other variables in the equation. We acknowledge that this relationship is not unidirectional, but due to the cross-sectional nature of the data we can only model one relationship. We have opted for the path from offending to problematic youth group involvement. We draw upon a selection effect to justify this hypothesized path, but keep in mind that problematic youth group involvement over time will intensify offending.

2   ANALYTICAL STRATEGY

The hypotheses will be evaluated against the empirical data. We used structural equation models for dichotomous and count-dependent variables to test the paths between the exogenous, endogenous, and dependent variables. We conducted all analyses using Mplus, version 7.12 (Muthén & Muthén, 2011). Structural equation models are considered common extensions of the linear path model (Jöreskog & Sörbom, 1993; Bollen, 1998) and have been introduced into the field of criminological enquiries before (e.g. Wikström et al. 2012). Path models, which combine dichotomous outcomes (such as PYG involvement) or count data (such as counts of offenses), with exogenous continuous variables can be handled with Mplus (Byrne, 2011). All scale scores were standardized before entering the equation. To test the hypotheses, we first ran all models taking into account the complex nature of the different measurement levels: this means that we first ran path models that combined negative binomial regression with logistic regression and linear regression. Then, the results were compared to a simplified model that combines linear modelling (maximum likelihood estimations) with logistic modelling. This allowed us to evaluate the models using the well-known model fit indices (like the RMSEA). It was an interesting exercise to compare the results of these different models. We stress that the results were highly identical. Therefore we have opted to present the simpler model.

Before progressing to the results section, some remarks are made regarding the use of statistical models. Statistical models are merely used to evaluate the hypotheses and only serve as guideline for the interpretation of the results. We acknowledge that the use of powerful statistical models, such as structural equation models, is no guarantee to demonstrate causal effects; we merely make the assumption that the existence of causal effects implies the existence of a certain covariance structure. Thus, statistical analysis guides the process of verification and falsification. While there is a great deal of discussion in the literature on the acceptability of 'causal talks,' we submit that thinking in causal mechanisms of importance from a theoretical point of view, both in the context of discovery and justification (Bunge, 2004). However, when the findings are discussed, effects need to be understood in mere statistical terms. Statistical relationships do not represent causation, they are in need of (causal) explanation.

3   MODELING THE RELATIONSHIP BETWEEN OFFENDING
AND PROBLEMATIC YOUTH GROUP PARTICIPATION

Classic theoretical perspectives provide no explication of the relationship between gang membership and offending. The three general theoretical frameworks proposed to explain the impact of gang membership on delinquent involvement are referred to as the selection, facilitation, and enhancement models (Thornberry et al., 1993). The **selection model** is consistent with theories that explain criminal behavior as the product of relatively stable differences in criminal propensity between individuals (Glueck & Glueck, 1950; Gottfredson & Hirschi, 1990; Hirschi, 1969). According to this view, the association between gang membership and delinquency is spurious, as a common set of factors explain both delinquency and gang involvement. The **facilitation model** is consistent with social learning and opportunity perspectives, whereby gang

membership influences attitudes, norms, and routine activities associated with delinquent behavior, which in turn increases individual criminal involvement. In this
model, gang membership is afforded a causal role in shaping delinquent behavior
both through a learning process similar to the one described by Akers (1998) as well
as by influencing and delimiting opportunities for delinquent and prosocial behavior.
Finally, the **enhancement model** blends the selection and facilitation models and suggests that gang members are more antisocial than non-gang youths even before gang
involvement, but that the gang context exacerbates these differences (Thornberry
et al., 1993; Thornberry et al., 2003). As Thornberry et al. (2003: 186) stated, "The
young men and women who join gangs have multiple deficits in many developmental domains and being a member of a street gang further impedes their prosocial
development." To date, findings consistent with the enhancement model have been
reported in American panel studies (Battin et al., 1998; Thornberry et al., 2003) as well
as in Norwegian (Bendixen, Endresen & Olweus, 2006) and Canadian samples (Gatti
et al., 2005).

The cross-sectional nature of the data does not allow us to make claims on the direction of the relation between offending and problematic youth group participation.
One way of assessing bidirectional effects is through the assessment of bidirectional
effects. This can be done in linear modeling only and is somewhat problematic in
models that combine count data and categorical-dependent variables (Muthén &
Muthén, 2011). Thus, a choice need to be made. We had a preference for modeling
offending as a proximate cause of problematic youth group involvement, as offending
was found to be reported by virtually all youths who participate in a problematic
youth group. However, we should bear in mind that we have no idea of previous
gang involvement of the youths who participated in the survey.

We underscore that it is quintessential to use stronger designs, such as panel data to
evaluate models that deal with the relationship between problematic youth group
involvement and offending. Longitudinal panel studies based on self-report data that
allow for testing theories developmentally are currently not being conducted in the Belgian context. One of the major reasons is the limited duration of research projects that
are funded by governments and the other reason is the expensive character of such data.

4   PATH MODEL IN THE GENERAL SAMPLE

This paragraph is concerned with the empirical test of the integrative micro-place con-
ditions-cognitions-controls-exposure model of problematic youth group involvement
and offending (Figure 19).

For reasons of parsimony, we present the results of the best fitting model and confront
this model directly with the hypotheses. There is a strong direct effect of micro-place
cumulative risk on cumulative low integration ($\beta = 0.27$), on external locus of control
($\beta = 0.20$), on low self-control ($\beta = 0.14$), and on lifestyle risk ($\beta = 0.29$). The effect of
cumulative micro-place risk on moral beliefs is fully mediated through external locus

Figure 19 Path model of the integrated conditions-controls-exposure model of problematic youth group involvement (general sample)

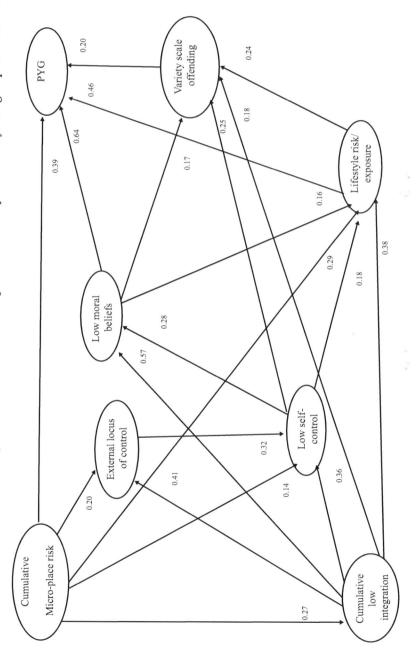

of control, low self-control, and cumulative low social integration. This makes sense from the theoretical framework: micro-place conditions may negatively affect cumulative social integration, which in turn promotes the installation of the learned belief of external locus of control, which in turn impedes the capacity to exercise self-control. The effect of cumulative micro-place risk on offending is also fully mediated through a number of intervening mechanisms: cumulative low social integration, external locus of control, low self-control, moral beliefs, and lifestyle risk. The effect of the micro-place conditions on offending is indirect, and that is supportive of the idea that micro-place social conditions are part of a social developmental model, as there is no direct effect on offending. However, there is a remaining direct effect of cumulative micro-place risk on problematic youth group participation that is not mediated through the intervening mechanisms of the theoretical framework.

Cumulative low integration has a direct effect on external locus of control ($\beta = 0.41$), moral beliefs ($\beta = 0.57$), lifestyle risk ($\beta = 0.38$), and low self-control ($\beta = 0.36$). There still is a small but substantial effect of cumulative social integration on offending ($\beta = 0.18$) that is not mediated. Thus, if social bonds are measured in a cumulative way, full mediation, as we have previously found when studying the effects of parental supervision, parental attachment, and the school social bond, is not observed. The cumulative effect is therefore much stronger related to offending than the effects of the separate control mechanisms. It is in line with our integrative theoretical framework that both micro-place conditions and low social integration are related to external locus of control. As stressed by the theory of Mirowsky and Ross, micro-place conditions may negatively affect control orientation, independent of informal control. It is important to stress that there is a direct relationship between micro-place conditions and external locus of control, independent of social integration, as classical disorganization theory stressed that the impact of detrimental micro-place conditions is realized especially via social controls. We hereby present some evidence that there is an alternative route through which micro-place conditions affect offending, albeit a highly indirect one. The direct effect of cumulative low social integration on external locus of control is also of relevance for control theories, as the findings suggest that social integration may impede the installation of external locus of control.

External locus of control has a direct effect on low self-control ($\beta = 0.32$). In line with the theoretical framework, the installation of an external locus of control has a strong detrimental impact on the capability to exercise self-control. There are no other direct effects of external locus of control. Thus, external locus of control is a mediator in the explanation of individual differences in problematic youth group participation and offending.

Low self-control has a direct effect on moral beliefs ($\beta = 0.28$), offending ($\beta = 0.25$), and exposure ($\beta = 0.18$). The effect of low self-control can be understood as a selection effect: individuals low in self-control select risky settings. There is no direct effect of low self-control on PYG involvement, once the other mechanisms are taken into account. This suggests that the effect of low self-control on problematic youth group involvement is indirect and fully mediated by one's moral standards. There remains a strong direct effect of low self-control on offending

Moral beliefs are directly related to lifestyle risk ($\beta = 0.16$), offending ($\beta = 0.17$), and problematic youth group involvement (log-odds = 0.64). This finding is consistent with the earlier discussed rationale developed in lifestyle theories and the routine activities theory of general deviance. Exposure is related to both offending ($\beta = 0.24$) and problematic youth group involvement (log-odds = 0.46).[1]

There is a direct effect of offending on problematic youth group involvement (log-odds = 0.20).

Of the mechanisms that directly are related to both offending and problematic youth group involvement, two of them are playing a key role in situational action theory: exposure and low morality. Low self-control is exclusively directly related to problematic youth group involvement, when offending is taken into account, and micro-place cumulative risk is exclusively related to problematic youth group involvement when offending is taken into account.

The idea that theories should distinguish between proximate mechanisms, which are defined as direct causes of offending in the integrative framework, and between distal causes of offending, which are especially important with regard to the development of moral standards, low self-control, and exposure, finds empirical support, if one is willing to see mediation effects as empirical evidence. The model fit was highly acceptable (<0.03).

5   TESTING THE INTEGRATED CONDITIONS-CONTROLS-EXPOSURE
         MODEL BY GENDER AND SEX DIFFERENCES

By ways of critically assessing the stability of the model, we reanalyzed the path model in subsamples by gender and immigrant background combined. In this paragraph, we discuss in brief the same path analysis as given for the general sample, but split up by gender and immigrant background. Overall, the logic of the model seems to be empirically supported. There are however some small differences, mostly regarding direct effects of distal mechanisms, so these differences are not a threat

---

1. One important criticism of our proposed model that studies the relationship between lifestyle risk (exposure to criminogenic moral settings) and violent youth group involvement would be that the relationship is tautological. A relationship is tautological when it involves a certain degree of circular reasoning. Although we acknowledge the fact that lifestyle risk and violent youth group involvement are closely related concepts, they are conceptually (and empirically) different. Our lifestyle risk measure is a combined measure that consists of routines and peer delinquency as indicators of a risky lifestyle. Lifestyle risk is constructed as an overall summation index, which only takes the risk ends of the distribution of each aspect into account. Violent youth group involvement refers to belonging to a violent youth group, explicitly using a conjunctive criterion, which is explained further (see measurements of constructs). Both concepts are measured using different questions. From our standpoint, one may see lifestyle risk as both a predictor and outcome of violent youth group involvement. Indeed, the relationship between both concepts is not one-directional but probably reciprocal in nature. In cross-sectional studies such issues cannot be dealt with adequately.

to the key reasoning of the causal model. We present the best fitting models, which all had a highly acceptable model fit (RMSEA < 0.05).

a   *Belgian Males*

We can observe direct effects of micro-place cumulative risk on cumulative low integration (β = 0.27), on external locus of control (β = 0.38), on low self-control (β = 0.10), on lifestyle risk (β = 0.29), and on problematic youth group participation (log-odds = 0.66). The effect of cumulative micro-place risk on moral beliefs is fully mediated through external locus of control, low self-control, and cumulative low social integration. The effect of cumulative micro-place risk on offending is also fully mediated through a number of intervening mechanisms: cumulative low social integration, external locus of control, low self-control, moral beliefs, and life-style risk (Figure 20).

Let us now turn to the presentation of the findings with regard to the causes of the causes, i.e. the developmental ecological framework. Cumulative low integration has a direct effect on external locus of control (β = 0.41), moral beliefs (β = 0.54), life-style risk (β = 0.29), and low self-control (β = 0.33). There still is a small but substantial effect of cumulative social integration on offending (β = 0.21) that is not mediated. External locus of control has a direct effect on low self-control (β = 0.35). There are no other direct effects of external locus of control. Thus, external locus of control is a mediator in the explanation of problematic youth group participation and offending. Low self-control has a direct effect on moral beliefs (β = 0.28), offending (β = 0.22), and lifestyle risk (β = 0.12). There is no direct effect of low self-control on PYG involvement, once the other mechanisms are taken into account. Moral beliefs is directly related to lifestyle risk (β = 0.18), offending (β = 0.17), and PYG involvement (log-odds = 0.97). There is a direct effect of offending on PYG involvement (log-odds = 0.42).

b   *Immigrant males*

We can observe direct effects of micro-place cumulative risk on cumulative low integration (β = 0.25), on external locus of control (β = 0.38), on low self-control (β = 0.14), on lifestyle risk (β = 0.23), and on PYG involvement (log-odds = 0.28). The effect of cumulative micro-place risk on moral beliefs is fully mediated through external locus of control, low self-control, and cumulative low social integration. The effect of cumulative micro-place risk on offending is also fully mediated through a number of intervening mechanisms: cumulative low social integration, external locus of control, low self-control, moral beliefs, and lifestyle risk. Cumulative low integration has a direct effect on external locus of control (β = 0.41), moral beliefs (β = 0.60), lifestyle risk (β = 0.25), and low self-control (β = 0.31). There are still substantial effects of cumulative social integration on offending (β = 0.23) and on PYG involvement (log-odds = 0.47) that are not mediated. External locus of control has a direct effect on low self-control (β = 0.31). There are no other direct effects of external locus of

Figure 20 Path model of the integrated conditions-controls-exposure model of problematic youth group involvement (Belgian males)

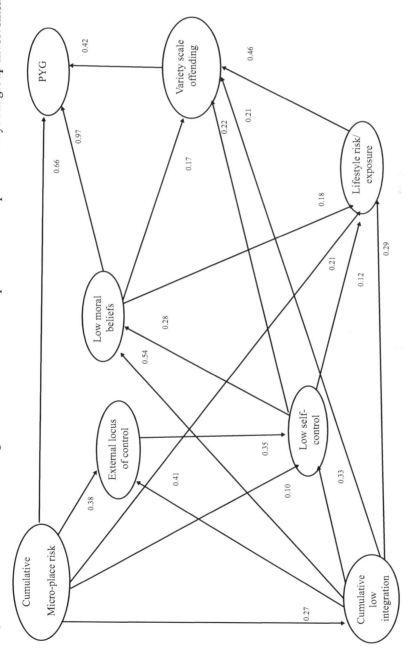

control. Thus, external locus of control is a mediator in the explanation of PYG involvement and offending. Low self-control has a direct effect on moral beliefs ($\beta = 0.28$), offending ($\beta = 0.27$), and lifestyle risk ($\beta = 0.17$). There is no direct effect of low self-control on PYG involvement, once the other mechanisms are taken into account. Moral beliefs is directly related to offending ($\beta = 0.11$) and PYG involvement (log-odds = 0.36). There is no direct effect of offending on PYG involvement in the subsample of immigrant males. The results in the immigrant male sample suggest that the relationship between offending and problematic youth group involvement has two common causes: moral beliefs and lifestyle risk/exposure. However, caution is warranted. This interpretation is the consequence of the fact that moral beliefs and lifestyle risk are the only direct effects that problematic youth group involvement and offending have in common, combined with the finding that, in this subsample, there is no direct relationship between offending and problematic youth group involvement (Figure 21).

c   *Belgian females*

We can observe direct effects of micro-place cumulative risk on cumulative low integration ($\beta = 0.23$), on external locus of control ($\beta = 0.39$), on low self-control ($\beta = 0.12$), and on lifestyle risk ($\beta = 0.19$). Among Belgian females, we did not find a direct effect of micro-place cumulative risk on problematic youth group partic-ipation. The effect of cumulative micro-place risk on moral beliefs is fully mediated through external locus of control, low self-control, and cumulative low social inte-gration. The effect of cumulative micro-place risk on offending is also fully medi-ated through a number of intervening mechanisms: cumulative low social integration, external locus of control, low self-control, moral beliefs, and lifestyle risk. Cumulative low integration has a direct effect on external locus of control ($\beta = 0.41$), moral beliefs ($\beta = 0.58$), lifestyle risk ($\beta = 0.29$), and low self-control ($\beta = 0.32$). There still is a rather strong effect of cumulative social integration on offending ($\beta = 0.46$) that is not mediated. External locus of control has a direct effect on low self-control ($\beta = 0.43$). There are no other direct effects of external locus of control. Thus, external locus of control is a mediator in the explanation of PYG involvement and offending. Low self-control has a direct effect on moral beliefs ($\beta = 0.25$), offending ($\beta = 0.23$), and lifestyle risk ($\beta = 0.14$). There is no direct effect of low self-control on PYG involvement, once the other mechanisms are taken into account. Moral beliefs are only directly related to lifestyle risk ($\beta = 0.18$). There is no direct effect of offen-ding on PYG involvement (Figure 22).

d   *Immigrant females*

We can observe direct effects of micro-place cumulative risk on cumulative low inte-gration ($\beta = 0.23$), on external locus of control ($\beta = 0.39$), on low self-control ($\beta = 0.18$), on lifestyle risk ($\beta = 0.21$), and on PYG involvement (log-odds = 0.39). The effect of cumulative micro-place risk on moral beliefs is fully mediated through external locus of control, low self-control, and cumulative low social integration. The effect of

Figure 21   Path model of the integrated conditions-controls-exposure model of problematic youth group involvement (immigrant males)

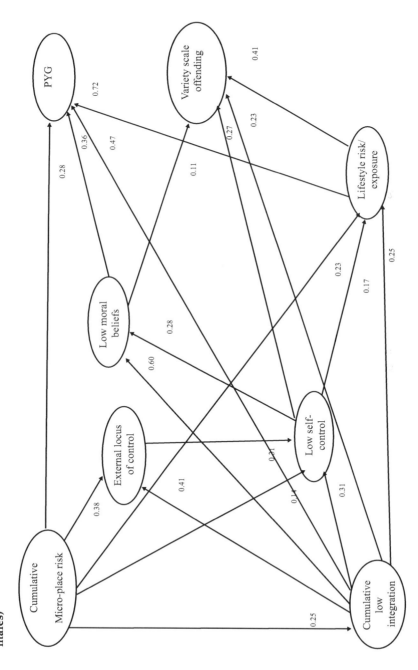

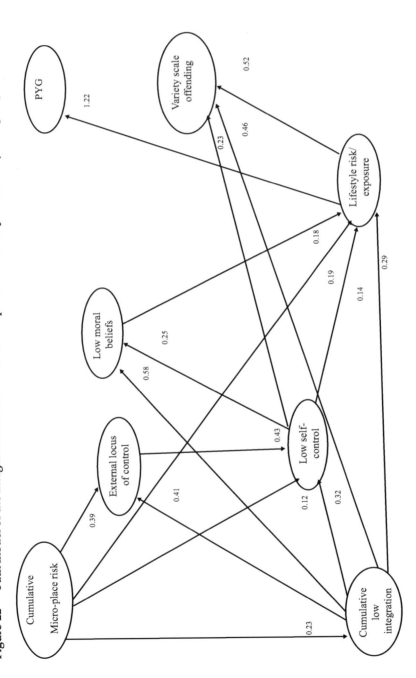

Figure 22   Path model of the integrated conditions-controls-exposure model of problematic youth group involvement (Belgian females)

cumulative micro-place risk on offending is also fully mediated through a number of intervening mechanisms: cumulative low social integration, external locus of control, low self-control, moral beliefs, and lifestyle risk (Figure 23).

Cumulative low integration has a direct effect on external locus of control ($\beta = 0.42$), moral beliefs ($\beta = 0.56$), lifestyle risk ($\beta = 0.29$), and low self-control ($\beta = 0.41$). There still is a substantial effect of cumulative social integration on offending ($\beta = 0.28$) that is not mediated.

External locus of control has a direct effect on low self-control ($\beta = 0.25$). There are no other direct effects of external locus of control. Thus, external locus of control is a mediator in the explanation of PYG involvement and offending. Low self-control has a direct effect on moral beliefs ($\beta = 0.25$), offending ($\beta = 0.32$), and lifestyle risk ($\beta = 0.10$). There is no direct effect of low self-control on PYG involvement, once the other mechanisms are taken into account. Moral beliefs are directly related to offending ($\beta = 0.21$) and PYG involvement (log-odds = 0.80). There is no direct effect of offending on PYG involvement.

6   DISCUSSION ON THE FINDINGS

There exist multiple routes through which micro-place conditions are related to problematic youth group involvement. Two distinct routes were distinguished: the cumulative social integration route (which is derived from control theory) and the external low social control route, which is derived from alienation theory. It seems that both routes are statistically significant and are also sequentially related: micro-place disorganization has an indirect effect through low social integration. Why youths from disorganized micro-places have *cumulatively* lower levels of social integration on different domains (the family and the school) should be scrutinized as a separate research topic to distinguish causal mechanisms from selection mechanisms and mechanisms of stigmatization. Cumulative low social integration had multiple effects on offending and problematic youth group participation, both direct and indirect. This finding is in line with much criminological research on social bonds and crime. The effect of external locus of control is entirely mediated by moral beliefs and low self-control. Thus, having learned belief the belief that one is not in control has detrimental consequences for one's capacity to exercise self-control and for one's moral beliefs. Low moral beliefs seemed to be a crucial mediator for the effect of low social integration. Previously we studied the effects of different informal controls on problematic youth group involvement separately (Pauwels & Svensson, 2013; Pauwels & Svensson, 2014), while this study examined the cumulative effect of low social integration. The cumulative effects seem to be much stronger than the effects of parental attachment, parental control, and the school social bond separately. Contrary to previous studies, this study did not find any direct effects of low self-control on problematic youth group participation. Lifestyle risk is one of the strongest situational

Figure 23 Path model of the integrated conditions-controls-exposure model of problematic youth group involvement (immigrant females)

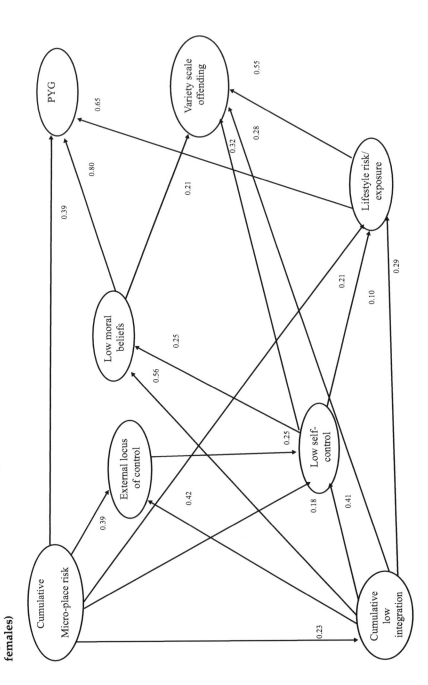

predictors of both problematic youth group participation and offending. Lifestyle risk is partially a common cause of the relationship between offending and problematic youth group involvement.

These findings have important consequences for further theoretical development and practice. The implication of our finding for theories of problematic youth group involvement is that we have shown that the relationship between observations of micro-place disorganization (low efficacy, high levels of disorder, and unsupervised youths) and PYG involvement/offending is not just a matter of social controls, self-control, and lifestyle risk but also a matter of personal-control orientation. As Ross and Mirowsky (2001, 2009) and Ross, Mirowsky, and Pribesh (2001, 2002) correctly observed, external locus control is higher in micro-places that are characterized by high levels of disorder and low levels of collective efficacy. This finding has also implications for Colvin's theory of coercion, which is one of the few contemporary theories that explicitly argues that an external locus of control is related to The negative world view that one is not in control (fatalism/control orientation) is an additional factor in the development of low moral beliefs and low self-control, which in turn has strong consequences for offending and problematic youth group involvement. Early models of disorganization did not take locus of control into account. Thus, we have pointed to an additional mediating mechanism, external locus of control, which has previously been neglected in much of the empirical literature on adolescent offending and problematic youth group involvement. It has been neglected because of the fact that direct effects have not been demonstratively shown. This study clearly demonstrates that the effect is indirect and therefore is one of the factors that is relevant for understanding the causes of the causes of problematic youth group involvement. Understanding the causes of the causes is as important as understanding the proximate causes of offending. Of course, there are some limitations that need to be taken into account. This study raises a number of questions with regard to the nature of the relationship between external locus of control, informal controls, PYG involvement, and offending over time. We have some concerns with regard to the unidirectional nature of the relationships that were tested. In line with arguments derived from Thornberry et al.'s (2003) interactional model, we acknowledge that feedback loops may exist between external locus of control and mechanisms of control and between low moral beliefs and lifestyles. We do not wish to exclude feedback loops at all, especially not in the life course differential susceptibility model that explains why youths are different with regard to their moral beliefs, self-control, and lifestyles. Whether cross-lagged effects exist, there is both a theoretical and empirical issue. People's individual moral beliefs are definitely not static, as have been demonstratively shown by longitudinal studies and changes may have consequences for one's level of social integration. Scholars should always reflect on the causal paths they hypothesize, e.g. in explaining the causes of the causes. A highly complex issue is the role of exposure (e.g. to delinquent peers) in the life course. While it may be plausible to hypothesize that low social bonds set the stage for delinquent bonding in childhood, it should also be acknowledged that delinquent bonding in turn may affect the quality of the parental bonds and the school social bonds. Thus, the causal ordering of the relationship between bonds and peers may be age graded. Changes in problematic youth group participation can also be related to changes in attitudes and moral beliefs. Being in a problematic youth group is about much more than just passive exposure and learning to justify offending. It is about group processes that have been thoroughly studied from within social psychological theories, such as self-categorization theory (Turner et al., 1987; Abrams et al., 1990) and social identity theory (Turner & Onorato, 1999). With regard to the situational model, we argue that changes in offending should be explained by changes in exposure (lifestyles) and moral beliefs.

This study went beyond the classic analyses that compared males versus females or immigrants versus nonimmigrants by testing the integrated theory for different subgroups: Belgian males, immigrant males, Belgian females, and immigrant females. For all subgroups we observed significant direct effects of micro-place disorganization on cumulative low social integration, external locus of control, low self-control, and lifestyle risk/exposure. With the exception of Belgian females, we could also observe direct effects of cumulative micro-place risk on problematic youth group participation, independent of offending.

All subgroups show direct effects of cumulative low integration on external locus of control, moral beliefs, low self-control, lifestyle risk/exposure, and offending. However, the subgroup of immigrant males is unique in the way that cumulative low integration directly affects PYG involvement.

For all subgroups, we observed direct effects of external locus of control on low self-control and direct effects of low self-control on moral beliefs, offending, and lifestyle risk/exposure.

Moral beliefs are directly related to lifestyle risk in the groups of Belgian males and Belgian females and to offending and PYG involvement in the groups of Belgian males, immigrant males, and immigrant females.

We could only observe a direct effect of offending on PYG involvement in the group of Belgian males.

| # Key findings and their explanation

1   The context of the study

This study gives a snapshot in time of 12- to 15-year-old adolescents' individual characteristics, their social environments (neighborhoods and micro-places), social controls, personal controls situational exposure, and problematic youth group involvement and offending in a large city (Antwerp). The study focuses on current offending and problematic youth group involvement as they relate to the youth's individual characteristics. Since this is a cross-sectional study, we do not know these adolescents' past-childhood development and we do not how they have evolved since they participated in the study. Therefore, we cannot explain how these individual differences have emerged and cannot say how their current crime and youth group involvement will affect their future lives. However, it is entirely reasonable to argue that we actually can use the findings from existing longitudinal studies to help in the interpretation of the findings and patterns of problematic youth group involvement and crime involvement in the present study.

A particular strength of this study is its simultaneous focus on the youths' situational contexts as represented by their lifestyles/routines, their control orientation, social controls and self-control, the micro-place conditions, and the interactions between key individual characteristics and situational characteristics. This aspect has become more and more common in the past years, without doubt under the influence of recent theories of offending, such as situational action theory. We have paid a lot of attention to the study of the effects of the micro-place context. This is of course due to the very fact that problematic youth group involvement has a long tradition in the community theories of the Chicago School. Our study revealed that micro-places are of importance as causes of the causes of problematic youth group involvement, not only via its effect on social bonds but also indirectly via its effect on control orientation. The micro-place context is the context that we can observe with our sense and is therefore more meaningful than large ecological settings.

2   Problematic youth group involvement

Only a small percentage of the adolescents self-reported being involved in a problematic youth group while offending (like an act of violence or theft) is more widespread among adolescents. Virtually all youths who participate in a problematic youth group have offended. This is in accordance with what has been found in previous studies of self-reported offending and troublesome youth group involvement. There is a huge difference between those youths involved in a problematic youth group and those who are not involved: the frequency of offending is a lot higher, as could be seen from a comparison of the prevalence of offending per offense: with the exception of burglary, those involved in a problematic youth group were much more active than those who did not participate in a problematic youth group.

Youths who are involved in a problematic youth group are versatile in their offending, and this versatility does not only include committing more acts of violence but also more serious acts of crime that were measured in our study. Within the problematic youth group, differences in offending between males and females turn smaller, as do differences between immigrants and nonimmigrants. This suggests that a problematic youth group may be a specific behavioral context in itself. However, not all individuals who self-report problematic youth group involvement are serious offenders; many of them are high-frequency offenders. We may expect that these youths have had an imposing personal history of antisocial behavior and negative life events. From the analyses of the social bonds, it became clear that an accumulation of low family attachment, poor parental control, low-class integration, and poor school social bond all are very strongly related to problematic youth group involvement. Poor social bonds virtually explained the relationship between the effects of street segment low efficacy. It is of great importance to stress that not all those who have been engaged in a problematic youth group have committed violent crimes. Some youths may simply be attracted to the group, as it may help in fulfilling needs such as belonging somewhere. In fact, this study has shown that only five percent of the youths involved in a violent youth group reported not to have committed any crime ever.

3   EXPLANATORY FACTORS OF PROBLEMATIC YOUTH GROUP
         INVOLVEMENT

What factors cause individuals to participate in gangs? While much qualitative studies have provided in-depth insights into the motives, large-scale quantitative studies take a look at mechanisms that explain the differences. The motives that are often discussed in qualitative studies (e.g. protection, excitement, looking for affection, and a peer network) are reflected in the effects of low self-control (excitement) and low social bonds. We argue that the study of motives is interesting and necessary, but motives are not causes: motives create a motivation to act, but motives develop in social contexts and before motives can be translated into problematic youth group involvement or offending, they need to be evaluated through the lens of one's moral beliefs. Thus, both approaches are complementary and both contribute to our understanding of the 'cogs and wheels' of problematic youth group involvement.

Problematic youth group involvement may probably best interpreted as a consequence of the perception of the problematic youth group as a 'lifestyle alternative'
and the consideration of the balance between what the problematic group may offer
the individual versus the broader society's offer not to engage in a problematic youth
group. The considerations of becoming involved in a problematic group should be
interpreted against the background of the interplay between the youth's individual
background characteristics and his or her behavioral contexts, as could be seen from
the strong interactions between personal and situational characteristics.

While engagement in a problematic youth group will necessarily involve some influence of the individual and some influences of the behavioral settings, it is plausible to
think of any other influence as indirect effects, i.e. as more distant causal factors,
whose effect should go through the proximate factors, an argument that we have integrated in our integrative micro-place conditions-controls-exposure model, which is
fully compatible with situational action theory. This means that in turn to understand
any effects of more distant factors (like family social position and immigrant status),
we should focus our efforts on improving our understanding of the social mechanisms through which structural disadvantage impacts the individual and lifestyle-
related characteristics that are involved in the process of becoming engaged in a problematic youth group. In the present study, we have applied this way of theorizing
with regard to the explanation of the engagement in a problematic youth group, primarily as a lifestyle alternative, which includes distant and proximate causes. Informal controls play without doubt a crucial role in the understanding of how
adolescents develop their crime propensities and lifestyles. This could already be
noticed in the path models.

3.1   Structural background characteristics

The impact of structural background characteristics is at best very modest. Neither
family disadvantage nor family structure has a direct effect on problematic youth
group involvement. These factors do not have a major impact on the youths' individual propensities and lifestyles. This is congruent with the assumption that structural
factors have a distant and indirect effect on problematic youth group involvement.
Even the accumulation of disadvantage and split family is weakly related to problematic youth group involvement and offending. There is however a small impact on the
social bonds. Problematic youth group involvement is not a particular lower-class
phenomenon. Earlier, Wikström and Butterworth (2006) and Wikström et al. (2012)
have documented that adolescent offending is not a lower-class phenomenon. That
does not mean that we ignore social class within criminology; we simply mean that
social class is not the major factor in the etiology of problematic youth group involvement in early adolescence.

The youths' immigrant background does not have a major impact on problematic
youth group involvement. Immigrant background seemed to be somewhat more
related to problematic youth group involvement than to offending. The relation

between immigrant background and problematic youth group involvement can be partially explained by social bonds and can entirely be explained by the individual differences in lifestyles.

3.2   *Community and micro-place characteristics*

The impact of community characteristics has often been the subject of debate. The community context has been widely accepted as a breeding ground (i.e. a context of development) for problematic youth group involvement and offending, partly because of the geographic clustering of offenders and youths who are involved in a problematic youth group in disadvantaged areas. However, this ecological correlation can be misleading, as has been previously shown in many studies. The impact of larger ecological units, such as neighborhood clusters, is entirely compositional and can be fully explained by the structural characteristics of the adolescents in these areas. However, when we take a look at the environment at a smaller level, the street segment level, a different picture arises: low social cohesion with neighbors, low collective efficacy, and observed disorder are related to problematic youth group involvement and offending. The effect of social processes at the street segment level is strongest when a cumulative risk measure is used to predict problematic youth group involvement and self-reported offending: street segments exhibit their strongest effect when the effects of poor collective efficacy, the presence of unsupervised youths, and disorder are treated like 'Guttman type of scales' or 'Mokken type of scales.' We argue it is important to see micro-places as a combination of control and criminogenic moral climate. Micro-places differ, just like individuals, on a risk-protective continuum, and their effect is most likely to be more pronounced when all organizational forces have vanished and disorganization processes are present. That is also congruent with the idea of Shaw and McKay (1942) that negative social capital may invade a neighborhood. At any given time, neighborhoods can be ranked on the basis of these theoretically relevant characteristics. Our treatment of neighborhoods as small ecological units, which differ in terms of cumulative risk, is also congruent with the idea that neighborhoods differ in their 'developmental trajectories': some are on their way down, as crime and disorder are invading these local settings, and others are on their way up. While being 'on the way up' or 'on the way down' may matter in the long run, and while informal control and neighborhood social ties may be causally related to crime and disorder in time, that does not matter in a cross-sectional study like this one, where the only thing we can do is treat the setting as a snap shot and study (1) what is going on at that very moment and (2) how that different picture affects neighborhood residents. Studies of neighborhood effects should definitely continue their efforts to focus on small areas in future inquiries. This study provided additional insight in the mechanisms that link cumulative setting risk to problematic youth group involvement.

3.3 Individual characteristics

While scholars predominantly have pointed to the importance of informal control and social bonds as mediators of the neighborhood-crime link, we find evidence for an additional link between low collective efficacy of the setting of residence and offending/problematic youth group involvement, which is subjective powerlessness or subjective alienation. The effect of subjective powerlessness on problematic youth group involvement and self-reported offending is however entirely indirect and mediated by social bonds.

Social bonds have a very strong effect on both problematic youth group involvement and self-reported offending. The key components of informal controls are parental monitoring and the school social bond. When the effects of low social bonds are studied combined, the effects of low social bonding become even more obvious.

The strongest predictors of problematic youth group involvement and self-reported offending are the individual propensity and lifestyle risk. First we discuss our findings with regard to propensity. Propensity was measured as the combination of low moral beliefs, using items that first appeared in Sampson and Bartusch's (1998) legal cynicism scale and poor self-control. Both concepts are significantly related to problematic youth group involvement and self-reported offending. With regard to problematic youth group involvement, it was striking that about half of the self-declared problematic youth group members were at risk at the poor self-control scale and legal cynicism scale.

Both problematic youth group involvement and self-reported offending are strongly related to differences in lifestyle risk. There were virtually no youths who were involved in a problematic youth group who were situated at the protective end of the distribution of lifestyle risk and propensity. That means that problematic youth group members are all quite different than average youths. Propensity and lifestyle risk have both independent effects on problematic youth group involvement and offending. Youths at the high-risk end of the propensity distribution differ from medium- and low-propensity youths at any level of exposure. Perhaps, even more important with regard to the dynamic nature of relationships between 'causes and effects,' future studies of the effects of lifestyle risk and problematic youth group involvement may benefit from distinguishing between exit and entry of problematic youth groups and between short-term and long-term effects. Emerging research on gang membership (e.g. Melde & Esbensen, 2011) reveals that joining and leaving such a group affect offending for the worse (entry) and for the better (exit). Our regression models merely illustrate independent effects of lifestyle risk on problematic youth group involvement and the independent effect of problematic youth group involvement and lifestyle risk on self-reported offending.

4 THEORETICAL REFLECTIONS

The micro-place conditions-controls-exposure model is an integrative framework (that is still in continuous development and in need for further testing), which aims

at integrating an ecological developmental model and situational model of the expla-
nation of why young adolescents offend and participate a problematic youth group.
At the meta-theoretical level, the integrative model is an application of an integrative
research program that has is deeply influenced in:
- Scientific realism (Psillos, 1999; 2008; Bunge, 1999)
- Sociological action theories (analytical sociology) and Opp's broad version of RCT
- Philosophy of causation, Bunge's emergentist systemism (Bunge, 2001)

At the theoretical level, it is conceptually inspired by the situational action theory, the
routine activities theory of general deviance, social bonding theory, alienation theory,
and micro-ecological applications of social disorganization/collective efficacy theory.
Because of the many similarities between problematic youth group participation and
offending, we are strongly convinced that it may be useful to additionally apply ideas
of action theories that have not been designed to explain individual differences in
problematic youth group participation. The fact that we successfully implemented
key ideas developed in the situational action theory in an integrated model that
explains problematic youth group involvement provides evidence of its broad usefulness. The basic idea is that integrative theoretical models of problematic youth group
participation serve two different purposes:
The *situational model* explains individual differences in problematic youth group participation and offending; both can be seen as results of processes of deliberation,
which are affected by propensity measures and measures of exposure, and the *social
developmental model* explains why individuals come to have the propensities that
increase the risk of problematic youth group participation and offending.

*A situational model (situated choice model of problematic youth group involvement
and offending)*
A situational model explains the role of situational instigations that play a role when
individuals perceive action alternatives and choose to commit an offense. Situational
instigation refers to the situational effects of exposure to criminogenic moral settings
(people in places). That has been the logic in the routine activities theory of general
deviance and more recently in the situational action theory. Not only have we found
empirical evidence for the use of an integrative model that fits both offending and
problematic youth group participation as explanandum, we have also found that both
problematic youth group participation and offending are the result of an interaction
between propensity and exposure.
We submit that joining a problematic youth group can elementarily be seen as a process that results from processes of deliberation (which we do not interpret from a
rational choice perspective; we just acknowledge that action includes elements of
moral deliberation and merely assumes a reasonable actor). The process of deliberation merely refers to the theoretical view on human nature: individuals have agency,

and agency is defined as the possibility to realize goals. Individuals are not merely puppets on a string but take active part in their lives.

Deliberation means that people outweigh pros and cons in a given situation; i.e. people perceive alternatives, based on a moral evaluation, and not based on self-control. Recall that self-control had no direct effects in our study.

While previous studies have found independent effects of self-control, the outcome of such studies usually reveals that the independent effects of indicators of morality are much stronger than measures of self-control (Kissner & Pyrooz, 2009; Pauwels & Svensson, 2013). A motivational process is started as an intersection of desires, beliefs, opportunities, and constraints (Elster, 2007). Offending plays a role as offending brings individuals in contact with gang members and it increases the likelihood of recruitment

A life course developmental model of moral beliefs, the ability to exercise self-control, and a risky lifestyle

A life course developmental model explains the causes of the causes of why people participate in a problematic youth group: why do adolescents develop a risky lifestyle, or put in other terms, why are adolescents differentially exposed to criminogenic moral settings, and why do adolescents develop deviant moral beliefs and low self-control?

The results are suggestive for the fact that there are long-term effects that emerge in the life course from being exposed to adverse micro-place conditions, low social integration, and a lack of personal control, a low capability to exercise self-control (immediate gratification and anger management), and low moral beliefs. The present study made it clear how control orientation plays a role in a broader causal chain toward the adaptation of deviant moral beliefs and low self-control. An external locus of control is a learnt belief that has its origins in developmental exposure to disruptive processes. Experiencing a lack of social integration (social bonds in the family and school) has negative effects for control orientation, moral beliefs, self-control, and the individual lifestyle. Exposure to criminogenic micro-place conditions (both criminogenic moral beliefs and the absence of cues of social control) is related to social integration and, together with social integration, exposure to criminogenic micro-place conditions helps to install the an external locus of control, the sense of fatalism which was mentioned, but not fully developed by early gang theorists.

Exposure to micro-place disorder, social controls in the family, and eternal locus of control have negative consequences for the executive functions (in the present study measured combined as low self-control, i.e. inhibitory executive function-impulse control/anger management), moral beliefs, and lifestyle risk.

The development of a risky lifestyle in the life course is seen as a consequence of moral beliefs, poor functioning of the inhibitory executive functions, and negative micro-place conditions and is the strongest predictor of offending and problematic youth group involvement. Problematic youth group involvement can be seen as a complex situated choice, a result of the interplay between situational exposure (as has been argued in the routine activities theory of general deviance) and individual character-istics (low moral beliefs in combination with a low capacity to resist temptation and provocation).

The mechanisms involved in the situational model fit Hedström's DBO scheme
Desires or preferences: an individual desires to be member of a problematic youth group. The concept of desires must be understood as a necessary but insufficient cause: desires may arise from temptations or provocations (e.g. youths being harassed and therefore decide to join a problematic youth group, or youths being tempted to become member of a problematic youth group, thereby making new friends, gaining status, power). The point made here is that desires are triggered by contextual clues in the environment, and different individuals react differently toward the same clues. Beliefs: there is clearly a strong interaction between propensity and situational expo-sure, and that means that individual beliefs (low morality) and opportunities (unstructured routines and peers) interact to bring about the situated choice. The DBO theory therefore can be said to build upon the situational logic of Popper, while more explicitly taking into account the role of individual differences. However, DBO schemes are organizing principles, not concrete theories.

The path model seemed to perform well in the general sample as well as in the sub-samples. However, there are of course a number of restrictions that need to be taken into account. Since this was a cross-sectional study, we do not know these adoles-cents' past childhood development, and we do not how they have developed since they participated in the study. Therefore, we cannot explain how these individual differences have emerged and cannot say how their current crime and problematic youth group involvement will affect their future lives. By studying cumulative risks in these developmental domains, we can say something about the effects of cumu-lative (dis)advantage.

5   FUTURE DEVELOPMENTS OF A CONDITIONS-CONTROLS-EXPOSURE
         MODEL

We have outlined the blueprint of a conditions-controls-exposure model. We have given a limited interpretation of the key concepts conditions, controls, and expo-sure. This interpretation was tailored to the explanation of problematic youth group participation and offending of young adolescents. Therefore, the mechanisms involved were adapted to the world of young adolescents. The theoretical frame-work should be expanded and integrated over time (from a life course developmen-tal perspective) to incorporate the effects of problematic youth group involvement on offending, thereby trying to disentangle the group processes that are playing a major role.

While we have presented a model that accounts for individual differences in problematic youth group involvement, it remains important to study the processes of disengagement: why do people leave problematic youth groups? What are the effects of the problematic lifestyle on the long run? What are the effects of official intervention (arrest, official sanctions, etc.). How do official sanctions knife off future possibilities of re-establishing a structured lifestyle, away from the peer group? Are there long-term effects of these negative effects on control orientation? In that case, feedback loops emerge between reaction and action, through the reinforcement of fatalism. These are empirical questions, which deserve to be studied. It would make sense to hypothesize that the effect of control orientation will increase with age, and that adults who have developed a criminal career become increasingly fatalistic about the future, which in turn reinforces deviant beliefs and restrains the individual to attempt to resist temptation and provocation and thus brings about the same interactive propensity-exposure mechanism. On the long run, control systems also get seriously affected by substance use. This has only been briefly addressed in the present study.

With this book, we have tried to demonstrate that integrative theories are useful and that concepts from theories are linked in a logical way. Formulated in a rather abstract way, conditions-controls-exposure models provide many opportunities for testing the core principles in different domains and different stages of the life course. While the content of conditions and controls may be somewhat different, the logic remains unchanged. That is what we meant when we stressed the importance of semi-general models. We do not submit the thesis that our theoretical model should be the only one. We do not apply the general principle of subsuming all theories under one overarching umbrella. It remains an interesting question: "how are theoretical integrations going to develop?" "Is there a future for a full-fletched integrative theories that includes other elements that have been omitted in this study, like genetics and other biological mechanisms?" The reason why we pose this question is the following: some important causal mechanisms (like the ability to exercise self-control and moral emotions, which are integral part of one's morality but whose effects have not been studied in the present enquiry) clearly have a genetic component. It is highly plausible that some scholars will continue to work in their paradigm, regardless of new developments in the field. We are convinced that further integration is a fruitful enterprise, if a distinction is made between the situational logic of explaining situated choice and the developmental logic of explaining criminal propensities and lifestyles. A full-fledged integration might be very useful to further disentangle the person-environment interactions in the development of moral beliefs, self-control, and lifestyles/situational exposure. A full-fledged integration can incorporate biological markers as causes of the causes. Whether such biopsychosocial and developmental integrations will be successful in the study of problematic youth group involvement is to be seen. It is argued that truth is the daughter of time. Time will also tell whether criminologists who are interested in the study of causes and development of problematic youth group involvement and offending will be working from different schools of thought in the next decades or whether they will try to integrate their findings, based on a sound philosophy of causation and mechanisms. If criminologist choose to build strong integrated models, than our analytical crime causation science framework, the emergentist systemist approach might be worth considering.

REFERENCES

Abrams, D., Wetherell, M., Cochrane, S., Hogg, M. A., & Turner, J. C. (1990). Knowing what to think by knowing who you are: Self-categorization and the nature of norm formation, conformity and group polarization. *British Journal of Social Psychology*, 29(2), 97-119.

Agnew, R. (2011). *Toward a unified criminology: Integrating assumptions about crime, people and society*. New York: NYU Press.

Akers, R. (2008 [1998]). *Social Structure and Social Learning*. Boston: Northeastern University Press.

Akers, R. L., & Sellers, C. S. (2004). *Criminological theory*. Los Angeles: Roxbury.

Bandura, A. (2001). Social cognitive theory: An agentic perspective. *Annual Review of Psychology*, 52(1), 1-26.

Battin, S. R., Hill, K. G., Abbott, R. D., Catalano, R. F., & Hawkins, J. D. (1998). The Contribution Of Gang Membership To Delinquency Beyond Delinquent Friends. *Criminology*, 36(1), 93-116.

Beaver, K. M., & Walsh, A. (Eds.). (2013). *The Ashgate research companion to biosocial theories of crime*. Burlington: Ashgate Publishing, Ltd.

Beaver, K. M., Ratchford, M., & Ferguson, C. J. (2009). Evidence of genetic and environmental effects on the development of low self-control. *Criminal Justice and Behavior*, 36, 1158-1172.

Bernard, T. J. (1990). Twenty years of testing theories: What have we learned and why? *Journal of Research in Crime and Delinquency*, 27(4), 325-347.

Bernard, T. J., & Snipes, J. B. (1996). Theoretical integration in criminology. *Crime and Justice*, 20, 301-348.

Bjerregaard, B., & Lizotte, A. J. (1995). Gun ownership and gang membership. *Journal of Criminal Law and Criminology*, 86, 37-58.

Bjørgo, T., & Haaland, T. (2001). *Vold, konflikter og gjenger. En undersøkelse blant ungdomsskoleelever i Skedsmo kommune*. NIBR-notat 2001:103.

Boghossian, P. (2006). *Fear of knowledge: Against relativism and constructivism*. Oxford: Oxford University Press.

Boisvert, D., Wright, J. P., Knopik, V., & Vaske, J. (2012). Genetic and environmental overlap between low self-control and delinquency. *Journal of Quantitative Criminology*, 28(3), 477-507.

Boudon, R. (1989). Subjective rationality and the explanation of social behavior. *Rationality and Society*, 1(2), 173-196.

Bourdieu, P. (1986). The forms of capital. In: J. G. Richardson (Ed.), *Handbook of theory and research for the sociology of education* (pp. 241-260). New York, NY: Greenwood.

Bronfenbrenner, U. (1992). *Ecological systems theory*. London: Jessica Kingsley Publishers.

Bruinsma, G. J., & Lissenberg, E. (1987). *Vrouwen als daders. Vrouw en criminaliteit, vrouwen als plegers en slachtoffers van criminaliteit*. Amsterdam, The Netherlands: Boom Appel.

Bruinsma, G. J., Pauwels, L. J., Weerman, F. M., & Bernasco, W. (2013). Social disorganization, social capital, collective efficacy and the spatial distribution of crime and offenders an empirical test of six neighbourhood models for a Dutch city. *British Journal of Criminology, 53*, 942-963.

Brutsaert, H. (2001). *Co-educatie: Studiekansen en kwaliteit van het schoolleven*. Antwerpen: Garant.

Bunge, M. (1979). *Causality in Modern Science*. New York, NY: Dover Publications.

Bunge, M. (1999). *Social science under debate: a philosophical perspective*. University of Toronto Press.

Bunge, M. (1999). *The sociology-philosophy connection*. New York: Transaction Publishers.

Bunge, M. (2004). How does it work? The search for explanatory mechanisms. *Philosophy of the Social Sciences, 34*, 182-210.

Bunge, M. (2006). *Chasing reality: Strife over realism*. Toronto: University of Toronto Press.

Bunge, M. (2006). A systemic perspective on crime. In: Wikström, P. O. H, & Sampson, R. J. *The explanation of crime: Context, mechanisms, and development* (pp. 8-30). Cambridge: Cambridge University Press.

Bunge, M. A. (2001). *Philosophy in crisis: The need for reconstruction*. New York: Prometheus Books.

Bursik, R. J. (1988). Social disorganization and theories of crime and delinquency: Problems and prospects. *Criminology, 26*(4), 519-552.

Bursik, R. J., & Grasmick, H. G. (1993). Economic deprivation and neighborhood crime rates, 1960-1980. *Law & Society Review, 27*(2), 263-283.

Byrne, B. M. (2011). *Structural equation modeling with Mplus: Basic concepts, applications, and programming*. New York, NY: Routledge Academic.

Byrne, J. M., & Sampson, R. J. (Eds.). (1986). *The social ecology of crime*. New York, NY: Springer-Verlag.

Campbell, D. T. (1955). The informant in quantitative research. *American Journal of Sociology, 60*, 339-342.

Chapple, C. L., & Hope, T. L. (2003). An analysis of the self-control and criminal versatility of gang and dating violence offenders. *Violence and victims, 18*(6), 671-690.

Cloward, R. A., & Ohlin, L. E. (1960). *Delinquency and Opportunity*. New York, NY: Free Press.

Cohen, A. (1955). *Delinquent boys: The culture of the gang*. Glencoe, IL: The Free Press.

Coleman, J. S. (1986). Social theory, social research, and a theory of action. *American Journal of Sociology, 91*, 1309-1335.

Colvin, M. (2000). *Crime and coercion: An integrated theory of chronic criminality*. New York, NY: St. Martin's Press.

Colvin, M., Cullen, F. T., & Ven, T. V. (2002). Coercion, social support, and crime: An emerging theoretical consensus. *Criminology, 40*(1), 19-42.

Cornish, D., & Clarke, R. (2008). The rational choice perspective. In R. Wortley & L. Mazerolle (Eds.), *Environmental criminology and crime analysis* (pp. 21-47). Oxon: Routledge.

Cullen, F. T. (1994). Social support as an organizing concept for criminology: Presidential address to the Academy of Criminal Justice Sciences. *Justice Quarterly, 11*(4), 527-559.

Curry, G. D., & Spergel, I. A. (1988). Gang homicide, delinquency, and community. *Criminology, 26*(3), 381-406.

Curry, G. D., Decker, S. H., & Egley Jr, A. (2002). Gang involvement and delinquency in a middle school population. *Justice Quarterly, 19*(2), 275-292.

Curry, G. D., Decker, S. H., & Pyrooz, D. (2003). *Confronting gangs: Crime and community*. Oxford: Oxford University Press.

De Witte, H., Hooge, N., & Walgrave, L. (2000). *Jongeren in Vlaanderen: gemeten en geteld. 12-tot 18-jarigen over hun leefwereld en toekomst*. Leuven: Universitaire Pers Leuven.

De Wree, E., Vermeulen, G., & Christiaens, J. (2006). *Strafbare overlast door jongerengroepen in het kader van openbaar vervoer. Fenomeen, dadergroep, onveiligheidsbeleving, beleidsevaluatie en – aanbeveling.* Antwerpen, Belgium: Maklu.

Decker, S. H., & Weerman, F. M. (Eds.). (2005). *European street gangs and troublesome youth groups (Volume 3).* Oxford: AltaMira press.

Dietz, R. D. (2002). The estimation of neighborhood effects in the social sciences: An interdisciplinary approach. *Social science research*, 31(4), 539-575.

Duke, M. P., & Fenhagen, E. (1975). Self-parental alienation and locus of control in delinquent girls. *Journal of Genetic Psychology*, 127, 103-107.

Durkheim, E. (2014). *The division of labor in society.* New York: Simon and Schuster.

Elliott, D. S. (1985). The assumption that theories can be combined with increased explanatory power: Theoretical integrations. In: Meier, R. F. (Ed.). (1985). *Theoretical methods in criminology* (pp. 123-149). Beverly Hills, CA: Sage.

Elster, J. (1989). *Nuts and bolts for the social sciences.* Cambridge, UK: Cambridge University Press.

Elster, J. (2007). *Explaining social behavior: More nuts and bolts for the social sciences.* Cambridge: Cambridge University Press.

Emery, C. R., Jolley, J. M., & Wu, S. (2011). Desistance from intimate partner violence: The role of legal cynicism, collective efficacy, and social disorganization in Chicago neighborhoods. *American Journal of Community Psychology*, 48(3-4), 373-383.

Esbensen, F. A., & Maxson, C. L. (Eds.). (2011). *Youth gangs in international perspective: results from the Eurogang program of research.* New York: Springer Science & Business Media.

Esbensen, F. A., & Weerman, F. M. (2005). Youth gangs and troublesome youth groups in the United States and the Netherlands: A cross-national comparison. *European Journal of Criminology*, 2, 5-37.

Esbensen, F. A., Peterson, D., Taylor, T. J., & Freng, A. (2010). *Youth violence: Sex and race differences in offending, victimization, and gang membership.* Temple, PA: Temple University Press.

Esser, H. (1994), Explanatory Sociology. *Journal of the Deutsche Gesellschaft für Soziologie*, 84, 177–190, Special Edition.

Felson, M., & Boba, R. L. (Eds.). (2010). *Crime and everyday life.* (4th edition). Thousand Oaks, CA: Sage.

Fishbein, M., & Ajzen, I. (2010). *Predicting and changing behavior: The reasoned action approach.* New York: Taylor & Francis.

Fleisher, M. S. (1998). *Dead end kids: Gang girls and the boys they know.* Wisconsin: University of Wisconsin Press.

Glueck, S., & Glueck, E. (1950). *Unraveling juvenile delinquency.* New York, NY: The Free Press. Wolfgang.

Goldthorpe, J. H. (2000). *On sociology: Numbers, narratives, and the integration of research and theory.* Cambridge, Oxford: Oxford University Press.

Gottfredson, M., & Hirschi, T. (1990). *A General Theory of Crime.* Stanford, CA: Stanford California Press.

Granovetter, M. (1985). Economic action and social structure: the problem of embeddedness. *American Journal of Sociology*, 91, 481-510.

Gurr, T. R. (1970). *Why Men Rebel. Princeton.* Princeton: Princeton University Press.

Haaland, T. (2000). *Vold – konflikt og gjengdannelse : en undersøkelse blant ungdom i fire byer.* NIBR-rapport 2000:14. Oslo: NIBR.

Hacking, I. (1999). *The social construction of what?* Harvard: Harvard University Press.

Hawdon, J. E. (1996). Deviant lifestyles: The social control of daily routines. *Youth & Society*, 28(2), 162-188.

Hedström, P. (2005). *Dissecting the social. On the principles of analytical sociology.* Cambridge, UK: Cambridge University Press.

Hedström, P., & Swedberg, R. (Eds.). (1998). *Social mechanisms: an analytical approach to social theory.* Cambridge, UK: Cambridge University Press.

Hedström, P., & Ylikoski, P. (2010). Causal mechanisms in the social sciences. *Annual Review of Sociology,* 36, 49-67.

Hedström, P., Swedberg, R., & Udehn, L. (1998). Popper's situational analysis and contemporary sociology. *Philosophy of the Social Sciences,* 28(3), 339-364.

Heitmeyer, W., Collmann, B., Conrads, J., Matuschek, I., Kraul, D., Kühnel, W., Möller, R., & Ulbrich-Hermann, M. (1995). *Gewalt: Schattenseiten der Individualisierung bei Jugendlichen aus unterschiedlichen Milieus.* München: Juventa.

Herrnstein, R. J. (1991). Experiments on stable suboptimality in individual behavior. *The American Economic Review,* 81, 360-364.

Hess, R. D., & Holloway, S. D. (1984). Family and school as educational-institutions. *Review of Child Development Research,* 7, 179-222.

Hill, K. G., Howell, J. C., Hawkins, J. D., & Battin-Pearson, S. R. (1999). Childhood risk factors for adolescent gang membership: Results from the Seattle Social Development Project. *Journal of Research in Crime and Delinquency,* 36(3), 300-322.

Hindelang, H. J., Gottfredson, M. R., & Garofalo, S. (1978), *Victims of personal crime: An empirical foundation for a theory of personal victimization,* Cambridge, UK: Ballinger Publishing Company.

Hipp, J. R., & Boessen, A. (2013). Egohoods as waves washing across the city: a new measure of "neighborhoods". *Criminology,* 51(2), 287-327.

Hirschi, T. (1969). *Causes of delinquency.* New Brunswick, NJ: Transaction Publishers.

Hirschi, T. (1979). Separate and unequal is better. *Journal of Research in Crime and Delinquency,* 16(1), 34-38.

Hirtenlehner, H., Pauwels, L. J. R., & Mesko, G. (2014). Is the effect of perceived deterrence on juvenile offending contingent on the level of self-control? Results from three countries. *British Journal of Criminology,* 01/2014, doi:10.1093/bjc/azt053.

Hope, T. L., & Damphousse, K. R. (2002). Applying self-control theory to gang membership in a non-urban setting. *Journal of Gang Research,* 9, 41–61.

Howell, J. C., & Egley, A. (2005). Moving risk factors into developmental theories of gang membership. *Youth Violence and Juvenile Justice,* 3(4), 334-354.

Jean, P. K. B. St. (2008). *Pockets of crime: Broken windows, collective efficacy, and the criminal point of view.* Chicago, IL: University of Chicago Press.

Jepperson, R., & Meyer, J. W. (2011). Multiple Levels of Analysis and the Limitations of Methodological Individualisms. *Sociological Theory,* 29(1), 54-73.

Johnson, R. E. (1979). *Juvenile delinquency and its origins: An integrated theoretical approach.* Cambridge: Cambridge University Press

Jones, S., & Lynam, D. R. (2009). In the eye of the impulsive beholder the interaction between impulsivity and perceived informal social control on offending. *Criminal Justice and Behavior,* 36(3), 307-321.

Junger-Tas, J., Marshall, I. H., & Ribeaud, D. (2003). *Delinquency in an international perspective. The International Self-Reported Delinquency Study (ISRD),* Amsterdam: Kugler.

Jurkovic, G. J. (1980). The juvenile delinquent as a moral philosopher: A structural-developmental perspective. *Psychological Bulletin,* 88, 709-727.

Katz, C. M., & Fox, A. M. (2010). Risk and protective factors associated with gang-involved youth in Trinidad and Tobago. *Revista Panamericana Salud Publica*, 27(3), 187-202.

Kempf, K. L. (1993). The Empirical Status Of Hirschi's Control Theory. In: Adler, F., & Laufer, W. S. (Eds). *New Directions In Criminological Theory, Advances In Criminological Theory* (pp. 143-185), Vol. 4. New Brunswick: Transaction Publishers.

Kirk, D. S., & Matsuda, M. (2011). Legal cynicism, collective efficacy, and the ecology of arrest. *Criminology*, 49(2), 443-472.

Kirk, D. S., & Papachristos, A. V. (2011). Cultural mechanisms and the persistence of neighborhood violence. *American Journal of Sociology*, 116(4), 1190-1233.

Kissner, J., & Pyrooz, D. C. (2009). Self-control, differential association, and gang membership: A theoretical and empirical extension of the literature. *Journal of Criminal Justice*, 37(5), 478-487.

Kivivuori, J. (2011). *Discovery of hidden crime: Self-report delinquency surveys in criminal policy context*. Oxford: Oxford University Press.

Klein, M. W. (1971). *Street gangs and street workers*. Englewood Cliffs, NJ: Prentice-Hall.

Klein, M. W., & Maxson, C. L. (2006). *Street gang patterns and policies*. Oxford, UK: Oxford University Press.

Klein, M. W., Weerman, F. M., & Thornberry, T. P. (2006). Street gang violence in Europe. *European Journal of Criminology*, 3, 413-437.

Kornhauser, R. R. (1978). *Social sources of delinquency*. Chicago, IL: University of Chicago Press.

Kubrin, C. E., & Weitzer, R. (2003). New directions in social disorganization theory. *Journal of Research in Crime and Delinquency*, 40(4), 374-402.

Lahey, B. B., Gordon, R. A., Loeber, R., Stouthamer-Loeber, M., & Farrington, D. P. (1999). Boys who join gangs: A prospective study of predictors of first gang entry. *Journal of Abnormal Child Psychology*, 27(4), 261-276.

Lau, S., & Leung, K. (1990). Self-concept, delinquency, relations with parents and school and Chinese adolescents' perception of personal control. *Personality and Individual Differences*, 13(5), 615-622.

Laub, J. H., & Sampson, R. J. (1993). Turning points in the life course: Why change matters to the study of crime. *Criminology*, 31(3), 301-325.

Laub, J. H., & Sampson, R. J. (2003). *Shared beginnings, divergent lives: Delinquent boys to age 70*. Cambridge: Harvard University Press.

Lefcourt, H. M (Ed.). (1982). Locus of control: Current trends in theory and research. London: Psychology Press.

Lewin, K. (1951). *Field theory in social science: selected theoretical papers* (Edited by Dorwin Cartwright.). Harper Torchbooks: The Academy Library.

Lilly, J. R., Cullen, F. T., & Ball, R. A. (2014). *Criminological theory: Context and consequences*. New York: Sage Publications.

Little, D. (1991). *Varieties of social explanation: An introduction to the philosophy of social science*. Boulder, Colorado (U.S.): Westview Press.

Little, D. (1998). *Microfoundations, method, and causation: On the philosophy of the social sciences*. New Brunswick: Transaction Publishers.

Liu, X., & Kaplan, H. B. (1999). Explaining the gender difference in adolescent delinquent behavior: A longitudinal test of mediating mechanisms. *Criminology*, 37(1), 195-216.

Lizotte, A. J., Krohn, M. D., Howell, J. C., Tobin, K., & Howard, G. J. (2000). Factors influencing gun carrying among young urban males over the adolescent-young adult life course. *Criminology*, 38(3), 811-834.

Longshore, D., Chang, E., & Messina, N. (2005). Self-control and social bonds: A combined control perspective on juvenile offending. *Journal of Quantitative Criminology*, 21(4), 419-437

Lynam, D., Moffitt, T., & Stouthamer-Loeber, M. (1993). Explaining the relation between IQ and delinquency: Class, race, test motivation, school failure, or self-control? *Journal of Abnormal Psychology*, 102(2), 187-196.

Lynam, D. R., Caspi, A., Moffitt, T. E., Wikström, P.-O. H., Loeber, R., & Novak, S. (2000). The interaction between impulsivity and neighborhood context on offending: The effects of impulsivity are stronger in poorer neighborhoods. *Journal of Abnormal Psychology*, 109, 563-574.

Manzo, G. (2007). Progrès et «urgence» de la modélisation en sociologie. du concept de «modèle générateur» et de sa mise en Œuvre. *L'Année sociologique*, 57(1), 13-61.

Martens, P. L. (1990). Criminal behaviour among young people with immigrant background. crime and measures against crime in the city. In: Wikström, P.-O. H. (Ed.). *Crime and measures against crime in the city* (pp. 47-72). Stockholm (Sweden) BRA-Report, 5.

Matsueda, R. L. (2006). Differential social organization, collective action, and crime. *Crime, Law and Social Change*, 46(1-2), 3-33.

Maxson, C. L., & Klein, M. W. (1995). Investigating gang structures. *Journal of Gang Research*, 3(1), 33-40.

Melde, C., & Esbensen, F. A. (2011). Gang membership as a turning point in the life course. *Criminology*, 49 (2), 513-552.

Mellgren, C., Pauwels, L., & Torstensson-Levander, M. (2010). Neighbourhood disorder and worry about criminal victimization in the neighbourhood. *International Review of Victimology*, 17(3), 207-226.

Merton, R. K. (1968). Social structure and anomie. *American Sociological Review*, 3(5), 672-682.

Messner, S. F., Krohn, M. D., & Liska, A. E. (Eds.). (1989). *Theoretical integration in the study of deviance and crime: Problems and prospects*. New York, NY: SUNY Press.

Miller, J. (2001). *One of the guys: Girls, gangs, and gender*. New York, NY: Oxford University Press.

Miller, W. (1958). Lower class culture as a generating milieu of gang delinquency. *Journal of Social Issues*, 14, 5-20.

Mirowsky, J., & Ross, C. E. (2003). *Social causes of psychological distress* (2nd edition). Hawthorne, NY: Aldine De Gruyter.

Moffitt, T. E. (1993). Adolescence-limited and life-course-persistent antisocial behavior: a developmental taxonomy. *Psychological Review*, 100(4), 674.

Moffitt, T. E., & Caspi, A. (2001). Childhood predictors differentiate life-course persistent and adolescence-limited antisocial pathways among males and females. *Development and Psychopathology*, 13(02), 355-375.

Morenoff, J. D., Sampson, R. J., & Raudenbush, S. W. (2001). Neighborhood inequality, collective efficacy, and the spatial dynamics of urban violence. *Criminology*, 39, 517-560.

Morris, T. (1957). *The criminal area: A study in social ecology* (Vol. 4). London: Routledge.

Muthén, L. K., & Muthén, B. (2011). *Mplus user's guide* (6th ed.). Los Angeles, CA: Muthén and Muthén

Nofziger, S., & Kurtz, D. (2005). Violent lives: A life style model linking exposure to violence to juvenile violent offending. *Journal of Research in Crime and Delinquency*, 42, 3-26.

Oberwittler, D. (2004). A multilevel analysis of neighbourhood contextual effects on serious juvenile offending the role of subcultural values and social disorganization. *European Journal of Ccriminology*, 1(2), 201-235.

Oberwittler, D., & Wikström, P. H. (2009). Why small is better: Advancing the study of the role of behavioral contexts in crime causation. In: D. Weisburd, W. Bernasco, & G. Bruinsma (Eds.), *Putting crime in its place* (pp. 35-59). New York, NY: Springer.

Oberwittler, D., Rabold, S., & Baier, D. (2013). Städtische Armutsquartiere – Kriminelle Lebenswelten. In: *Studien zu sozialräumlichen Kontexteffekten auf Jugendkriminalität und Kriminalitätswahrnehmungen*. Wiesbaden, Germany: Springer.

Op de Beeck, H. (2011). *Strain en jeugddelinquentie: een dynamische relatie? Een toets van twee centrale verklaringsmechanismen uit Agnews General Strain Theory*. Boom Lemma uitgevers.

Opp, K. D. (1999). Contending conceptions of the theory of rational action. *Journal of Theoretical Politics*, 11 (2), 171-202.

Opp, K. D. (2001). How do norms emerge? An outline of a theory. *Mind & Society*, 2(1), 101-128.

Opp, K. D. (2005). Explanations by mechanisms in the social sciences. Problems, advantages and alternatives. *Mind & Society*, 4(2), 163-178.

Opp, K. D. (2009). *Theories of political protest and social movements: A multidisciplinary introduction, critique, and synthesis*. New York: Routledge.

Osgood, D. W., & Anderson, A. L. (2004). Unstructured socializing and rates of delinquency. *Criminology*, 42 (3), 519-550.

Osgood, D. W., Wilson, J. K., O'Malley, P. M, Bachman, J. G., & Johnston, L. D. (1996). Routine activities and individual deviant behavior. *American Sociological Review*, 61, 635-655.

Papachristos, A. V., & Kirk, D. S. (2006). Neighborhood effects and street gang behavior. In: Short, J. F., & Hughes, L. A. (Eds.), *Studying youth gangs*. Lanham, MD: Alta Mira.

Papachristos, A. V., Hureau, D. M., & Braga, A. A. (2013). The corner and the crew: The influence of geography and social networks on gang violence. *American Sociological Review*, 78, 3: pp. 417-447.

Parrot, A. C., & Strongman, K. T. (1984). Locus of control and delinquency. *Adolescence*, 19, 459-471.

Parsons, T., & Shils, E. (Eds.). (1951). *Towards a General Theory of Action*. Cambridge: Harvard University Press.

Pauwels, L. (2006). Ecologische betrouwbaarheid en constructvaliditeit van "sociale desorganisatieconstructen" op basis van de methode van key informant analysis, *Panopticon*, 27, 34-55.

Pauwels, L. (2007). *Buurtinvloeden En Jeugddelinquentie: Een Toets Van De Sociale Desorganisatietheorie*. The Hague, The Netherlands: Boom Juridische Uitgevers.

Pauwels, L. (2008). Geweld in groepsverband onder Antwerpse jongeren: De rol van schoolcontext en leefstijl, *Tijdschrift Voor Criminologie*, 50, 3-16.

Pauwels, L. (2012). How similar is the interaction between low self-control and deviant moral beliefs in the explanation of adolescent offending? An inquiry in sub groups by genderand immigrant background. In: Fruili, A. S., & Veneto, L. D. (Eds.), *Psychology of morality*, New York, NY: Nova Publishers.

Pauwels, L., & Hardyns, W. (2009). Measuring community (dis)organizational processes through key informant analysis. *European Journal of Criminology*, 6(5), 401-417.

Pauwels, L., & Pleysier, S. (2009). Self-Report Studies in Belgium and The Netherlands. In: Zauberman, R. (Ed.), *Self-reported crime and deviance studies in Europe* (pp. 51-76). Brussels, Belgium: VUB-Press

Pauwels, L., & Svensson, R. (2013). Troublesome Youth Group Involvement, Self-reported Offending and Victimization: An Empirical Assessment of an Integrated Informal Control/Lifestyle Model. *European Journal of Criminal Policy & Research*, 19, 369–386. doi: 10.1007/s10610-013-9205-7.

Pauwels, L. J., & Svensson, R. (2013). Violent youth group involvement, self-reported offending and victimisation: An empirical assessment of an integrated informal control/lifestyle model. *European Journal on Criminal Policy and Research*, 19(4), 369-386.

Pauwels, L., & Svensson, R. (2014). Micro-place disorder, subjective powerlessness and violent youth group involvement: Testing an integrative control theory. *International Journal of Criminology and Sociology*, 3, 200-221. DOI: http://dx.doi.org/10.6000/1929-4409.2014.03.18

Pauwels, L. J. R., Hardyns,W., & Van de Velde, M. (2010). *Social disorganisation, offending, fear and victimisation: findings from Belgian studies on the urban context of crime*. The Hague, The Netherlands: Boom Legal Publishers.

Pauwels, L., Ponsaers, P., & Svensson, R. (2010). An analytical perspective on the study of crime at multiple levels. In: Pauwels, L., Hardyns, W., & Van de Velde, M. (Ed.), *Social disorganisation, offending, fear and victimisation. Findings from Belgian studies on the urban context of crime*. Den Haag, The Netherlands: Boom Juridische Uitgevers.

Pauwels, L., Vettenburg, N., Gavray, C., & Brondeel, R. (2011). Societal vulnerability and troublesome youth group involvement: The mediating role of violent values and low self-control. *Journal of International Criminal Justice*, 21, 283-296.

Peeples, F., & Loeber, R. (1994). Do individual factors and neighborhood context explain ethnic differences in juvenile delinquency? *Journal of Quantitative Criminology*, 10(2), 141-157.

Piquero, A. R., Jennings, W. G., & Farrington, D. P. (2009). On themalleability of self-control: Theoretical and policy implications regarding a General Theory of Crime. *Justice Quarterly*, 27, 803-834.

Pizarro, J. M., & McGloin, J. M. (2006). Explaining gang homicides in Newark, New Jersey: Collective behavior or social disorganization? *Journal of Criminal Justice*, 34(2), 195-207.

Popper, K. R. (1959). *The logic of scientific discovery*. New York, NY: Hutchingson & Co.

Popper, K. R. (1972). *Objective knowledge*. Oxford, UK: Oxford University Press.

Psillos, S. (1999). *Scientific realism: How science tracks truth*. Routledge.

Psillos, S. (2009). *Knowing the structure of nature: Essays on realism and explanation*. Palgrave Macmillan.

Ransford, H. E. (1968). Isolation, powerlessness, and violence: A study of attitudes and participation in the Watts riot. *American Journal of Sociology*, 73, 581-591.

Raudenbush, S. W., & Sampson, R. J. (1999). Ecometrics: Toward a science of assessing ecological settings, with application to the systematic social observation of neighborhoods. *Sociological Methodology*, 29(1), 1-41.

Raudenbush, S. W., Bryk, A., & Congdon, R. (2004). *HLM6: Hierarchical linear and nonlinear modelling*. Chicago, IL: Scientific Software International.

Reckless, W. C. (1961). New theory of delinquency and crime. *Federal Probation*, 25, 42-46.

Reiss, A. J. (1951). Delinquency as the failure of personal and social controls. *American Sociological Review*, 16, 196-207.

Riley, D. (1987). Time and crime: the link between teenager lifestyle and delinquency. *Journal of Quantitative Criminology*, 3(4), 339-354.

Robinson, M. B. & Beaver, K. M. (2009). *Why crime? An interdisciplinary approach to explaining criminal behavior*. Durham, NC: Carolina Academic Press.

Robinson, W. S. (1950). Ecological correlations and the behavior of individuals. *American Sociological Review*, 15(3), 351-357.

Ross, C. E., & Mirowsky, J. (1987). Normlessness, powerlessness, and trouble with the law. *Criminology*, 25, 257-278.

Ross, C. E., & Mirowsky, J. (2001). Neighborhood disadvantage, disorder, and health. *Journal of Health and Social Behavior*, 42, 258-276. (PMID: 11668773).

Ross, C. E., & Mirowsky, J. (2009). Neighborhood disorder, subjective alienation, and distress. *Journal of Health and Social Behavior, 50,* 49-64.

Ross, C. E., Mirowsky, J., & Pribesh, S. (2001). Powerlessness and the amplification of threat: Neighborhood disadvantage, disorder, and mistrust. *American Sociological Review, 66,* 568-591.

Ross, C. E., Mirowsky, J., & Pribesh, S. (2002). Disadvantage, disorder and urban mistrust. *City and Community, 1,* 59-82.

Rotter, J. B. (1966). Generalized expectancies of internal versus external control of reinforcements. *Psychological Monographs, 80*(1, Whole No. 609).

Rovers, G. B. (1997). *De buurt een broeinest? Een onderzoek naar de invloed van woonomgeving op jeugdcriminaliteit.* Nijmegen: Ars Aequi Libri.

Sampson, R. J. (2012). *Great American city: Chicago and the enduring neighborhood effect.* Chicago: University of Chicago Press.

Sampson, R. J., & Bartusch, D. J. (1998). Legal cynicism and (subcultural?) tolerance of deviance: The neighborhood context of racial differences. *Law and Society Review, 32,* 777-804.

Sampson, R. J., & Groves, W. B. (1989). Community structure and crime: Testing social-disorganization theory. *The American Journal of Sociology, 94,* 774-802.

Sampson, R. J., & Laub, J. H. (2003). Life-Course Desisters? Trajectories Of Crime Among Delinquent Boys Followed To Age 70. *Criminology, 41*(3), 555-592.

Sampson, R. J., Morenoff, J. D., & Gannon-Rowley, T. (2002). Assessing neighbourhood effects: Social processes and new directions in research. *Annual Review of Sociology, 28,* 443-478.

Sampson, R. J., Raudenbush, S. W., & Earls, F. (1997). Neighborhoods and violent crime: A multilevel study of collective efficacy. *Science, 277,* 918-924.

Schils, N., & Pauwels, L. (2014). How Invariant is the interaction between extremist propensity and exposure to extremist moral settings in sub groups by gender and immigrant background? Testing a leading hypothesis of SAT. *Journal of Strategic Security, 7*(3), 27-47.

Seeman, M. (1959). On the meaning of alienation. *American Sociological Review, 24*(6), 783-791.

Sharp, C., Aldridge, J., & Medina, J. (2006). *Delinquent youth groups and offending behaviour: Findings from the 2004 Offending, Crime and Justice Survey.* Home Office Online Report 14/06, London, UK: Home Office.

Shaw, C., & Mckay, H. (1942). *Juvenile delinquency and urban areas.* Chicago, IL: University of Chicago Press.

Shaw, C., Zorbaugh, F. M., Mckay, H. D., & Cotrell, L. S. (1929). *Delinquency areas, a study of the geographic distribution of school truants, juvenile delinquents, and adult offenders in Chicago.* Chicago, IL: University of Chicago Press.

Shaw, J. M., & Scott, W. A. (1991). Influence of parent discipline style on delinquent behaviour: The mediating role of control orientation. *Australian Journal of Psychology, 43*(2), 61-67.

Shonkoff, J. P., & Phillips, D. A. (2000). *From neurons to neighborhoods: The science of early childhood development.* Washington, DC: National Academy Press.

Siegel, L. J., & McCormick, C. R. (2006). *Criminology in Canada: Theories, patterns, and typologies.* Toronto, ON: Thomson Nelson.

Simcha-Fagan, O. M., & Schwartz, J. E. (1986). Neighborhood and delinquency: An assessment of contextual effects. *Criminology, 24*(4), 667-699.

Simon, H. A. (1991). Bounded rationality and organizational learning. *Organization science, 2*(1), 125-134.

Sims, C. R., Neth, H., Jacobs, R. A., & Gray, W. D. (2013). Melioration as rational choice: Sequential decision making in uncertain environments. *Psychological Review*, 120(1), 139.

Skarðhamar, T. (2005). *Lovbruddskarrierer og levekår: En analyse av fødselskullet 1977*. Statistisk sentralbyrå.

Srole, L. (1956). Social integration and certain corollaries: An exploratory study. *American Sociological Review*, 21, 709-716.

Steenbeek, W., & Hipp, J. R. (2011). A longitudinal test of social disorganization theory: Feedback effects among cohesion, social control, and disorder. *Criminology*, 49(3), 833-871.

Sutherland, E. H. (1939). *Principles of criminology* (3rd edition). New York, NY: Macmillan.

Svensson, R. (2003). Gender differences in adolescent drug use the impact of parental monitoring and peer deviance. *Youth & Society*, 34(3), 300-329.

Svensson, R. (2004). Shame as a consequence of the parent-child relationship a study of gender differences in juvenile delinquency. *European Journal of Criminology*, 1(4), 477-504.

Svensson, R., & Oberwittler, D. (2010). It's not the time they spend, it's what they do: The interaction between delinquent friends and unstructured routine activity on delinquency: Findings from two countries. *Journal of Criminal Justice*, 38(5), 1006-1014.

Svensson, R., & Pauwels, L. (2010). Is a risky lifestyle always "risky"? The interaction between individual propensity and lifestyle risk in adolescent offending: A test in two urban samples. *Crime & Delinquency*, 56(4), 608-626.

Svensson, R., Bruinsma, G., Pauwels, L. J. R., & Bernasco, W. (2013). Moral emotions and offending: Do feelings of anticipated shame and guilt mediate the effect of socialization on offending? *European Journal of Criminology*, 10(1), 22-39.

Svensson, R., Pauwels, L., & Weerman, F. M. (2010). Does the effect of self-control on adolescent offending vary by level of morality? A test in three countries. *Criminal Justice and Behavior*, 37(6), 732-743.

Thomas, W. I., & Znaniecki, F. (Edited By Eli Zaretsky) (1996) [1920]. *The Polish Peasant in Europe and America. A classical work in immigration history*. Urbana, IL: University Of Illinois Press.

Thornberry, T. P. (1989). Reflections on the advantages and disadvantages of theoretical integration. In: Messner, S., & Krohn, M. (Eds.). *Theoretical integration in the study of deviance and crime: Problems and prospects*, 51-60. New York: SUNY Press.

Thornberry, T. P., Krohn, M. D., Lizotte, A. J., & Chard-Wierschem, D. (1993). The role of juvenile gangs in facilitating delinquent behavior. *Journal of Research in Crime and Delinquency*, 30, 55-87.

Thornberry, T. P., Krohn, M. D., Lizotte, A. J., Smith, C., & Tobin, K. (2003). *Gangs and delinquency in developmental perspective*. Cambridge, UK: Cambridge University Press.

Thrasher, F. M. (1927). *The gang*. Chicago, IL: University of Chicago Press.

Tita, G., Riley, J. K., & Greenwood, P. (2002). From Boston to Boyle heights: The process and prospects of a "Pulling Levers" strategy in a Los Angeles Barrio. In: Decker, S. (Ed.), *Gangs, youth violence and community policing*. Belmont, MA: Wadsworth Press.

Tolan, P. H., Gorman-Smith, D., & Henry, D. (2003). The Developmental-ecology of influences on urban males youth violence. *Developmental Psychology*, 39(2), 274-291.

Turner, J. C., Hogg, M. A., Oakes, P. J., Reicher, S. D., & Wetherell, M. S. (1987). *Rediscovering the social group: A self-categorization theory*. Oxford & New York: Basil Blackwell

Udehn, L. (2002). The changing face of methodological individualism. *Annual Review of Sociology*, 28, 479-507.

Van Der Put, C. E., Dekoviᐧ, M., Stams, G. J. J., Van Der Laan, P. H., Hoeve, M., & Van Amelsfort, L. (2011). Changes in risk factors during adolescence implications for risk assessment. *Criminal Justice and Behavior*, 38(3), 248-262.

Vazsonyi, A. T., & Huang, L. (2010). Where self-control comes from: On the development of self-control and its relationship to deviance over time. *Developmental Psychology*, 46, 245-257.

Vohs, K. D., & Baumeister, R. F. (Eds.). (2011). *Handbook of self-regulation: Research, theory, and applications.* New York: Guilford Press.

Vynckier, G., & Pauwels, L. (2010). Exploring the role of exposure to offending and deviant lifestyles in explaining offending, victimisation and the strength of the association between offending and victimisation. In: Cools, M., Ruyver, De B., Easton, M., Pauwels, L., Ponsaers, P., Vande Walle, G., Vander Beken, T., Vander Laenen, F., Vermeulen, G., & Vynckier, G. (Eds.), *Governance of security research papers series III, new empirical data, theories and analyses on security, societal problems and citizens' perceptions.* Antwerp, Belgium: Maklu.

Walsh, A. (2014). *Biosociology: Bridging the biology-sociology divide.* New Brunswick: Transaction Publishers.

Wan, P. Y. Z. (2011). *Reframing the social: emergentist systemism and social theory.* Burlington: Ashgate Publishing, Ltd.

Warr, M. (2002). *Companions in crime: The social aspects of criminal conduct.* Cambridge: Cambridge University Press.

Weerman, F. M. (2011). Delinquent peers in context: A longitudinal network analysis of selection and influence effects. *Criminology*, 49(1), 253-286.

Weerman, F. M., Maxson, C. L., Esbensen, F., Aldridge, J., Medina, J., & Van Gemert, F. (2009). *Eurogang program manual background, development, and use of the Eurogang instruments in multi-site, multi-method comparative research.* Retrieved from the Eurogang Network website: <http://www.umsl.du/~ccj/eurogang/Eurogang_20Manual.pdf>.

Weisburd, D. L., Groff, E. R., & Yang, S. M. (2014). *The criminology of place: Street segments and our understanding of the crime problem.* Oxford University Press.

Wikström, P.O.H. (1991). *Urban crime, criminals, and victims.* New York: Springer Science & Business Media.

Wikström, P.-O. H. (2004). Crime as alternative: towards a cross-level situational action theory of crime causation. In: Mc Coard, J., (Ed.), *Beyond empiricism: institutions and intentions in the study of crime* (pp. 1-37). New Brunswick, NJ: Transaction.

Wikström, P. O. (2007). In search of causes and explanations of crime. In: Kin, R., & Wincup, E. (Eds.), *Doing research on crime and justice.* Oxford: Oxford University Press.

Wikström, P.-O. H. (2010). *Situational action theory.* Oxford Bibliographies Online. Oxford University Press.

Wikström, P.-O. H., & Butterworth, D. (2006). *Adolescent crime: Individuals differences and lifestyles.* Devon: Willan Publishing.

Wikström, P. O. H., & Sampson, R. J. (2003). Social mechanisms of community influences on crime and pathways in criminality. In: Lahey, B. B., Moffitt, T. E., & Caspi, A. (Eds.). *Causes of conduct disorder and juvenile delinquency* (pp. 118-148). Guilford Press.

Wikström, P.-O. H., & Svensson, R. (2008). Why are English youths more violent than Swedish youths? A comparative study of the role of crime propensity, lifestyles and their interactions. *European Journal of Criminology*, 5(3), 309-330.

Wikström, P.-O. H., & Treiber, K. (2007). The role of self-control in crime causation: Beyond Gottfredson & Hirschi's General Theory of Crime. *European Journal of Criminology*, 4, 237-264.

Wikström, P. O. H., Oberwittler, D., Treiber, K., & Hardie, B. (2012). *Breaking rules: The social and situational dynamics of young people's urban crime*. Oxford: Oxford University Press.

Wilson, W. J. (1987). *The truly disadvantaged: The inner city, the underclass, and public policy*. Chicago, IL: University of Chicago Press.

Wong, T. M. L. (2012). *Girl delinquency: A study on sex differences in (risk factors for) delinquency*. Doctoral dissertation. VU Amsterdam, The Netherlands.

Wright, J. P., Cullen, F. T., & Miller, J. T. (2001). Family social capital and delinquent involvement. *Journal of criminal Justice*, 29(1), 1-9.

Ylikoski, P. (2011). Social mechanisms and explanatory relevance. In: Demeulenaere, P., (Ed.), *Analytical sociology and social mechanisms* (pp. 154-172). Cambridge: Cambridge University Press.

APPENDIX: MEASUREMENT OF KEY CONSTRUCTS

1 INTRODUCTION

The present appendix contains information on all scales that were used in different chapters of the book. We have chosen to present all measurement issues in one separate appendix, instead of spending time on discussing measurement issues throughout the text. The basic argument is that this book should be readable by students, practitioners, and scholars of different levels. Readers who do not have a strong statistical background can skip this appendix, while scholars who are interested in the reliability scores, factor loadings, and so on can find it all presented here. All technical information is presented per data set, i.e. the youth survey, the key informant survey, and register data (police-recorded crime data and administrative data on structural characteristics).

2 SCALES DERIVED FROM THE YOUTH SURVEY

2.1 Background variables

Gender is coded as zero for girls and one for boys. *Immigrant background* is coded zero when both parents are native and one if at least one of the parents was born abroad. Additional measures were created: immigrant status (born in Belgium, first generation, second integration) and finally a variable that is coded zero if both parents are Belgian, coded one if parent has a non-EU background, and coded two is both parents have a non-EU background. Since the youth survey is conducted in 2005, the EU classification variable of 2005 has been used. This is important as Antwerp has undergone some changes, especially with regard to migration from former Eastern European countries. *Split family* is coded as zero if the respondent is living with two parents and one if the respondent is living in a split family. Family structural risk is the combination of split family and low SES. The result is a risk score that ranges from zero to two. School failure is coded zero if the student has not repeated a year and one if the student has ever repeated a year.

2.2   *Social bonds*

Scale construct	Used items	Factor loading	ALPHA value
Parents	*5-point scale: totally agree till totally disagree*		
Parental attachment	I can get along well with my parents/caretakers.	0.730	0.810
	I find the remarks from my parents important.	0.740	
	I like to be with my parents in my free time.	0.740	
	I can talk well with my parents/caretakers.	0.701	
Parental monitoring	My parents/caretakers know with whom I hang around with, when I am not at home.	0.645	0.709
	My parents/caretakers know where I am, when I am not at home.	0.743	
	My parents/caretakers know how I behave, when I am not home.	0.625	
	When I have to go to school next day, I need to be in bed on time.	0.439	
	If I am with friends, I need to be home at an agreed hour.	0.454	
School	*5-point scale: totally agree till totally disagree*		
School social bond (items were recoded for scale construction)	I do not do a serious effort to do homework.	0.601	0.652
	I don't care for the remarks of my teachers.	0.519	
	I am not interested in getting high grades.	0.539	
Class integration	I can get along easily with pupils in my class.	0.674	0.773
	I have the feeling that I belong in this class.	0.810	
	I can count on pupils in my class.	0.706	

The social bonds constructs were used to additionally create an overall cumulative social bonds risk scale. Median dichotomization per scale was used. The risk scale ranges from zero to four.

2.3   *Individual cognitions and individual dispositions*

Volatile temper and impulsiveness have been added to create the low self-control scale. Low moral beliefs and external locus of controls are used separately in most of the analyses. However, in the analysis of the cumulative effects of risk factors, low moral beliefs and external locus of control are taken together and referred to as subjective alienation, in line with the alienation theories of the 1960s.

2.4   *Lifestyle*

To create the lifestyle risk exposure scale, we recoded the peer delinquency scale into a variable containing three categories (based on the cut-points of +1 and −1 std). The same was done for two additional survey questions on unstructured routines

Scale construct	Used items	Factor loading	ALPHA value
	5-point scale: completely disagree to completely agree.		
Volatile temper	When I am angry, others can better stay out of my way.	0.63	0.67
	When I am angry with someone, I'd rather hit then talk.	0.61	
	I get angry easily.	0.65	
Impulsiveness	I often do things without thinking.	0.58	0.71
	If I can have fun immediately, I'll do it, even if I get in trouble later.	0.66	
	I say what I think, even if it is not smart.	0.58	
	I often do immediately what I feel like doing.	0.66	
Low moral beliefs/(items taken from the legal cynicism scale)	Rules are made to be broken.	0.66	0.78
	It is okay to break rules, as long as you do not get caught.	0.77	
	It is okay to fight, if you are challenged.	0.63	
	If I do not succeed using honest methods, then I use unfair methods.	0.68	
External locus of control/ subjective powerlessness	I often have the feeling of getting into trouble.	0.56	0.58
	Planning does not guarantee success.	0.61	
	It is useless to work hard, one seldom get rewarded for that matter.	0.52	
Relative deprivation	I have enough pocket money to buy what I want.	0.624	0.58
	I am satisfied with the clothes I am wearing.	0.503	
	If I want something nice, my parents/caretakers buy it most of the time.	0.590	

The legal cynicism scale used by Sampson and Bartusch is multidimensional; it measures cynicism about the law and cynicism about other rules (e.g. rules that apply within the family context). Clearly, only the items that refer to how morally right or wrong something are relevant for this study.

Peer delinquency 5-point scale	Factor loading	ALPHA value
How many of your friends have ever stolen something or taken away money?	0.697	0.719
How many of your friends have ever hit someone with the consequence that this person needed medical care?	0.684	
How many of your friends have ever destroyed or damaged something?	0.682	

(spending time on the streets and spending time in parks, street corners, etc.) The result is an overall lifestyle risk score (ranging from −3 to +3). Inspiration was found in Loeber and Wikström (2000) and Wikström and Butterworth (2006).

2.5   *Street-level social processes*

Constructs		Factor loadings	ALPHA value
	4-point scale: never, sometimes, often, very often.		
Observed micro-place disorder and crime	Neighborhood inhabitants quarrelling on the street.	0.549	0.841
	Elder people are angry with youth.	0.515	
	Someone tries to hide something in a shopping bag in a local store to steal it.	0.612	
	Garbage and/or dirt on the sidewalk.	0.515	
	A group of local youths harasses someone to get money or something else of value.	0.698	
	House fronts, doors, etc. covered with graffiti.	0.467	
	A couple of men drink alcohol (beer, …) in the street (e.g. at a bus-stop or local supermarket).	0.605	
	Someone is selling drugs (hash, marihuana, …) on the streets.	0.671	
	Someone is being threatened with a weapon on the street (fire arm, knife, …).	0.662	
	A youngster starts a fight because he has been challenged by other youth.	0.669	
Unsupervised youth	Many youths in my neighborhood are engaged in things that are dangerous.	0.713	0.852
	Many youths in my neighborhood do things that are forbidden.	0.790	
	Many youths in my neighborhood sometimes skip classes without a valid reason.	0.648	
	Many youths in my neighborhood harass people on the street.	0.671	
Informal control (inter-generational closure)	How many adults in your neighborhood know you by name?	0.628	0.769
	How frequently do you associate with youths from your neighborhood?	0.706	
	How many peers in your neighborhood do you know by name?	0.849	
Social trust	It is easy to come in contact with my neighbors.	0.757	0.832
	My neighbors are very friendly to me in general.	0.804	
	My neighbors are prepared to help me if you ask them.	0.813	

3   RELIABILITY AND VALIDITY OF THE KEY INFORMANT SURVEY
           MEASURES

Measurement can be described as the systematic assignment of numbers to variables to represent features of persons, objects, or events. In ecological research, one's aim is to measure characteristics of ecological settings. Ecometrics is *the art of measuring* characteristics of ecological units (Raudenbush & Sampson, 1999).[1] Ecological settings involve street blocks, neighborhoods, postal code areas, or units at a higher level of analysis. One major issue in ecological research is the question of how close we can get to measuring characteristics of ecological units, rather than measuring characteristics of respondents answering observational questions about ecological units. After all, individual respondents are providing data to assess characteristics measured at higher levels of aggregation. The perception of individuals determines the ecological survey-based measure. To what extent is it possible to express social processes such as social trust and disorder in numbers?

It is clear that specific criteria are needed to evaluate sociological properties. So far, this has been done in the psychometrical tradition by using (a) reliable and valid measures at the respondent's level and (b) multilevel modeling to evaluate the ecological reliability of measurement scales created at the individual level (Raudenbush & Sampson, 1999). Although multilevel modeling has become much more integrated in quantitative analyses, we highlight the difference between psychometric and ecological reliability. A *reliable psychometric scale consists of a set of items that meet the demands of internal consistency*. This can be checked by factor analysis of the observational questions and by computing Cronbach's alpha, one of the most well-known estimators of scale reliability. To assess ecological reliability, Raudenbush and Sampson introduced the *lambda parameter* (Raudenbush & Sampson, 1999).

A reliable measure is not necessary a valid measure; accordingly it is necessary to test the ecological validity of area level aggregates. Validity refers to the absence of systematic bias: the measure should measure what it claims to measure. We bear in mind the construct validity of measures. However, the principle of construct validity seems so simple that it can be misleading. Construct validity is achieved when ecological measures correlate as highly as would be expected based on theoretical expectations. Within criminological research, the validity of a measure is often demonstrated by looking at correlations between constructs; thus, construct validity is often limited to correlational validity or convergent validity. In this contribution, we will evaluate the ecological reliability and validity of measures of social trust and disorder using the key informant analysis technique.

3.1   *Sample and methodology*

In the Antwerp survey, communities were defined as census tract clusters. The survey was carried out in all 42 official neighborhood clusters of the city of Antwerp.

---

1. Ever since the publication of this influential contribution, more attention has been paid to developing reliable and valid measures of community processes in European studies (Wittebrood, 2000; Oberwittler, 2001, 2004; Pauwels, 2006).

Antwerp is the second largest city of Belgium with a population of approximately 470,000 residents and a surface area of 205 km² (Table 71).

In total, 321 key informants were interviewed in the Antwerp key informant survey.[2] Face-to-face interviews and self-administrated questionnaires were used. The 42 combined census tracts are insufficient to conduct multivariate analyses on the relationships between community characteristics, but this was not the goal of this research. This contribution is restricted to testing the ecological reliability and validity of constructs obtained through a number of well-informed key informants. The key informants were selected on the criterion of self-selection. In addition, the interviewers were instructed to maximize the diversity of the sample. Table 72 presents descriptive statistics relating to the demographic and professional background characteristics of the informants.

In the Antwerp expert survey of professional key informants, social trust was measured by asking respondents to what extent they agreed with following items:

- it is easy to come into contact with the residents of this neighborhood.
- in general, the residents of this neighborhood are very friendly.
- the majority of this neighborhood's residents are prepared to help if you ask them.

Cronbach's alpha is 0.73.

Disorder was measured by asking respondents how many times they observed the following in their neighborhood:

- homeless people in the streets;
- drunks in the streets;
- visible signs of vandalism (e.g. broken windows, damaged public phone cells, graffiti on walls, and so on);
- people complaining about noise pollution;
- litter on the streets; and
- people being harassed on the streets.

Table 71   Descriptive characteristics of neighborhood clusters in the Antwerp expert survey

Antwerp survey (2004) Neighborhood cluster level	Minimum	Maximum	Mean
Number of key informants per area	5	15	7.64
km²	0.31	8.43	1.98
Inhabitants	1211	39,979	10,331.69

Cronbach's alpha is 0.78.

---

2. The fieldwork for the Ghent survey was conducted between October and November 2007; in Antwerp, the fieldwork was conducted between October and November 2004. Under the supervision of the authors, 153 and 236 criminology students from Ghent University interviewed the key informants within the framework of methodology classes. Students were given interviewer instructions and information on the objectives of the assignment.

Table 72   Descriptive statistics of samples

Background characteristics	Antwerp survey (2004) Neighborhood cluster level Number of units: 42	
	Absolute counts	%
Professional background		
Local shops and catering industry	131	40.8
Social work and medical doctors' offices	67	20.9
Local governance	73	22.7
Local police and private security	50	15.6
Total	*321*	*100*
Gender		
Male	174	54.2
Female	147	45.8
Total	*321*	*100*
Age		
18-25	20	6.2
26-35	77	24.0
36-45	108	33.6
46-60	95	29.6
60+	21	6.5
Total	*321*	*100*

Disorganization was measured by asking respondents how many times they observed the following in their neighborhood:
- How many times do neighborhood quarrels happen according to you?
- How many times do you experience tensions between younger and elder inhabitants of this neighborhood?
- Adolescents are hanging around on the streets a lot in this neighborhood.

3.2   *Ecological reliability of organizational processes*

To assess ecological reliability, lambda values and ICCs were calculated using random intercept models. To evaluate the ecological, neighborhood-level reliability of the scales, the first step within multilevel modeling is to compute ICCs in a so-called 'empty model,' i.e. without any individual-level predictors, comparable to variance decomposition in a conventional analysis of variance. As reported in Table 73, about 12% of the variance of social trust is due to differences between output areas, both in the Antwerp (neighborhood clusters) and in the Ghent study (postal code areas). Weighted by the number of respondents, this ICC translates to lambdas for social trust of, respectively, 0.50 and 0.80. Whereas the result for the latter scale is very good, the value of the latter is at best satisfactory. We can conclude that the social trust scale

Table 73   Reliability measures (lambda values and intraclass correlation coefficients (ICCs)) of constructs

	Social trust Antwerp census tract survey	Disorder Antwerp census tract survey
Lambda[+] (ecological reliability)	0.50*	0.81*
Intraclass Correlation Coefficient (ICC)[++]	12.41%	38.36%

+ = empty random intercept models of informants nested within ecological areas.
++ = intraclass correlation coefficient = [variance at the aggregate level/(variance at the individual level + variance at the aggregate level)]*100.
* = $p < 0.05$.

used in the Ghent study and extracted from the work of Sampson and his colleagues (1997) leads to a much more reliable measurement at the postal code area level than the social trust scale used in the Antwerp study at the neighborhood cluster level. Furthermore, 38% and 34%, respectively, of the variance of disorder is due to differences between the neighborhood clusters in the Antwerp study and postal code areas in the Ghent study. Weighted by the number of respondents, these percentages translate to lambdas for disorder of 0.81 and 0.94 respectively. All parameters in this study significantly differ from zero. Both lambdas point to a high level of reliability at the ecological level of analysis. Once again the lambda for the study at the postal code area level exceeds the lambda for the neighborhood cluster level. It is striking that respondents seem more in agreement in terms of their perception of disorder in their geographical area, than in terms of their impressions of social trust.

These results are similar to the reliability values obtained by Raudenbush and Sampson (1999) when they used representative samples of neighborhood residents in Chicago. Oberwittler and Wikström (2009) demonstrated the ecological reliability of resident-based survey measures. The findings of this study corroborate earlier findings on the potential of using key informants when measuring organizational processes. The method seems to produce reliable measures in both ecological settings (neighborhood clusters and postal code areas). However, the lower lambda value of social trust suggests that differences between respondents are somewhat higher than differences between ecological settings. It seems that it is easier to measure the consequences of lack of cohesion than social trust, at least using the key informant technique. Previous studies (Raudenbush and Sampson, 1999; Oberwittler, 2001) have found that measurements of organizational processes (social trust/cohesion) are less reliable than those of organizational processes (disorder). Thus, the use of key informants does not seem to solve that problem.

3.3   *Ecological construct validity of organizational processes*

Let us first of all look at the construct validity of social organizational processes. Social trust, as a dimension of cohesion, refers to informal control in geographical areas.

Disorder is commonly believed to be a negative outcome of lack of social control. We should therefore expect strong negative associations between these measures. The ecological level measures are simply the aggregates of the individual level measures (by using mean scores) and represent sociometric characteristics of neighborhood clusters and postal code areas rather than psychometric characteristics of individuals. After calculating the ecological level correlations (Pearson's r) between the constructs, it can be concluded that the ecological construct validity is very high. The correlation between social trust and disorder is significantly negative in the Antwerp study (−0.48).

We now turn to the ecological correlations between organizational processes and structural characteristics. These characteristics are considered to be major structural causes of crime and disorder concentrations in certain areas. Selected structural characteristics are population density, single-person households, and the unemployment rate. The results are summarized in Table 74. It should be stressed that, in this exploratory research, it can be as just interesting to study strength and direction of the correlation coefficients rather than only focusing on the significant levels.
The ecological correlations between social trust and the selected structural characteristics are without exception negative, but not statistically significant in each case. The strongest negative correlations can be found between social trust and population density, both in the Antwerp study (−0.43). Other significant correlations can be observed between social trust and unemployment rate in the Antwerp study (−0.35). Some ecological characteristics (single-person households at the neighborhood cluster level and unemployment rate at the postal code area level) do not correlate significantly with social trust. This finding deserves attention. At present, it cannot be determined whether this is a consequence of validity problems of these scales measured, as they were, by questionnaires with key informants. Furthermore, all ecological correlations between disorder and the structural characteristics are strong to very strong (and statistically significant). Unemployment rate shows the highest correlation with disorder both in the Antwerp study (0.66). Population density and single-person households also correlate strongly with disorder in the Antwerp study (respectively, 0.48 and 0.42). Taken together, we can be positive about the convergent validity of the scales measured through key informants' perceptions.

Table 74   Correlations between community structure and organizational processes

	Antwerp census tract survey N = 42 neighborhood clusters	
	Social trust	Disorder
Population density	−0.428**	0.483**
Single-person households	−0.184	0.419**
Unemployment rate	−0.352*	0.659***

***p < 0.001, **p < 0.01, *p < 0.05.

4   MEASUREMENT OF NEIGHBORHOOD STRUCTURAL CHARACTERISTICS

Neighborhood disadvantage was measured by a compound measure of income, percent unemployed, percent of non-Belgians (inhabitants who do not have the Belgian nationality), and unoccupied dwellings.

In the present study, many structural neighborhood characteristics were used in different parts of the book. Below is the list of all variables used to create risk scores.

Variable	Definition	Source
Disadvantage	Factor scores of median income, percentage of unemployed, percentage of non-Belgian citizens, and percentage of unoccupied dwellings (factor loadings, respectively: −0.875, 0.892, 0.908, 0.671)	Municipality of Antwerp (1990, 2001, 2010)
Violent crime rate	All violent offenses against persons (excluded partner violence) per 10.000 inhabitants	Local Police (2001)
Violent theft rate	All theft that were accompanied by violence per 10.000 inhabitants	Local Police (2001)
Car theft rate	Registered car thefts per 10.000 inhabitants	Local Police (2001)
Theft from cars rate	Registered theft from cars per 10.000 inhabitants	Local Police (2001)
Theft of handbags	Registered theft from per 10.000 inhabitants	Local Police (2001)
Vandalism rate	Reported violence against property per 10.000 inhabitants	Local Police (2001)
Burglary rate	Registered burglaries per 10.000 inhabitants	Local Police (2001)
Owner-occupied dwellings	% of home owing households	Census (1991)*
Offender rate per 100 inhabitants	% of all police suspects	Local Police (2001)
Juvenile arrest rate per 100 Inhabitants	% of juvenile police suspects (11-17 years)	Local Police Antwerp (2001)
% unoccupied dwellings	% of unoccupied dwellings in total number of dwellings	Municipality of Antwerp (2001)
Median income	Median household income	Municipality of Antwerp (2001)
Unemployment rate 1990	% of unemployed of working population	Municipality of Antwerp (2001)
Unemployment rate 2001	% of unemployed of working population	Municipality of Antwerp (2001)
Unemployment rate 2012	% of unemployed of working population	Municipality of Antwerp (2001)
% non-Belgian citizens 1990	% of inhabitants who are officially registered as non-Belgians of total number inhabitants	Census (1990)
% non-Belgian citizens 2001	% of inhabitants who are officially registered as non-Belgians of total number inhabitants	Municipality of Antwerp (2001)
% non-Belgian citizens 2012	% of inhabitants who are officially registered as non-Belgians of total number inhabitants	Municipality of Antwerp (2012)
Population density 2001	Number of inhabitants per hectare	Municipality of Antwerp (2001)
Residential stability	% of residents who lived at the same address for 5 years or more	Census (1991)

To validate the data, we calculated the census tract correlation of the disadvantage measure with other indicators derived from official data (Table 75).

From Table 76, it can be seen that neighborhood disadvantage is strongly correlated with official data on juvenile delinquency (population density, police arrest rates per 1000, and the percent of owner-occupied dwellings).

Finally, factor analysis was used to create an overall measure of registered crime. This measure was used to study the relationship between crime rates in the neighborhood and violent youth group involvement.

Table 75   Ecological correlates of disadvantage (census tract level)

	Disadvantage
Population density	0.521**
Owner-occupied housing	−0.688**
Disorganization	0.402**
Number of juvenile arrests 2001	0.541**

**$p < 0.01$ (2-tailed).
*$p < 0.05$ (2-tailed).

Table 76   Factor loadings of street crime based on police records (neighborhood cluster level)

Antwerp indicators (2001)	Crime factor loading
Violence against persons/km^2	0.983
Violent theft/km^2	0.938
Car theft/km^2	0.925
Theft from car/km^2	0.905
Theft of handbags/km^2	0.845
Vandalism buildings/1000 buildings	0.802
Burglaries/1000 households	0.608